D0986375

Date: 6/27/19

BIO TUTTLE
Tuttle, Connie L.,
A gracious heresy : the queer
calling of an unlikely prophet /

PALM BEACH COUNTY
LIBRARY SYSTEM
3650 SUMMIT BLVD.
WEST PALM BEACH, FL 33406

# A Gracious Heresy

# A Gracious Heresy

*The Queer Calling of an Unlikely Prophet*

Connie L. Tuttle

RESOURCE *Publications* · Eugene, Oregon

A GRACIOUS HERESY
The Queer Calling of an Unlikely Prophet

Copyright © 2018 Connie L. Tuttle. All rights reserved. Except for brief quotations in critical publications or reviews, no part of this book may be reproduced in any manner without prior written permission from the publisher. Write: Permissions, Wipf and Stock Publishers, 199 W. 8th Ave., Suite 3, Eugene, OR 97401.

Resource Publications
An Imprint of Wipf and Stock Publishers
199 W. 8th Ave., Suite 3
Eugene, OR 97401

www.wipfandstock.com

PAPERBACK ISBN: 978-1-5326-5572-2
HARDCOVER ISBN: 978-1-5326-5573-9
EBOOK ISBN: 978-1-5326-5574-6

Manufactured in the U.S.A.

This book is dedicated to the memory of my father, M.Sgt. (ret) Charles Lenny Tuttle, who taught me what it means to be brave; and of my mother, Barbara Jane Tuttle, who showed me what it means to love without borders. And in honor of my daughter, Tanya, who is the conduit of so much grace.

# Author's Note and Acknowledgements

THIS STORY IS COBBLED together from my memories—and it is precisely that: memories and mine. In the writing of this, I began to wonder how we know what is true and what is myth. I have come to believe that memories wed facts with truth and myth emerges.

The conversations reported are not necessarily verbatim but are essence of my recollections. Some names have been changed. There are no villains in this story. I experienced some of the actors as villains and relate this tale from the immediacy of my feelings at the time. The players who represented and perpetuated the oppressive status quo were the windmills at which I tilted and the dragons I felt called to vanquish.

Though I would not choose to live my life differently, I have learned that sometimes the dragon wins. And sometimes, over time, the dragon transforms.

Writing this part of my story has only been possible because of those who encouraged and supported me.

Many thanks to Loreen and Janice, my writing group pals, who offered insight and encouragement, critiqued and tweeked until something cohesive was birthed.

I am grateful to Hedgebrook and all the opportunities that amazing retreat (or, as Gloria Steinem says, "advance") provided, and to the wonderful teachers and mentors I met there: Faith Adiele, Ruth Ozeki, and Jane Hamilton. A special thanks to Faith who story edited my manuscript and gave me invaluable input. To Amy, Vito, Julie, Diane, and Kathy, who offer radical hospitality to writers: thank you for the magical space and the gift of time.

Thank you to Linda Bryant for copy editing this work in what was an act of love and friendship.

Thanks to my family and my spiritual community for their support during this long process, even when I walked through some very difficult personal times. Thank you to my sister, Sherry, who believes I am better than I really am.

As I contemplate putting my self and my life out in the world with agonizing honesty, my hope is that I can add something to understanding the history behind changes in the church, to contemporary theological conversations, and to questions about who can be considered faithful or spiritual or even legitimate.

# Contents

gra·cious *adjective* \ˈgrā-shəs\
    **1a** *obsolete* : godly

her·e·sy *noun* \ˈher-ə-sē, ˈhe-rə-\
    **1c** : an opinion or doctrine contrary to church dogma

*Miriam Webster Dictionary*


# Chapter 1    *Are you kidding me?*


A PROPHET? ARE YOU kidding me? Thirty years ago I would have been right there with you. Believe me, I would never have called myself a prophet. Prophets are special. I am not. They have a direct line to God and the go-ahead and where-with-all to do all kinds of miraculous things. I do not. They rail at people for being idiots. Well, sometimes. They declare impending doom. The most I can claim about impending doom is that I'm often scared. Prophets occasionally foretell the future. Not me. They are righteous in the extreme and above the fray and trials of this messy business we call life. Again, not me. Not in any lifetime. Not on any planet.

Boy, was I wrong. In seminary I learned just how wrong I was. I discovered that prophets are wonderfully flawed and chaotic people. Just like me. Folks often thought they were crazy. True here. Eventually I got to know the prophets as chums who spoke passionately and acted hyperbolically. I identified. I am not above the bedlam of life. I am neither a soothsayer who predicts the future nor a miracle worker. I am not particularly righteous, though I have been known to be self-righteous. To be honest I am a flock of flaws, surrounded by a majesty of misunderstandings, hobbled together with an impediment of imperfections. I am not special in any way to anyone except, maybe, to my mom and dad and daughter. I don't have a direct line to God and when the party line *is* open, I often don't hear—or more truthfully, don't listen—to what God is saying. I am strong willed and sometimes lazy. I get stuff wrong. A lot.

But I am in good company. The thing about prophets is that when God calls they head the other way. Take Jonah. "God, you're knocking on the wrong door." Moses told God "Let someone else do it, maybe my brother Aaron. He is a much better choice and besides, I stutter." Jeremiah came right out and said, "I don't want to. People make fun of me and don't invite me to their parties. They think I'm crazy . . . but (damn it) there is a fire burning inside me and I can't shut up." Or, like me. "I'm busy and there are lots of other things I want to do and besides, I'm mad at the church over the Viet Nam War, civil rights, and the women's movement. I want to act and write and have sex. You've really got this one wrong, God."

Becoming a prophet is not a career option. Children will tell you they want to be a teacher, doctor, lawyer, or firefighter when they grow up but never, as far as I know, a prophet. When you get right down to it, there is nowhere to go to fill out an application. It's a call. An irritating and irresistible call. And if I have in any way lived a prophetic life I have to admit that only some of it has been responding to God's call. The rest has been giving in. Let me repeat, I am not very good either at responding or giving in.

Prophets love people and they're pissed off. Their appeals to repentance are for the community to return to its source. To love God. To do justice. To remember who they are to God and to one another. Sure, they're bitchy and angry. Injustice makes them angrier than a bee swarm in a tornado. Prophets tend to make people uncomfortable. They irritate, intimidate, challenge, and enrage the general population. Actually, those are things at which I excel.

A prophet will stir up a shit storm or stand against one—and always on the side of the oppressed. They champion unpopular causes. The passion of their anger and grief makes them hard to be around. They are hair-brained vision-holders who refuse to give up on God's dream for us and who we can be as a people of justice and compassion. Prophets challenge the certainty of doctrine with the uncertainty of what happens when God is unleashed. They offer hope. I only pray my witness offers hope, advocates for justice, insists on compassion. If it does, then that must be enough because I have come to understand that faithfulness is not tied to measurable outcomes.

I tell you all this to give context to my story of a queer calling that took years to untangle. I speak out for justice for the LGBT, and later QI, community both in the church and out of it. I spent years banging on sacred doors hollering, "Let me in!"

Frankly, I am the very last person you would consider to be a prophet. Even writing that feels grandiose. My life is untidy. I don't always do my best. There are times I've wanted to give up. More times than I'd like to admit. And even though I am driven by grace I can be harsh in my opinions of others and harsher in estimations of myself. Or worse, I give myself a pass but find it hard to allow for the frailty of others. And there are times I get so pissed off at God I could spit. I am like Jonah who sat under that bush and groused because God extended compassion to the people he despised.

The following tale is a story about how I got myself—or God got me—into the heresy of challenging the church to justice over doctrine and compassion over polity. You might think I'm a heretic and you might be right. I've been called worse.

Here is a story about the gracious heresy of my life and an unlikely call to prophetic ministry. Nothing grand. Nothing large. Mostly it's a story about the risk and the price of being faithful and learning to trust that somehow it makes a difference.

Here's one thing
you must understand
about this blessing:
it is not
for you alone.

It is stubborn
about this.
Do not even try
to lay hold of it
if you are by yourself,
thinking you can carry it
on your own.

To bear this blessing,
you must first take yourself
to a place where everyone
does not look like you
or think like you,
a place where they do not
believe precisely as you believe,
where their thoughts
and ideas and gestures
are not exact echoes
of your own.

Bring your sorrow.
Bring your grief.
Bring your fear.
Bring your weariness,
your pain,
your disgust at how broken
the world is,
how fractured,
how fragmented
by its fighting,

its wars,
its hungers,
its penchant for power,
its ceaseless repetition
of the history it refuses
to rise above.

I will not tell you
this blessing will fix all that.
But in the place
where you have gathered,
wait.
Watch.
Listen.
Lay aside your inability
to be surprised,
your resistance to what you
do not understand.

See then whether this blessing
turns to flame on your tongue,
sets you to speaking
what you cannot fathom

or opens your ear
to a language
beyond your imagining
that comes as a knowing
in your bones,
a clarity
in your heart
that tells you

this is the reason
we were made:

. . .

—©Jan L. Richardson, from "This Grace That Scorches Us" in *Circle of Grace: A Book of Blessings for the Seasons.* Used by permission. janrichardson.com

# Chapter 2  *Battle Lines Being Drawn . . .*

"A SOLDIER IN A nameless war, a pawn on the battlefield . . ." A line of an obscure poem runs through my mind as I slide into the next to the last pew and position myself to take in the unfolding scene. I give a surreptitious pull to my purple polyester dress. It's my only dress. I'd worn it to every committee meeting I was commanded to attend at seminary. Meetings about what courses I would or would not be allowed to take. Meetings about what placements I would or would not be allowed to accept. Meetings about what degree I would or would not be allowed to pursue. Today I am wearing that same worn out, unofficial uniform to a meeting of a church governing body where a vote will be taken about whether I—or any other gay or lesbian candidate for ministry—will be permitted to be ordained.

I am an army brat and I imagine the day before me as yet another battle. I clutch my seminary degree, a Masters of Divinity, wearing it like an invisible combat infantry badge. I fought hard for this degree and am I proud I survived, though sometimes I wonder if the hill was worth taking.

I nod to people as they pass on their way to take their seats. Most of them have no idea who I am or why I am here. In truth, my presence will most likely be as ineffectual as a jammed bazooka. Still, I am going to stand because it is the right thing to do.

Sometimes my kid self wants to kick the back of the pew and whine, "I don't like them anyway." And I know I am trying to protect myself from being hurt. This is the place you are supposed to belong if you are baptized. This is the beloved community Martin Luther King, Jr. talked about. At the same time, I am all too aware that I am not a "cradle Presbyterian." I wasn't born into this denomination and I don't have a spiritual pedigree that goes back generations. I am more like an immigrant who enlisted in the army and is trying to get citizenship. I'm a recruit and *you* need bodies but you're telling me I am only good enough to peel potatoes and scrub latrines.

Slowly I rise. My knees shudder as I curl my hand over the back of the pew. I am silent. Erect. Defiant.

The Atlanta Presbytery gathered that spring day in 1994 to debate an amendment to *The Book of Order*, their constitution, that would allow for the ordination of gay men and lesbians to the Ministry of Word and Sacrament. Every presbytery in the nation would debate and vote on this

5

amendment by the end of the year. The rules of the meeting, which are the rules of every presbytery meeting, state:

1) Only those ordained could speak.

2) Gays and lesbians could not be ordained.

Tears I refuse to shed pressure the backs of my eyes. I desperately want my presence, my silence, my standing, my witness, to make a difference. I am putting my body on the line. Not like my dad, who risked life and limb during battle, but I put my "self-ness" at the front. I am exposing a truth that many urged me to conceal. Not for my sake only but because I have the strength to do it. Or if not the strength, at least the determination, *and* this damn call. My body shakes a little from fear and anger. My body wrapped in a dress whose hem was stitched with safety pins. *Am I good enough? Brave enough? Strong enough? Will it matter?*

Outside, azaleas unfurl coral and white blossoms, small magenta flowers peek from under the leaves of redbud trees, and dogwoods open their creamy petals like so many earthbound stars. I fidget with the hem of my dress again and slide one shoe off under the pew in front of me.

A minister makes his way to the podium and calls the meeting to prayer. I bow my head. It is hard to pray. I brace myself against real or imagined hostility. As the prayer begins, a bitter metallic taste rises in my throat. I. Will. Not. Cry. I tense then force myself to unclench. I want to be brave and righteous and faithful. I want to make a difference, to will justice into existence just like I willed my muscles to release. I refuse to give in to anger or hopelessness, set my jaw, and breathe into my own prayer. *Please be with me. Please give me strength. Please let me feel you here with me. Please. Please. Please.* I stifle a giggle. My prayer sounds a little too much like James Brown. Imagining myself in a cape of ermine and scarlet, throwing myself to my knees by the altar, and begging in a gravelly voice for the presbytery, the church, the world, to please—please—please . . . My breath slowly returns to normal and I pray again. *Let me be brave. Let me be a hero. Let taking a stand in this skirmish somehow make a difference.*

The minister in front keeps praying and I keep praying and I don't know what to pray for anymore so I give over to wordless yearning for connection. For strength. For courage.

Light drizzles through the stained glass windows and splashes across my face as the sun leans towards noon. The presence of the Holy fills me, fills the room, the air, the light.

And then I am running, running, running. Running through the long sweep of wheat fields that stretches toward a copse of trees down by a river bottom and angles back, churning past the barn, listing to the horizon. Knees pumping, heels kicking. Running through the scent of yellow. Warm, pre-bread yellow. Yellow, and the black of loamy earth. The smells rise like an offering in the afternoon heat. A breeze pushes the next wave across the fields, small wheat hands swirl and my outstretched arms graze the curl of rolling waves in a sea of yellow. The quiet swish-swish of wheat whispers unfathomable secrets.

Grandma and Grandpa lived in an old two-story farmhouse, nestled on a slope of farmland, heated by a wood stove in the kitchen. On winter mornings, I would grab my clothes, run downstairs and shiver them on in front of the stove that my grandmother, who rose before any of us, fed and stoked until it blasted heat that made my skin glow pink.

For me, everything was about God—wind and kites, calves and swimming holes, snails and cherry trees. Mysterious and magical, it filled me up. Somehow the big feelings I had about God were also all about my grandmother.

In late winter, I helped Grandma start seedlings in the greenhouse. A small heater whirred in the background and the drip, drip of water counted time. The smell of possibilities drifted up from the rich, black dirt. As soon as the first snow fell, out came sleds and ice skates. And after the last frost we planted the flowers in the front yard that we had started from seed.

In the summer, after morning chores, Grandma packed a picnic lunch and we traipsed down to the river bottom for the afternoon. And every day there were pancakes and sugar and fresh milk, thick with cream brought up from the dairy. Sometimes Grandma sent me out with a small pitcher and Grandpa skimmed cream off the top of the vat. I would tramp back to the kitchen, careful not to spill a drop of delight. We drenched our first course of oatmeal with that fresh, still-warm cream.

Few people are left who know the deep sensual pleasure of milk fresh and warm from the cow: its sweet richness, the complexity of its scent, and the comfort of its smoothness. I tasted God in those glasses of milk. It was my first holy meal.

Sundays on the farm included a new form of worship. We drove to Good Shepherd Catholic Church in Sheridan, a small town between the farm and McMinnville, Oregon. For the first time I experienced the majesty of the Latin Mass. I didn't understand the language but the cadences of the priest's invocations were powerful and mysterious. I did my best to follow the unfamiliar script: sit, kneel, stand. The very strangeness enchanted me. Even after it became familiar I didn't belong to it. I was not allowed to re-ceive communion because I was not Catholic. It made me ache with long-ing. I was sure God would be okay with me taking communion, but row after row of congregants passed, skirts rustling and shoes squeaking, while Mom and I sat silent in the pew.

The day before, my grandmother brought flowers from her garden to adorn the altar for Mass. The riot of gladiolas smelling of sunshine and damp earth, whose stems had been lovingly cut, rolled into wet newspapers, then again into dry ones for the long ride into town, their green tang permeating the air. When we arrived the church was empty and grand. Our footsteps and whispers echoed as we made our way through the sanctuary to the altar. Light cascaded in dusty shafts and statues in their niches gazed at my grandmother while she arranged the tall, vibrant glads into vases.

It was my grandmother who worked God's magic. When I returned to church for mass the next day I didn't recognize the flowers. Overnight they transformed into icons, the blossoms seeming to burn with a holy light.

It was my mother who introduced me to the joy of soaring church music. She took me to church concerts and sat enraptured beside me as voices blended, organs boasted and groaned, and pianos splashed fountains of notes onto my untutored ears.

It was my mother who taught me about Jesus. As we drove in the car to church she sang in her sweet, slightly off-key voice:

> Jesus loves the little children
>
> All the children of the world,
>
> Red and yellow, black and white,
>
> They are precious in his sight,
>
> Jesus loves the little children of the world!"

I joined in, sometimes imitating her soft tones, sometimes bellowing the words as I bounced in the back seat of our 1956 Chevy, too excited by the idea of all this love to sit still. I heard the story in the song and I believed it. It is the gospel I internalized, the truth I distilled.

How wonderful it would be when Jesus came back! It set my small heart on fire. I prayed so hard, "Please, please, God, let me be here when Jesus comes back!" My body filled with wanting, like wanting Christmas morning to come, like wanting a new puppy: the anticipation as lovely and powerful as the possibility of the event itself. I breathed hard and squinched my eyes closed "Please, please, please." I begged. My first lesson on love without boundaries grabbed me up and did not let go.

When Jesus came back there would be joy—like singing alleluias real loud, or rolling in fresh grass and pine needles until you smelled like heaven, or swinging so high your toes touched the clouds. And love. There would be love as good as when my heart hugged the hums of bumblebees. Love as good as snuggling in my mother's lap and breathing in and out together until we breathed one breath.

It was women who opened a world beyond words, who taught me that God is experienced, that the Sacred resides in every thing and every moment: in songs, in empty sanctuaries, and in gardens crowded with blossoms.

Light shifts and I emerged from the visions of my childhood to find myself once again in the stultifying present. The sanctuary, that I might have once thought beautiful, closes around me, bearing down with the weight of both form and formality. It doesn't matter. I have always been in love with God.

The peace and sureness of my memories center me. I stand at attention, no longer feeling the discomfort of my body. I remember who I am.

Bring it on.

The mind that is the prisoner of conventional ideas, and the will that is the captive of its own desire, cannot accept the seeds of an unfamiliar truth and a supernatural desire . . . I must learn therefore to let go of the familiar and the usual and consent to what is new and unknown to me. I must learn to 'leave myself' in order to find myself by yielding to the love of God.

—Thomas Merton, <u>New Seeds of Contemplation</u>

## Chapter 3  *Brave Little Soldier*

BRING IT ON. I can take it. Bring on your dusty theology wrapped up in frayed scraps of piety. I am not afraid. Bring on your misinformation, your hatred. Your fear. I know who I am. "Bring it on," I say to myself, my bravado contradicting the fluttering tension in my chest.

I careen between cynicism and hope, feeling first powerful, then powerless. Is this what battle feels like? I think of my soldier dad and the battles he fought, the wars he endured and survived, the humor he used to live with the unlivable. I recall my mom who loved without borders, a testament to the unflinching courage of her faith.

A straggle of people is still taking their seats, waving and calling out to friends. The energy in the room tightens as the chatter winds down. We are about to begin. My body rebels. Bile burns my throat and a sheen of sweat threatens to melt my dutifully applied makeup.

"Who are these homosexuals and what do they want with our church?" A man at the microphone asks.

Anxiety thrums in my chest and I am knock kneed with premature fatigue. This will not do. I come from better stock than this. I buttress my knees and stiffen my spine, hoping that I am like my parents. I really don't believe you want to know who I am. But I will tell you anyway. I'll tell the truth the best I can, just in case you listen.

My name is Connie Lee Tuttle, but you can call me slumgullion.

During the War, my mom worked as a ship welder and burner building ships for the U.S. Navy in Portland, Oregon. The day before payday, my mom and her neighbors dumped all their leftovers into a common pot and heated it up for dinner. They called it slumgullion. You might see peas swimming with tomatoes, meatloaf un-chunked into small meatballs, macaroni noodles with the cheese dissolving into the larger broth. Sometimes, I hear, it was tasty. Sometimes, merely tolerable. But always, always, it was a party. Hard times transformed by laughter and food.

So call me slumgullion because I, too, am made up of bits and pieces thrown together. I am part French, part German, part Southern, part army brat, part mother, part daughter, part sister, part lesbian. Call me slumgullion because sometimes my story is tasty, a meal for the senses. Unexpected. Graceful. And sometimes it is merely edible, offering only what is necessary to survive. And you can call me slumgullion because my life, my theology, my story is always transformed by sharing food and making community.

My first name is *not* Constance; it's Connie. Mom said if she wanted to call me Constance she would have named me Constance. Still, my name in the diminutive means the same thing: constancy, loyalty. And I am both constant and loyal.

My middle name is Lee. It kind of makes me Southern. I was named after my Aunt Hattie Lee, who was my dad's oldest sister. The only time either my mom or dad used that name was when I was in trouble. And it was always a triptych, never just my first and middle name. In fact, "Lee" may not exist without my first and last names tied to each end. As in, "Connie Lee Tuttle, get down here right now!"

My last name is Tuttle. It's a Scot-English name. There aren't many Tuttles where I live, in the South, but there are all up and down the New England seaboard. Dad's family is from Kentucky. We are related to Abraham Lincoln. Third great cousins or maybe fourth great. It is a fact I am proud of and it inspired a passion for justice in me quite early. Having Abraham Lincoln as your great cousin (even if no one believes you) is an, impressive legacy to carry on.

I am from all over, a citizen of the planet, a third culture kid. That means the life I lived in the other countries overlays the culture of the nation of my birth. I see connections between people while celebrating differences.

Because my father was a career military man, our family's history is segmented by wars, near wars, and conflicts: World War II, the Korean War, the Cuban Missile Crisis, and the Viet Nam War. They defined our lives as my father was sent around the world in the service of the interests of the United States. That meant our interests—homes, birthdays, and rites of passage—are all geographically aligned with strife.

I was an unplanned child, conceived during my parents' stop in Hardin County, Kentucky, on a visit to my Aunt Hattie Lee. Hardin County is in the middle of coal country. Hilly, green, and sparsely populated, farms dotted the countryside and crossroads sprouted scattered corner stores, gas stations, the obligatory post office, and sometimes, a feed and seed. Wealth and poverty, hard work and gentility, coal miners and blue grass thorough-breds, all called Kentucky home.

Aunt Hattie was a farmwoman who lived on a working farm. She washed her clothes in a caldron suspended over a wood fire and there was a two-hole outhouse in the back. The story my mom is willing to tell is that while she and Dad were visiting, fed up with the lack of privacy and hungry for one another after Dad's long stint in Korea, they met up in the outhouse.

When I visited Aunt Hattie I slept in a large old cast iron bed with a bottomless down mattress. When my mom told me that I was conceived at Aunt Hattie's, I imagined it was in that glorious feather bed. The truth is closer to how my life has played out: with passion, often unplanned, and unexpected in both grace and hardship.

Nine months later, eleven years after my only sibling and sister was born, they welcomed me to the family. I was born in Camp Gordon, Georgia, after two world wars and before the advent of air conditioning, nurtured on Southern soil, that deep red clay that bakes hard in the summer and both absorbs and radiates heat. My mother laid me under an old shade tree and I soaked up the heat and damp and smells of Southern summers. I now imagine that those scents were of humidity, human sweat, heavy perfumes, cool baths, and clean, crisp cotton. I like to think that for the rest of my life the scents and sensations of southern summers have coursed in my veins.

Not long after, Dad shipped overseas to his new station in Verdun, France. I was six months old when Mom, Sherry, and I received our orders to follow him. We were to fly to Paris and my father would meet us there. Mom bundled up Sherry and me and drove to New York City from Georgia to board the plane. As the plane taxied and rose skyward, my identity as an American and quasi-Southerner faded into the blue-white sky. We headed to a new land that would shape my unformed consciousness and beget an expansive understanding of both the world and myself.

You want to know who I am? I'm a woman who was taught that my possibilities were limitless. In Ft. Lewis, Washington, Dad was assigned to the 22nd Infantry Division to train troops. His men admired him. I adored him. Every evening I watched from the window for him to come up the walk to our quarters. I raced to the door and he squatted down to greet me as I launched myself into his embrace.

"Whose girl are you?" he asked as he swung me around in a flying arc.

"Daddy's girl!" I squealed throwing my arms around his neck and burying my face in his collar. I breathed in the faint smell of starch mingling with a fading scent of Aqua Velva aftershave that clung to his fatigues. It was our daily ritual.

Daddy was infinitely patient. I would sit in his lap twirling and combing his hair that, though close on the sides, had delicious curls at the crown. His benign tolerance encouraged me. I became fearless. I became a sassy and somewhat willful, child whose world was safe enough to nurture a passionate, loving heart.

"I'm running away from home!"

Mom had just told me to do who-knows-what. I refused, ran out of my room, and stomped down the stairs.

"Catch her!" my mom hollered down to Dad, who sat reading the paper in the living room.

I stood on the bottom step, my hands on my hips and tried to glare at him.

"Come here," he commanded.

"No," I said, inching down the last step.

"Come here."

It is not for nothing that my father trained troops. I sidled over to his chair.

"Bend over my knee."

I didn't connect "bend over my knee" with the possibility of a spanking. *Okay. This was a little weird.* I bent over his knee, realizing at the last moment the vulnerability of my position. I looked over my shoulder. He held his newspaper, rolled into a tight tube.

"Yell," he whispered as he began walloping the side of his chair with the newspaper.

I still didn't get it. Finally it dawned on me. I began to yell, not knowing what I was supposed to sound like. "Ouch! Ouch!" I bellowed, getting into the spirit of the thing. My dad kept thrashing the side of his chair.

"Don't. Ever. Talk. To. Your. Mother. Like. That. Again."

We looked up at the same time to see my mom, arms akimbo, standing motionless on the bottom step. I looked at Mom, then Dad, then back at Mom. A beat of silence, then the cackle of laughter. I laughed with them but I didn't get the joke.

My dad was a feminist. He would have never used that word to describe himself. Nonetheless. He nursed me through the night every time I got sick. Wise and careful. Tender and reassuring. He knew the country remedies he learned from *his* mom. He knew how to bring down my fever when it spiked (he bathed my pulse points with rubbing alcohol and if it got really bad, he would gently ease me into a lukewarm bath, not heeding my screams and pleading whines), how to ease my coughs (warm whiskey, honey and lemon juice), how to bring boils to a head (the membrane peeled from the inside of an eggshell and placed over the ulcer), and how to lull me to sleep with soft songs hummed under his breath.

Mom took care of me during the day in the way it is with mothers. She kept me quiet, brought dry toast and juice, took me to the doctor, and changed my sweaty sheets. She read aloud to me for hours. Dad relieved her when he came in from work. Before he changed out of his fatigues and removed the faint odor of starch and brass polish that said "Dad", he would come and place his coarse hand on my forehead. If I were really sick he watched over me through the night, sitting in a chair beside my bed.

I wasn't sick that often, and while those memories are the strongest, I remember the times he came home after work and played with me. Me and every other kid in the housing area. They all came by, "can Lenny come out and play?" He taught me how to ride a two-wheeler and played catch with me every night when I decided I would be the first girl to be a professional baseball player.

"You can be anything you want," he told me. I believed it.

Who I am, is shaped by the friendships of my youth as my family moved around the world. We were an amazing spectrum of colors and kinds, instinctively knowing that we were more alike than different. We all liked baseball and paper dolls, fireworks and hamburgers, riding our bikes and playing pretend. We didn't expect that we would all be the same and our differences didn't divide us. Our parents may have struggled with it when the Department of Defense ordered the complete integration of the military from housing to schools, medical facilities to swimming pools, companies to battalions. It was the way my life looked and I didn't know any different.

Life was an adventure where everywhere was safe.

"Come on!" I shouted to Peachy as I stomped through rain puddles on the way to school.

Peachy was Filipino, pale brown skin with exotic, tropical features and straight black hair. Heavy curtains diffused the light in Peachy's quarters. Useful in the Philippines, in island dwellings where bright light, the conduit of heat, was shut out. The muted interior was familiar to her family. Perhaps in the Pacific Northwest it served the purpose of holding heat in. It became another familiar thread in the tapestry of my experiences. Her grandma lived with her family, so instead of light, their home was filled with the aromas of ginger, garlic, onions, lemon grass, bay, and padan that her grandmother used in her cooking.

My new yellow rain boots were just dandy for making huge splashes. Peachy, more sedate and less enamored of the rain, trailed behind me trying to avoid the water splattering in all directions. The soggy brown hem of my dress hung below my slicker.

"Come on!" I yelled to Diane one spring day. I found a patch of daffodils and thought it would be wonderful to pick some for our mothers. Diane was my best friend and academic rival. Her mom was Japanese and her father was black. She shook her head no.

"I think someone planted them." She said.

"There's so many, they won't miss a few."

"I don't think so . . ."

I picked a dozen, more or less, enough for a huge fist full and headed home.

"Here, Mom, these are for you."

She gazed at me suspiciously. "Where did you get them?"

"Oh, I just found them growing." This wasn't going as well as I thought it would. I expected hugs and kisses.

"Sgt. Collins called me a little while ago."

Uh-oh.

"He said he saw you and Diane picking his flowers."

Uh-oh.

"Oh, Mom, Diane didn't pick any, only me. She was too chicken."

"I want you to take these flowers back to Sgt. Collin's quarters right now and apologize."

The mild guilt I felt when Diane tried to stop me turned into searing shame.

"Sgt. Collins, I'm Sgt. Tuttle's daughter and I stole your flowers. I'm sorry," I said through gulping sobs. If I was brave enough to steal I needed to be brave enough to face the consequences.

"Help me weed the garden next Saturday and we'll be even," he said.

"Come on!" I yelled to Rosita and Ivy on the playground during recess. Rosita's family was from Argentina. Her long straight black hair hung to her waist and her equally long legs galloped beside me as we pretended to be horses. Ivey galloped with us. I wanted blue-black skin like Ivey's. I wanted large black eyes with long lashes like Rosita's instead of my mousey brown hair and muddy hazel eyes.

"Let's sneak off the playground and pick wild strawberries." Those wild strawberries were enchanted fruit, their flavor more brilliant and untamed than cultivated ones.

"I don't know . . ." Rosita began.

"Come on—it'll be fun."

"Not me," Ivey retorted. "Last time we got in trouble."

Drawn into a world of imaginings and possibilities, I longed to discover the unknown. I was sure I was magic and that magic would find me.

"Come on!" I called to Vicky and Rosanne and Peachy. Vicky lived at the other end of our building. Her parents were Puerto Rican. Dinner at her house was a much of an adventure as it was at Peachy's. Peachy and Rosanne lived in the building facing ours.

"Let's go to the fort!"

Saturday we hiked single file through the massive forest behind the housing area to our special place. We discovered a tree felled by a storm whose upturned roots extended into the ground three feet and curved above ground another two feet. Natural ledges held our cups, flowers, balls, and sweaters. We swept the dirt with branches and played games of pretend. And we vowed to keep our special place secret from grown ups.

Sometimes I went alone. I packed my blue railroad scarf with a peanut butter and jelly sandwich, a Band-Aid, and an empty jar with a lid, bundled it up and tied it around a stick, then headed for the fort. Sometimes I used my jar to catch tadpoles. Sometimes I caught fat bumblebees lingering on clover blossoms. Occasionally dark would slip up on me as I trudged home after a day full of adventures and I would run into MPs (Military Police) searching for me.

In the summer of 1957, the Cold War raged, Jack Kerouac published *On the Road* and Governor of Arkansas, Orval Faubus, used National Guard troops to block court-ordered school integration. Three weeks later, one thousand soldiers of the 101st Airborne Division, escorted nine black students into the all-white Central High School in Little Rock. Meanwhile, Ft. Lewis, Washington, was a world away.

Who I am, sir, is a person of faith. I was nurtured in a church with no boundaries. Summer meant Vacation Bible School at the post chapel. A slew of kids were rounded up into general age groups and trotted from activity to activity. My favorite time was at the end of the day when we crowded into the auditorium to be led in singing by our music director.

"Now wider and wider our circle expands," he sang in his smoky baritone.

"Viva La Company!" we replied joyfully.

"We sing to our comrades in faraway lands," he continued then pointed to us.

"Viva la company!" we escalated our decibel level. And then the mighty chorus:

"Viva la, Viva la, Viva l'amour
Viva la, Viva la, Viva l'amour
Viva l'amour, viva l'amour
Viva La Company!"

Long live love, long live love, long live this company! Not exactly a song one thinks of connected with Vacation Bible School but we sang it full out as if the words were written for us. God was like that. Unabashed love connecting us in air we breathed, the songs we sang, and the gravity that held us to the earth. And God was in the friends who filled my days.

We all, Protestants, Catholics, and Jews shared the same worship space. Friday evening, the rabbi's assistant rolled out the Torah Ark and set the altar for the cantor and rabbi to lead the Shabbos service. Early mass was at eight a.m. Sunday morning. The Ark rolled back, the crucifix placed on the wall behind the altar and the fonts inside the door replenished with holy water.

After Sunday school, I hurried into the chapel to help our (Protestant) chaplain and his assistant take up the missals (the weekly service for mass) and put out the bulletins for our service. The assistant turned the crucified Christ on the cross toward the wall; an empty cross now faced the pews. We Protestants came from many traditions- Baptist, Methodist, Lutheran, Episcopalian, Presbyterian, Pentecostal—but we all worshipped together. The service took on the flavor of the chaplain du jour. We all knew where the Torah Ark was and that there were two sides to the cross. We shared spiritual space and it felt right, reinforcing the idea that we different and alike at the same time. It is still who I am—a person who believes all religions point to the same God.

My friends and I were in Brownies together. I don't remember one girl in my class who wasn't a Brownie. It was magical:

"Twist me and turn me and show me an elf.

I looked in the mirror and saw myself!"

I leaned over and peered into a mirror set on the floor and surrounded by plants to make it look like a pond in the middle of a forest. In it I spied

Rosita and Rosanne and Diane, and Peachy and Ivy and Vicky. I gazed in their faces and saw myself reflected there. Because they were my friends, I knew us to be beautiful in our differences. And because they were my friends, what is different isn't foreign. Because they were my friends, and because I loved them, God was very large.

I was nine years old when Soviet missiles based in Cuba, pointed at major targets in the United States. It was 1961. In school we practiced atomic bomb drills, crouching under our desks, trying to imagine exactly what an atom bomb might be like. I carefully followed the teacher's instructions, sure in my belief that if I did exactly what I was told I would be safe from nuclear peril. In pictures, the mushroom clouds always exploded on the distant horizon and after a while, the drills became an opportunity to daydream and chatter, while we all pretended that everything was fine. I worried in a private way that didn't have words. Vaguely uneasy, the threat of nuclear war slipped in and out of my consciousness.

At home, I overheard muffled conversations between my mom and dad about missiles in Cuba, and that Cuba was very, very close to the United States. My friends and I experienced the menace viscerally. If I remembered to think of the immediate threat of war, the world tilted off its axis. When I forgot, it shifted back into familiar patterns until the next time a word or image crashed into my awareness. Dad was shipped overseas to work with nuclear warheads in Europe because of his high security clearance.

I didn't mind when my father went away. I missed him, but he was doing his job. He was everything the United States was supposed to stand for: liberty and justice for all. There was no question that my father could and would protect the entire world from bad things.

The summer before he left to work with nuclear warheads in Europe, we went camping at Crater Lake, Oregon. My mom and dad and I had just settled down into our sleeping bags. Though mid-summer, it was chilly in that part of Oregon. The tent flap was up and moonlight washed over the sky-leaning trees. Wood smoke from the campfire infused our pajamas and I breathed deep to take it in as I dropped off to sleep.

Suddenly a giant filled the doorway. A grizzly, taller than our tent, stood on his hind legs and pawed the air. I didn't have enough sense to be afraid. Dad would handle it.

The scratch of flint against steel followed the hollow, metallic sound of his Zippo lighter flipping open. He touched the flame to a box of tissues. Curious, I watched as the carton caught fire. My dad stood, moved toward the opening and waved the flaming box. The grizzly thunked to the ground with a guttural "oof" and lumbered away.

Dad methodically stomped out the fire, then turned and said, "Remember, fire is the one thing all animals are afraid of."

My seminal truth was reinforced. Dad could protect us from anything. *Got it, Dad? Good.* I turned over and drifted off to sleep. My dad was a soldier: to my mind a cross between Daniel Boone and Superman. Bears, nuclear war; it was all the same. I wanted to be just like my dad.

I am not much like my dad in lots of ways. I am a Democrat for one thing. And I am a troublemaker. I don't always *plan* on making trouble. I just don't try to avoid it. Trouble seems to get made when I am trying to do "the next right thing" and, to be completely honest, it shows up when I do "the next wrong thing" with equal conviction. I am a thinker and a struggler but after I think and struggle, if I am moved by the spirit or passion or impelled by some holy fire or just plain stupid, I act. It's not the same thing as wisdom. Any wisdom I possess comes after I trip over many, and sometimes oft repeated, ill-conceived actions.

But I *am* like my dad in some ways. Or I try to be. Like him, I want to live my life in service to something greater than myself. I want to put myself on the line when it counts. I want to be bound to large ideas that make the world a better place, so tightly bound, so impassioned that I am willing to dig a foxhole. I am prepared to make choices that don't insure my personal, emotional, or financial safety. But maybe, just maybe, my choices will contribute to a greater good. Those are the ways I want to be like my dad.

So you want to know who I am? Who all these homosexuals are, acting like they belong in and to the church? We are as unique and varied as the stars of the Milky Way. You are not asking the right question, I think. The question I put to you is the same one the Ethiopian eunuch asked Philip, "What is to prevent me from being baptized?"

And by extension, I would ask you, "What is to prevent me from being ordained?"

The implication inherent in both questions is, "Nothing."

My legs are tired. I want to sit down so bad I think I can mentally elevate the pew to meet my hindquarters. How am I going to last the entire meeting? I am not important to the process. I won't even make it as a footnote, but I burn with the conviction that I need to bear witness. I am learning that conviction doesn't prevent sore feet, calm a churning stomach, or brace shaky knees. But I am determined and I *will* keep standing.

The outcome of the debate and the vote about to unfold will forever alter my relationship with the Presbyterian Church. If I can't be ordained, then what? If the church doesn't want me, who will? What the fuck are you thinking, God?

Part of me believes that my witness will change the church, though there is no supporting evidence. I hold onto hope, pushed by the firm hand of God to my backside. If this is where God wants me then this is where I am going to be. Like many prophets before me, and many who will come after, I discovered that living out one's call comes with a price. Most of all I learned not to assume that my understanding of success and God's are the same.

This meeting is personal to my core. I have been trying to answer God's prodding as faithfully as I can for as long as I can and I have reached an end that appears to be very much dead. I know it's not about me, but it is. It is also about many others, all those in the closet and in ministry and those out of the closet, pursuing ordination. Really, it's about more than ordination. It's about the people in the pews and their sons and daughters, uncles and aunts, cousins and friends being acceptable, no longer second-class spiritual citizens of the kingdom of God. The vote taken this day will be a matter of justice and I passionately believe that the church needs to be on the front line. It is also personal because some here have worked tirelessly to insure I would not be ordained and others have risked their reputations by supporting me.

There are many gray heads here today. Many men in suits and ties. The women are in suits, too, for the most part. Made up and coiffed as if they worked for a downtown corporation. Oh, wait. They do. The moderator is a lesbian. Not common knowledge. She is very well liked. Bred, born and raised in the Presbyterian Church. Her ministry is with the elderly and she is gifted at it. But I wouldn't want to be her, even if she is ordained, for the silent trauma she faces day in and day out. Today she will moderate the debate and hear the opinions of friends and colleagues one never wants to hear.

I recognize few other faces. Not many that I know well. I wonder if anyone will speak in favor of the ordination of gays and lesbians. I don't have to guess who will speak against. And I don't see anyone who might be equipped (and willing) to credibly defend the proposition. The debate might be fairly one sided.

I am pretty sure being faithful doesn't always look like success for prophets. At least not in the ways we usually think about it. I mean none of the Biblical prophets were rich. Even Jesus and the disciples lived off the generosity of others. Public prophetic success is changing people's hearts and minds. Personal success is responding faithfully to God's call. Neither is well paid.

I continue to stand, feeling powerless and alone and very much a failure. Then I remember my dad's faithfulness to an outcome he couldn't count on and how he persevered in the face of death and destruction because of his commitment to a larger idea. He taught me that there are things worth struggling and dying for. Good for me that struggling was all that was being asked.

Mary Boney Sheats, my professor and mentor in college, gently encouraged me saying, "You may not get there, but the ones to follow will be able to go further, and those after that even further, until the work is done." The longer I stood the more certain I became that I would never be called to a church. But I had to believe that, somehow, it mattered. Somehow, I was being faithful. Somehow, this small act was enough. That, somehow, I was a brave little soldier.

" . . . we ask all these things in the name of the Father, the Son and the Holy Spirit. Amen," the minister's prayer winds to close. The gavel comes down. The debate begins.

"To do the work of others is slavery. To do the work of God is true liberation."

—Anonymous

## Chapter 4  *The Call Thing*

TO MAKE CHANGE IN the Presbyterian Church always begins by commissioning a study. If you don't like the results of the study, you send out for another one. And another. This can take years that, truth be told, is the point. Put it off for as long as you can and when you can't put it off anymore, debate it, and take a vote. Much like an amendment to the U.S. constitution, it takes a majority vote of two thirds of the presbyteries. Presbyteries are the representative bodies of local churches to the national church. Kind of like the relationship of states to the federal government. The vote being taken today is to determine if they will ordain gay men and lesbians to the ministry.

But I'm putting the propellers before the cockpit. You have to do a lot more than say you are heterosexual to be ordained in the Presbyterian Church (USA). In theory, you first experience God's call in your life. Then you meet with the session, the group, elected from people in the congregation that manages the business of your local church. Then you go to seminary for a Masters of Divinity where you take Greek, Hebrew, theology, ethics, church history, church polity, and pastoral care. During that time, you come "under care" of your presbytery's "candidates committee" that meets with you multiple times during your seminary career and votes on whether or not they recommend you for ordination. Finally, after you graduate, pass a two-day ordination exam, assuming the faculty also recommends you for ordination, *and* you find a church willing to hire you, *then* you can be ordained to ministry.

But the first thing, before any other thing, is receiving a call from God. Call is experienced in many ways: as a slow unfolding, as a zap of lightning, or, sometimes, as openness to unanticipated discernment that arrives quietly but leaves you shaken. Responding to a call can take moments or decades. It all depends on the one being called and the call to which one is invited to respond. It can be as elegant as prayerful insight and as inelegant as a knockdown drag-out between you and God.

It's hard to define the concept of call. I've tried and come up with different answers at different times of my life. I can point to extravagant spiritual experiences that shouted at me, the wary un-listener. Or whispers in the night that enveloped me for the moment and faded in the light of day. Call is not so much words as it is feeling. Not the imposition of feeling but the rise of relationship beyond words. Those feelings, the beyond-word-ness, are central to my first memories.

Vilosnes sur Meuse tasted like stones and earth and wet sunshine. The small village of three hundred and fifty people layered centuries of history in its cobbled paths and ancient architecture. Lazy rivers gurgled and tripped over moss-covered stones and meandered under ancient bridges. River fishing, gardening, farming, and the rising of dough and baking of bread set the rhythm of life. The sharp clap of wood being split, the meow of a mouser, the solid opening and closing of ancient doors and the crunch of rocks underfoot blended into the jazz riff of sound that underscored every day. The smells of water, fish, and earth braided together and shifted with the changing of the seasons. It would be our home for the next four years.

Our apartment faced the road that led into the village. Its heavy wooden door, set back from the stone façade, led into a cozy interior. Rough plaster walls, yellowed lace curtains draped dramatically over ancient windows, and mismatched furniture crouched in every corner. Dim bulbs cast puddles of light, hinting at secrets waiting to be discovered. The faint scent of Madam Buvelo's (pronounced biv-a-low) cooking permeated every room. We lived next door to the Buvelos and visited and shared meals often. Madam Buvelo was a country French cook with a pot always on the back burner to which she added the odds and ends of vegetables and meat, creating a rich stock for the soups we ate with our evening meal. She took great care in choosing the ingredients for her soups and called the result *cuisine*. All this would become part of my everyday life. I learned the smells, colors, and textures of this world. It was my first real sense of home.

Susie was my one doll, a gift from my grandmother on my first birthday. I adored her and carried her everywhere. She was a black rag doll with yarn cornrows and a beatific smile, made for cuddling and important, private conversations. Madam Buvelo created a couture wardrobe for her. Mom and I visited Mm. B. in the afternoons and she would help me pick fabrics and styles and buttons for Susie's clothes. Scraps and leftovers of material from dresses made for me were fashioned into dresses for Susie. Madam Buvelo created beautiful frocks for my beloved friend. Her elaborate and extravagant designs, her care and attention to detail, were my first experiences of nurturing the creation of beauty. I came to understand beauty as necessary. Each morning Susie and I dressed together for the day and I proudly paraded her and her lovely wardrobe everywhere I went.

The dirt road in front of where we lived was dry and dusty, the color of 'suntans', a type of military uniform my Daddy wore in the summer time. The fabric was light, the crease of his trousers crisp, the short sleeves of his shirt hinted at a very slight relaxing of military protocol and signaled, to me, long evenings of sunshine and play.

"How much do you love me?" Daddy asked as he swung me in the air each evening when he arrived home from work.

I squealed and squinched up my face thinking hard, hard, hard "Four nine six and three little ones!" I declared, confident it was the biggest number in the world.

Monsieur Buvelo apprenticed me in gardening. He took me by the hand, a basket in his other large paw, and we walked to the end of the village to our garden. I hitched double and triple steps to keep up with him, though he was not moving fast. Monsieur Buvelo was a big man with a purpose.

Beside us ran one of the three rivers that passed through our fishing village. A soft gurgle greeted us as we followed its banks to our garden. Sometimes we would see, two rivers over, barges lumbering through the several locks that raised or lowered to give them passage to the next section to be travelled. The odor of river and the scent of fish permeated the village on warm days. Monsieur Buvelo was not only a gardener he was also the village baker. It did not leave him much time to fish. He also tended to the rabbits that lived in hutches behind the kitchen. I think we eat them, though I am never told.

Monsieur Buvelo lived out loud. He had thick black hair, much longer than my Dad's spit-shine haircut, and a long, luxuriously droopy mustache. Had he not had such large white teeth his exuberant smile might have been lost beneath its cascade.

We often strolled through the garden past rows of strawberries. Their perfume wafted up suggesting the ripeness we would discover under the bowed green leaves. He would lean over to harvest them, his baggy trousers rising above his scuffed black shoes, his suspenders straining, white shirt billowing, while I meandered through the patch, listening to his simple explanations of strawberry tending while popping the ripest ones into my mouth. Sunshine warmed my face. Turning toward its heat, a frisson of awareness shot through my body. Something large and wonderful and wholly loving held me for the briefest moment.

"Oh la!" Monsieur Buvelo yelled, "Come here, Coney!"

I trundled over to inspect the lifted strawberry leaves, "Escargot," he breathed, smiling with satisfaction. "Es-car-go," he repeated. He was teaching me a new word. I looked to where he pointed. A large snail, whose shell was bigger than my small fist, had set up housekeeping in the garden.

"Mmmm," he groaned as he grinned and rubbed his stomach. I was pretty sure that he was teasing.

Winter came and I was enormously proud of my new, red wool snowsuit. It was scratchy but beautiful. Every morning, when I was finally bundled into it, my mother walked me to the bakery a block away. Snow would be shoved against the buildings haphazardly. My breath fogged the air as I skipped ahead, my boots crunching ice crystals all the way.

I pushed open the door to the bakery and warm air rushed out carrying with it the rich, complex scent of freshly baked baguettes. "Mmmm," I moaned, imitating Monsieur Buvelo. He pulled bread out of the oven and I saw *my* bread, the small loaf he made just for me each morning. He smiled, took it from the paddle, and wrapped it in white paper. 'La,' he said, handing it to me. I unzipped my snowsuit, tucked the warm bread inside, the end peeping out from under my chin, and zipped back up almost to the top.

'Au revoir!" I called as I ran out the door to my waiting mother. The heat of the small loaf made me giddy. I lowered my nose to snuffle the smell of the bread, breathing deeply all the way home. This was the best part of breakfast.

My room was small and cold. In the winter Mom tucked me between icy sheets, a hot, towel-wrapped brick at my feet. It was matchless luxury. Warmth slowly spread up my limbs into my chest and all the way to my nose that was tucked beneath the covers. I breathed deeply and caught a faint hint of the morning's bread. Magic permeated the warm, elemental scent and flung me into the same wordless place that captured me in the garden. Embraced in delight, I snuggled down into a wordless place of connectedness and mystery.

Often I rode with my mom the twenty-seven kilometers from our village to post in Verdun to pick up my dad from work. No matter where we were on post everyone stopped when "Taps" played and the flag lowered at the onset of dusk. I got out of the car and stood next to my dad in the twilight, my hand over my heart until the flag was reverently folded and the last bugle note disappeared into the impending dark.

The moment drew us together as we silently acknowledged something greater than any one of us. Something connected us beyond words and lingered between us when we returned to ordinary time. My young heart yearned towards everyone who stopped with me expanding to take in the air, the sky, the disappearing sun, and the solid earth in those holy sundowns.

In late spring, the week of my third birthday, Mom posted a note on the heavy wooden door to our apartment that faced the street. The children of the village were all invited to come celebrate my birthday, Tuesday at noon. Cake and ice cream would be served. She figured the school-aged kids would be in school and only the preschool children would come.

A knock on the door heralded the arrival of the first three children, starched and pressed and ready to party. Another knock and another group of children. Another knock and it became clear that every child of every age was showing up at our doorstep. Within the hour all the children in the village—along with their parents—presented themselves at our door. The cake and ice cream didn't last long. Mom got the inspired idea to serve cans of peaches we had in the cupboard. When the peaches were gone she rifled through the pantry and served whatever she could find. What was planned as small afternoon entertainment for preschoolers became a party for the entire village. The *International Herald Tribune,* an English language Paris newspaper, did a write up on it that my mom carried around in her wallet for the longest time.

I consider myself French though I was born in the United States. I first learned to talk in France, often switching between French and English. My earliest memories are of Vilosnes sur Meuse. My first dog, Rheep, played with me there in the fields and by the riverbanks. I am French not only because I ate my first real food there, smelled soup simmering every day on Madam Buvelo's stove, saw rabbits munching happily in their hutches, fish splayed for perusal at the market, lettuce, fat and sweet, in the garden but because being there connected me to hundreds and hundreds of years of human history, culture, and belief. All the while, I remain an American filled with a sense of promise, destiny, and unlimited possibilities. My true hometown, however, will always be an obscure village in France where I first experienced family, community, God, and the vague feelings I later recognized as call.

What is to give light must endure burning.

—Viktor Frankl

# Chapter 5    *Encountering Evil on the Road*

THE THING YOU CAN'T avoid when getting it on with God is the question of evil. People of faith must acknowledge evil. Name it. Shame it. Smack it. Challenge it. It makes me a little twitchy sometimes when things are called evil that aren't really evil at all, but are just other than you. It's easy to call things that make us uncomfortable or that require complex thought, evil. I am completely aghast when true evil is ignored. Like racism, sexism, homophobia, ableism, ageism, (all the isms that dehumanize), genocide, people dying from hunger, lack of clean water, or lack of healthcare. Those kinds of things.

As a working and not an academic theologian, I'm going to define evil as that which dehumanizes or demeans another by the intent of morally conscious person and the arrogance of humanity in its destruction of creation. And for sin,—which is separate from evil—my working definition is the one we used in seminary: that which separates us from God. I understand sin to be breaking relationship, missing the mark, choosing separation.

Growing up rooted in the unfettered love of God didn't prepare me for the evil I encountered early and often. Or maybe it did. I unfolded in a world of innocence. Of joy. Of mystery. I trusted God. So when I encountered evil I didn't question God, I wondered how people could do such unspeakable things to one another.

In June of 1962, we headed to Germany to be with my dad. I would miss the Farm, where we stayed while we waited to join Dad, but I looked forward to getting back to my regular life. I was ten years old and the Cuban Missile Crisis was coming to an end. Mom and I received orders to ship overseas late that summer. The Army put our furniture in storage, packed our household goods, and sent them on ahead of us. Mom and I drove to Seattle to have our 1959 Chevy loaded onto a ship for Dad to pick up at the port in Germany.

Then we flew to Atlanta, the initial leg of our trip, to visit my only sibling, Sherry, eleven years my senior, and a WAF (Women's Air Force) until she married an Airman and was released from service. Back then married women were not allowed to serve. She and her husband were stationed at Maxwell Air Force Base in Montgomery.

Heat sucked the breath out of me when we exited the plane to the tarmac. We boarded the plane in Seattle with temperatures hovering in the 60's. We touched down in Atlanta to ninety-eight degrees of heat and humidity. I couldn't get into the air- conditioned airport fast enough. Sherry's husband, Bobby, picked us up and drove us the three hours to Montgomery. Bobby was as southern of a boy as you could get. His black hair looked like Elvis's when Elvis was in the service but he was stocky and solid, leaning to plump and lacking Elvis' natural grace. He hailed from Tallassee, Alabama and grew up dirt poor. The Air Force was his salvation.

I struggled to untangle his slow, syrupy drawl. He regaled us with the antics of my three nieces: one infant and two toddlers. I drifted out of the conversation, my head pressed against the window toward the passing landscape an unending parade of red clay and scrub pines that lined the road from Atlanta to Montgomery.

We stopped to fill up with gas shortly after we crossed the state line into Alabama. I crawled out of the back and made my way into the ramshackle station as the pump ticked off tenths of gallons of gas. Inside, a few candy bars were stacked haphazardly next to the register. A large fan whirred, circulating heat and dust, and the smoke from the attendant's cigarette. A thin layer of grease blanketed the isles of rickety metal shelves stacked with car oil, chewing tobacco, and pork rinds.

Rounding the end, I confronted twin notices hanging over two rust stained water fountains. One sign declared "whites only" the other, "coloreds only." They weren't hand-lettered, but very official looking for the dilapidated space they adorned. Things were definitely not right in the state of Alabama.

"Why can't everyone drink out of the same water fountain?" I demanded of my mom.

"Wait till we get to the car," she shushed me under her breath.

I couldn't understand. It made no sense. I expected her to take on what I now realize was a hundred years or so of entrenched racism. Well, if she wouldn't I would! In defiance I marched over to the water fountain labeled "colored" and drank.

Hadn't they heard of the Declaration of Independence or the Constitution in Alabama? Someone needed to make it a priority to inform the states about their federal obligations. After all, didn't I make that pledge every day in my classroom?

"... one nation, under God, indivisible, *with liberty and justice for ALL.*"

And I was just an ordinary citizen. I refused to believe that either document was ever intended to exclude any citizen from full partnership! The writings that established our country were as important to me as the Bible. I'm not even sure if I distinguished between the two. I still find both to be sacred, calling us to be our brightest, best, and deepest selves. If only water fountains were the extent of the evil our nation perpetrates. It would be years before I began to understand the insidious, systemic nature of racism.

A few days later Mom and I boarded the USS Rose in New York City and began our trans-Atlantic crossing to Bremerhaven, Germany. The ship was a lumbering, gray troop transport ship fitted for traveling dependents. We pulled away from the city that rose from the docks like a futuristic vision. Brown water lapped against the sides of the ship as the tug towed us out to open sea. We eased past the Statue of Liberty, elegant and full of promise. I was transfixed by the beauty and majesty of this testament to who we Americans claimed to be. This. Not the rusty filling station in rural Alabama. This.

I always feel a part of the whole. The whole country. The whole world. The whole church. Even when I am deeply connected to a particular place. It is all a part of me and I am a part of it, a two-way belonging that defines a life-long struggle. Born in the South, recently from the Pacific Northwest, early from France, and now plowing the waves to Germany.

"Seattle is mine, Mom." I declared as we watched the land recede. "And so is McMinnville and Portland and Atlanta."

"Chicago is yours, too," she joined in, "because Daddy was scouted by the Cubs there."

"So it's really, *really* mine!"

"Is New York yours?"

"New York and the Statue of Liberty. And Mount Rushmore and the Grand Canyon. It's all mine!"

I didn't have words to claim my tribe and the expansive sense that all of America is home for me. And I couldn't access in any real way what it might mean that Alabama was "mine." The shore receded and my heart ached with competing aches: the bitter ache of leaving home tangled with the sweet ache of going home to my dad. I am an American, defender of freedom and human rights. And yet I am from a land with complex, ancient, and textured histories, entwined with a culture, and anchored in an ethos America has yet to experience.

Before the day was out, we lost sight of land and the ocean stretched to the end of every horizon. Enchanted by the dancing water, I spent most of the day hanging over the rail, looking into the blue green depths of the sea, feeling the salty spray on my face, listening to the constant rush of steel cutting through water, my headscarf fluttering in the breeze. For a long while, seagulls followed us then turned back, their distant keening our last connection with land.

Our small cabin had two bunks; Mom let me have the top one. I lay on my stomach and stared out the brass porthole. Waves foamed as the ship plowed a furrow through the ocean. God was there and I knew it. Knew it more deeply than I had known anything before. Somewhere in the middle of the ocean I began letting go of small ideas about God. My heart stretched so wide I thought it would break into a thousand pieces. My thoughts opened beyond how I knew to think, like the mouth of a hungry baby bird. I stopped trying to understand. I fell in love with the dolphins that sometimes frolicked close to the ship. I held my breath each time we spotted a whale, a cord of connection spiraling between us.

Suddenly God was both near and far, expansive and intensely close. Knowable. Touchable. Infinitely mysterious and unfathomable but as close as my breath. I began to trust the buoyancy and to revel in the vastness that I called God. Like so much I experienced I was a part of it and it was a part of me and I wanted to be stay on the ocean forever.

" I'm going to join the Navy and be the captain of a ship," I told my Mom.

"Your Dad would be very unhappy if you joined the Navy," she responded, completely missing the point.

"Well, I want to live on a ship for the rest of my life and I want to drive it through the ocean! If that means I have to join the Navy then I will." A pause and a thought, "The Army doesn't have ships does it?"

I still love being near the ocean, hearing the hiss of waves as they hit shore and remove themselves back into the sea. I love the smell of salt and marine life, the stiff breezes, and the promise of vastness. But the ocean feels too anchored to the land at the beach. I crave deep-ocean, suspended between lands, where God is unleashed, not tied to the particulars of history or geography.

Every culture's experience of the Sacred is fascinating in their differences and dependent on their landscapes. Desert people experience the vastness of God and hear God's voice in the wind. Forest dwellers experience the lushness and nearness of God. I first saw God in a garden in Vilosnes, in the wheat fields of Oregon and the forests, and splendor of snow-capped Mount Rainier. Then I encountered God in the vast, daunting, joy of the ocean.

It was on board ship that I made the connection between spirituality and politics. I left the United States believing in the ideal of America with a fierce passion. America was supposed to be the land of freedom, fairness, and justice. We were the land of the underdog who made good. We were the people who weren't supposed to be afraid of freedom. We shared a commitment to those common values. And those ideals just happened to mirror my understanding of the teachings of Jesus.

I wanted to be president of the United States. It was my destiny. I wanted to be president not for fame or glory, but to lead my country into the future. One evening at supper I shyly shared my dream with my mother. The gentleman sharing our table chuckled, "There never has been and never will be a woman elected president."

"Why not?" I asked.

"Because girls can't be president."

"Is it in the Constitution that girls can't be president?"

"No, but it will never happen."

"Then I'll be the first," I declared, absolutely certain that neither God nor the Constitution discriminate.

That night I began writing my inaugural address on the back of paper bags that were slipped between the rails in the corridors for weak-stomached sea travelers. I wrote passionately about reforming prisons (prisoners would be educated and given the opportunities to work and live with dignity—and they would be treated with respect while in prison) and improving public education (schools would have more teachers and more special classes for anyone who needed them and students would be a part of the decision-making), and enough jobs so that everyone could make a decent living. I scribbled furiously about the importance of the United Nations (peace was an urgent concern in a time when the possibility of nuclear war was very real).

Last, but not least, I proposed an immediate, fully integrated society. I would be the first woman president of the United States and I would do something about that terrible situation in Alabama.

My first conscious experience of evil was racism. Horrified and sickened, I made a pact with myself to stand up to it wherever I could. My second encounter with evil was sexism, intensely personal, though too often seen as benign. I would experience this kind of not so subtle, pervasive sexism exponentially as I grew into womanhood. My next encounter with evil followed soon after.

Our ship pulled into port at Bremerhaven, Germany, and my heart began to race. We disembarked and were taken to the train station for the final leg of our journey. The train clattered and swayed along the tracks all night as we tossed in the sleeper. I couldn't wait to see my dad who had been deployed nearly a year before we joined him. And then there he was, standing straight and tall, familiar in his starched fatigues, watching for us from the platform. I abandoned Mom to gather our things, clambered down the steep train steps, and threw myself at him.

"You love me?" Dad asked as he hugged me close and swung me around.

"Yes!"

"How much?" This was our ritual.

"Four, nine, six and three little ones!" I laughed as I hung on to his neck. I was home.

Our quarters were part of a collection of large buildings. Two stairwells with wide banks of stairs and landings dominated each end. From the door at street level, going downstairs to a long open basement, a row of storage units, one chain-link compartment for each apartment, lined the entire length of the building. Bikes and sleds and things that didn't fit it the quarters but were too important to leave behind were stored here. Two communal washers huddled at one end. For four floors, identical metal doors stood sentry on each side of the landing leading into individual quarters.

The fifth floor landing was the entry into an enchanted territory. Like the basement, the attic also ran the length of the building. Pockets of light peeked in through dormer windows that peppered the backside of the building. The space became the repository of our collective imaginations, from footraces on rainy days to dreams of becoming superheroes as we leaned out the windows way-too-far. We shared our space with the clothesline that our moms used on rainy days, just incorporating the hanging clothes into our games. They became racing tracks or forests or ghosts.

Sometimes my friend, Edie, and I put down an army blanket in the fifth floor landing and played paper dolls. Not your cut-out-of-a-book paper dolls, but ones we drew ourselves. Mostly, it was a way to pretend. We invented stories. Sometimes Amelia Earhart and Abigail Adams would be friends. Other days it might be Dolly Madison and Florence Nightingale. Abigail Adams was my favorite. I read her biography and thought she was just great.

"Remember the Ladies," she wrote to her husband at the Constitutional Convention, "for all men would be tyrants if they could."

No matter how dire the circumstances we manufactured in our imaginations, our heroines saved the day.

The bröchen man drove around the housing area in his truck every day, selling fresh bread and treats. He doled out candies to the children for our few pfennigs. We poured out of our apartments, clutching the Deutsche marks our moms gave us to buy bread, the moment his bell tinkled.

"Gummi Bears, bitte." And he would take a paper cone from its stack and scoop multi-colored gummi bears into it for a few pfennings.

"Danke!" We sang, as we popped a white or red or green bear into our mouths, the flavors exploding between our teeth. "Danke!"

The entire housing area was surrounding by farmers' fields. Next to the school rows of cabbages, potatoes, and sugar beets proliferated. Sometimes the farmer planted small sections of green peas. We would sneak into the fields and eat sugar beets or peas after we scraped the dirt off on our jeans. If the farmer saw us he would run after us with a BB gun, scattering us in different directions. Vineyards surrounded the housing area on three sides, ascending a hill. At the top, an "eagle's nest" crouched among a scattering of trees, one of many Nazi lookouts throughout Germany that were named after Hitler's famed home.

In the summer I set up camp in the eight by eight, concrete bunker to keep a watch out for Nazis. The view took in most of Heilbronn, the city next to our base. Leaning over the half wall, you could see the Neckar River and the expanse of fields surrounding our housing area, heavy with produce in the summer and autumn. Marching neatly up the surrounding hills, grapes fell from their formalized vines in weighty clusters. I snitched some of those grapes, warm from the afternoon sun, and popped them between my teeth, spattering their intense juice into my mouth. A honey wagon, an open wagon heaped with manure-saturated hay, lumbered its way down a cobblestoned street toward the fields. The smell that rose from steaming cow patties at my grandparents' dairy farm was identical to the scent wafting from the honey wagon. Home and home intersected in scents and purpose. The languid odors of damp earth, sun drenched grapes, and 'honey wagons' permeated the bunker. And every day I climbed the hill to the eagle's nest to keep the world safe from Nazis.

Our first vacation was to the Army Recreation Area in Garmisch. Garmisch is a beautiful Alpine village in the section of Germany known as Bavaria, just across the border from Austria. Dad played golf every day and Mom and I went on tours. We hiked into Neuschwanstein; a magical castle built by Ludwig the II that stepped out of the pages of a fairytale. Inside, room size paintings, elaborate woodcarvings, mirrors, and gilded fixtures dazzled us.

We explored Oberammergau, wondering through shops filled with woodcarvings and cuckoo clocks. We visited local cheese makers and chocolatiers. And though it was not in season, we walked around the stage of the Passion Play, imagining the Biblical drama. We toured monasteries that made liqueurs and custom beers. Every night we came home tired and excited. My cup was full. The world was filled with amazing, beautiful, and fantastical things.

Another day we visited the original Eagle's Nest in Berchtesgaden.

"The Eagle's Nest was built for Adolf Hitler's fiftieth birthday by his personal secretary and head of the Nazi Party, Chancellery Martin Bormann," the tour guide intoned, "Hitler spend time here with his mistress, Eva Braun."

The house was nowhere near as extravagant as Ludwig's, but the view was spectacular. We walked through the house and grounds knowing that fewer than twenty years had gone by since Hitler stood in this place, looking out at the same panorama, planning to take over the world. Twenty years seemed like ancient history to me, as far removed as the Revolutionary War or even cave men.

And then I saw Dachau. Our bus pulled into a gravel parking area and we crowded out. The atmosphere changed from light-hearted laughter and animated conversations on the bus to harsh, colorless silence as we disembarked. The overcast sky, a solid gray, blended with the gray buildings and the drab yard between.

The guide herded us together and began, "When women came into the camps with babies, the guards ripped them from their arms and, while the mothers watched, broke the baby's back over their knees, (here our guide mimes the act, creating a nauseating visual) and tossed the howling babies into a pile." I looked in the direction our guide tossed the imaginary, broken-backed baby and pictured a heap of wailing infants. I heard mothers screaming as they are led away, unable to protect, rescue, or comfort their children. I groped for my mother's hand, needing to feel something solid, warm, and real.

Next we were led to a shed housing a pile of coats and shoes. "When the prisoners were first brought in they were stripped of all their clothes. The Nazi soldiers went through them, looking for hidden money and jewelry or anything of value. Then the prisoners were given thin pajama-like uniforms to wear." We looked over the black and white pictures of prisoners in their striped pajamas, their identities confiscated as surely as their clothes. I squeezed my momma's hand harder, tighter, until my fingers hurt. How could people do this to each other? I had walked into a nightmare.

Miniature flags lined the walls of the room outside the "showers", a bright, colorful display of many nations screaming in stark contrast to the oppressive gray.

"Women and men were stripped of their uniforms," our guide contin- ued. "Cold, humiliated, they were forced to abandon modesty as they were sent into the large room expecting the small luxury of a shower. Instead, gas poured in from the ceilings as they fought and clawed to find a way out. There was none."

As our group paraded through the gas chamber I searched in vain for any way out. The ceiling? Walls? Concrete. Windows? Barred. Doors? Metal. In my world, there were always possibilities, and it horrified me to imagine being that powerless. There must be a way out that they missed. I couldn't find one. I began to panic and for the first time in my life I experienced visceral fear. I sidled closer to my mom. The tour continued.

Pictures of "Muselmann," the word coined to describe prisoners whose souls were methodically destroyed by the nightmarish, dehumanization of the camps, lined the walls. The photographs showed vacant-eyed people covered with abscesses, skeletally thin, and gray skinned. The Muselmann suffered to the point that they lost all sense of self. Powerless to resist the atrocities to which they were subjected, they shut down spiritually, intel- lectually, and emotionally while their bodies deteriorated.

"They were living corpses," our guide informed us as if it were not self-evident.

The parade of photographs formed a wordless tribute to those who survived and those who had not. The horrifying images gave witness to the evil to which we humans can descend.

We were ushered through the Krematoriam where prisoners were re- quired to shovel dead friends and family into the ovens and later remove the ashes and remaining pieces of bone. Finally, there were pictures of the liberation of the camp, of American soldiers riding into the camp to rescue the prisoners.

My dad fought in the Pacific. He saw his own horrors. But I knew that this was who my dad was: a liberator. His job was to stop things like this from ever happening or, if they did happen, his job was to save people. My dad was my hero. That day I realized he was also the world's hero.

Could I be like my Daddy and risk my life to fight evil? Could I be a hero?

I leaned into my mother's warmth, hungry for the security she offered as I took in the pain and horror. Questions I would struggle with the rest of my life were forged in those moments. Forever, my questions about the Sa- cred and the human, history and theology, politics and prayer, seek answers in those grim, gray rooms filled with the remains of the innocent and the stench of intolerance.

That day I left the camp in the safety of my mother's embrace. It did not occur to me that she was like other mothers and that there were things from which she could not protect me. We passed through the gates of the camp returning to a world filled with magic and color and sunlight. I did not know then but Dachau will be a part of me until the day I die.

We returned home and over the next weeks and months, my fear and outrage receded to tolerable levels. Back in school, I turned to my studies and friendships.

Toward the end of November, I walked up the flight of stairs to the next landing to spend the night with my friend, Edie. I hoped her Oma (Grandma) would come by and let me practice German or teach us to knit. The smell of schnitzel beckoned to me the moment I entered their quarters. On the table were kartoffelkloesse, small potato dumplings flavored with fresh parsley and a hint of nutmeg, and braised red cabbage, tangy and sweet. Edie's mom brought the schnitzel and bröchen to the table and we commenced our feast. Bröchen is a small German bread, somewhat larger than a roll and smaller than a loaf. It reminded me of the baguette Monsieur Buvelot made for me each morning.

At nine o'clock, we went to bed giggling and talking under the covers. At eleven, the doorbell rang. It was my mother who called me over to her and said in hushed tones, "President Kennedy has been shot."

Edie and I started to cry while Mom spoke with Edie's parents. We scooted back to bed where we sat, tensed under the covers, each grasping a knitting needle, sure that we would be next.

The president of the United States shot and killed? Another certainty I didn't even know was a certainty, shattered. If this was true, that someone would assassinate our president, what else was true? If the possibility of nuclear war was true, what else is true? If it is true that people can be discriminated against because of the color of their skin, what else is true? If Dachau is true, what else is true?

Edie and I cried and talked. We held each other. Then I remembered the chain of command. There *were* things we could count on. There were ways to survive, to go on after something horrible happens. My dad told me that in the American army, it doesn't matter if you lose your commanding officer. Command moves down the chain of rank, each soldier enabled to take up the mantle of leadership, down to the lowest private. If that were true, then maybe we would make it through this.

President Kennedy's death was a blow to us all. Our communal grief was palpable. Any political event, especially one so large and tragic, put our troops both at home and around the world on heightened alert. Our nation was vulnerable. We needed to be ready for any threats. Soldiers and, by default, their families, geared up to high alert status. How long it lasted, I do not know. Once again, it became a way of life.

As a woman and a lesbian I wear the first hand scars of the injury done to my soul by sexism, heterosexism, and the not so subtle message that I am "less than." I also carry within me secondary scars of evil. As a white person, I the carry the secondary scars of racism, as a non-Jew, the secondary scars of Nazism. As a citizen, the secondary scars of violence. As a human being, the secondary scars of intolerance.

I guess I made that up, secondary scars, or maybe I heard it in another context, but what I mean is that I and we carry in our persons not only the consequences of evil that has been done to us but also the evil that is done to others. We are not separate from that which is perpetrated on others. We are injured either by our complicity or our compassion, whether conscious or not. It is those scars that make it impossible for me to remain silent on the behalf of others.

God calls us to confront evil with love and love seems like an awfully flimsy weapon given the depth of evil we are capable of perpetrating on one another. But the activity of love is justice and God enlists human souls to do justice and *be* justice as the antidote to evil.

Take the whole kit
with the caboodle
Experience life
don't deplore it
Shake hands with time
don't kill it
Open a lookout
Dance on a brink
Run with your wildfire
You are closer to glory
leaping an abyss
than upholstering a rut

—James Broughton

# Chapter 6    *Dancing on the Brink*

IS THERE ANY WAY to talk about call without talking about dancing on the brink? That probably should have been a statement instead of a question. My mom laughed when I told her I felt called to ministry because she had seen me make wild, unruly decisions and live into them. Sometimes with great success. Mostly, not so much. I make fierce choices wrapped in a swath of naïveté. I cannot tell my story truthfully if I do not share the times I danced and teetered on the brink.

We travelled in another troop transport ship on our way back to the States in the fall of 1965. Dad was assigned to Special Forces, the 101st Airborne, Ft. Bragg, North Carolina. The Viet Nam war escalated and the civil rights movement in the United States gathered momentum and power.

We settled into our quarters, a small brick, two-bedroom, one bath, house that I loved. Actually, I loved every home we lived in. Unpacking and rediscovering each item of household goods, every doll and puzzle, every book—and my bike! As I found a new home for each item on a nook or shelf, the house settled into that conundrum of unknown and familiar.

Now I was really in the South. Not just for a visit, but for the next while. My teacher spoke with a North Carolina drawl. I discovered there are differences between a low country South Carolina drawl, an Alabama lilt, a Tennessee twang, and a south Georgia slide. My mother tongue now included "sugah," honey, and darlin' right along with danke, bitte, petit poulet, and cherie.

Dorothy was my first new friend and she reminded me of Ivy, one of my special friends when we had been stationed in Ft. Lewis. Her dark skin shone with the lanolin rubbed into it by her mother, leaving a soft, unnameable perfume. I envied her thick braids and large doe eyes. She lived two houses down and we palled around after school most days.

Right before her dad was transferred to his next station of duty we went into downtown Raleigh to see a movie. It was a big adventure for us to go off base. We ambled up to the ticket window and asked for two tickets. The older man behind the glass stared at us long and hard then shook his head.

"We're sold out. Y'all go ahead on and git outta here."

Dorothy grabbed my hand and started to pull me away as the next person in line asked for a ticket. And got one!

"Hey!" I screeched. "You do too have tickets!"

"Come on." Dorothy urged, a tinge of panic in her voice.

I turned to her in disbelief. Why wouldn't this guy sell us tickets?

He leaned into the small portal where money was passed and said, "We do not let coloreds and whites to sit together. Now get along."

Dorothy was dragging me away while I kept bawling, "This is the United States of America! You can't do this! I'm calling the police!"

"Stop it." Dorothy begged. "Please."

I was angry, she was scared, and our whole day was ruined. Colored? Colored? So what! It's not FAIR! This was wrong! I huffed and yelled and worked myself into a righteous dervish by the time my mom picked us up and on the entire ride back to post. Dorothy got quieter and quieter. How little I knew about so much. I wanted her to be outraged with me. I wanted my mom to be outraged with me. I wanted the world to be outraged with me. I wanted my Dad to go down there and do something about it! I had absolutely no idea how frightening it was for my friend. I didn't know the history of violence and lynching in the South. I didn't know that I was powerless. I sure didn't believe my Dad was powerless.

Dorothy and her family were transferred overseas shortly after that. She never mentioned the incident and I took my cue from her. I think it was shame she felt and shame I felt, but for two very different reasons.

Merrill's family moved into their quarters. I wandered down and introduced myself.

"What grade are you in?" I asked.

"Seventh." Merrill replied, tossing her long dark hair. She had a wide smile and dark blue eyes. She was "developed," as my mom would say, filling out her blouse admirably. For the first time I felt the hint of attraction.

"Oh." I felt suddenly tongue-tied, not knowing why. "Maybe you'll be in my class."

So began the long days of summer. Merrill would come over and "lay out" in her two piece bathing suit and we would talk the afternoon away. She turned on her side and I gazed at the curve of her waist and the flare of her hip. I wanted to run my hand along those planes and caress the arcs of her shape. I think she knew it, but she never said. She teased me silently, gently, aware of her charms. It could be she was practicing on me. I didn't know what I was feeling and didn't try to figure it out. I just enjoyed the tension and lingered in the delight.

The next move would be ours. Merrill and her family stayed at Ft. Bragg when we packed for what would be our final move. I left Merrill and her lovely curves behind when we moved from Ft. Bragg to Columbus, Georgia, a move would prove more profound than any other. Yes, we moved our location, but the extreme remove was to living off post. We would not live on post again.

Dad retired from the Army at the end of 1965, the same year Casey Stengel retired from the Yankees, race riots erupted in Watts, and right before his outfit, the 101st Airborne, deployed to Viet Nam. Columbus, Georgia felt as foreign to me as anywhere we had travelled up to now. I wanted to love this place just like I had every new place we moved. I wanted to love the scrub pine and sand burrs in our yard, and the chorus of katydids rioting in the trees on summer nights. I wished I could learn to like sweat.

The difference was that now I lived permanently off base. I missed desperately the texture and colors of my previous life. I missed being around other kids with whom I shared experiences and expectations. Kids who weren't worried about class distinction or social standing. I missed being around kids who could make friends quickly, because we didn't have the luxury of time and generations of connections. I missed my life.

It was like the time Mom and I lived in McMinnville, Oregon and I went to a civilian school while we waited for the end of the Cuban Missile Crisis so we could travel to Europe and be with my dad. The kids had known each other since kindergarten. Their histories and contexts were generational. They didn't want or need to make new friends. They weren't interested in my stories about places they had never been to and things they had never done. It felt like their world was complete inside the bubble of their neighborhood and family.

My first day of school and the first time changing classes, rather than feeling grown up, I felt like I had landed another planet, more foreign than anywhere my dad had been stationed at home or abroad. Between classes a wash of pastels spilled from the classrooms into the hall, laughing, passing notes, busily negotiating an invisible maze. The boys, hair high and tight, postured in their khaki pants and short-sleeved Izods. The girls wore dresses with Peter Pan collars, cardigans draped across their shoulders, and pocketbooks that matched their penny loafers. I had never seen anything like it.

I, myself, wore a red and purple flowered miniskirt and go-go boots. Really nice ones. White leather ones that hugged my calves. Très chic. I walked down the beige corridors, my long hair swinging, and tried to orient myself. Where was my locker? And what was that combination? And what room number was I supposed to show up to next? Can I jimmy the page out of my notebook without dropping my books? And how do you work this dang combination lock and what *was* the combination anyway? Oh, yeah, I wrote it inside my notebook.

I jockeyed my books and pried open the blue cloth notebook to the inside page. I. Can't. Quite. Read. It. Just a half inch more . . . before I lost purchase of my books, my purse, *and* my notebook. Papers scattered from here to the lunchroom, fifty feet down the hall. My classmates, a school of salmon swimming mindlessly upstream, trampled the clean white paper scattering before them like so many flower petals after a spring storm. I stood quietly, isolated in a sea of sameness, aching in a way I had never before experienced.

After school, I got off the bus alone and walked the long the quarter of a mile to my new home, my armpits drenched with sweat, textbooks heavy in my arms. I was almost dizzy from the heat by the time I reached the front door. There is a subtle difference, only truly appreciated by Southerners, to enter a light-saturated room and know it to be shady. I've always thought that Southerners should have different words for different kinds of shade the same way the Inuit have names for different kinds of snow.

The whir of a fan and the promise of a cool drink eased me as I put down my books and sat at the kitchen table. Mom asked me about my day, about school. She knew I adapted easily. Wasn't she the one who taught me by her own love of travel, adventure, and meeting new people, learning new things? She waited to hear my story. What was it like, this new adventure we were on? She didn't anticipate me dropping my head to the table and wailing, "They're all white!"

In the middle of the year Florence came to school and my world made a turn for the better. Florence's dad was stationed at Ft. Benning but they lived off post so she came to the civilian school nearest her home. The minute I saw Florence my breath let out, my shoulders eased, and a grin erupted somewhere in my stomach. Florence's Japanese-American heritage sang out from her graceful features, her slight figure, and her straight black hair. I made my way to her table at lunch and introduced myself.

"Hi."

From that moment we were inseparable. We both loved the Beatles. We talked, obsessed, daydreamed and fantasized about them on the bus ride to and from school, on the phone and when we spent the night each weekend. We saved our lunch money for the entire year and bought tickets to their concert at the closest venue: Memphis, Tennessee. We were convinced that if we bought the tickets surely the miracle of a ride, hotel stay and meals would manifest.

My dad, our reluctant hero, drove us three hundred and eighty-seven miles to Memphis, arranged for our hotel room, and made sure we were fed. We felt we paid him back in trumps because we had purchased him a ticket. He shook his head as he watched the crowd, mostly girls, lose our collective minds. After the show, Dad took us to eat and let us rant and squeal with each other. Lost in the high of the moment, we forgot he was even there.

The kids at school thought we were strange. We wore matching Granny dresses on the same day, long dresses with long sleeves capped by a ruffle at the end. We made them for ourselves after a term in Home Ec. class. Florence changed her name to Jo-Jo. I continued to let my hair grow and to wear my stylish go-go boots.

One day we intentionally missed the bus after school so we could walk the three or so miles to my house together. It was early spring, listing from warm to hot. We were on an adventure. We made it home close to an hour after we would have arrived had we taken the bus. In that hour all hell had broken loose. It seems that it was against school policy for kids to walk home if they were "bus students." I was incensed. The next day I was called to the Dean's office. I volunteered in the office so we knew each other more than in passing. She motioned for me to sit.

"Connie, I'm concerned that your relationship with Florence might be inappropriate."

I waited for her to explain. She sat uncomfortably for a moment, shifting in her chair. "I think y'all are too close."

"What do you mean? We're best friends. We love each other! How can that be inappropriate?" I couldn't fathom what she was talking about.

She dropped the subject. "You girls should have known better than to walk all that way home from school. No one knew where you were and anything could have happened to you. I have to punish you for that because it can't happen again. I want you to write a one thousand word essay."

"One thousand words! About what?"

"Anything you want. Just be sure it's one thousand words and in my office by Friday."

My friendship with Jo-Jo was good and true and loving. *How dare she?* I went home and in two hours wrote a thousand-word essay. I wrote on the beauty of friendship, what it looked like, what it meant, how it manifested, and concluded with a diatribe against adults who not understand the meaning of real friendship and love.

The dean called me into her office the day after I turned it in. "Connie," she said, "this is really good, you should be a writer." She dismissed me without another word.

At the end of my freshman year in the high school we had been siphoned to, I dropped by her office to say hello. She smiled and opened her desk drawer, pulling out the essay I had written.

"I still have this, Connie. It is really good. Don't forget what I told you about writing."

I was surprised and pleased that she still had my essay, especially with all the students that filed through her office over the years. How many essays had she assigned? I felt a warm rush of pleasure. I now know these things: she never married and she lived with the PE teacher at my high school.

Everything changed in October after the Beatles' concert the previous August. Jo-Jo and I still spent the night every weekend. We began to be interested in boys more accessible than the Beatles. Not boys that went to our school, but guys who lived at the trailer park where Jo-Jo lived. Gradually, she became too busy for some of my phone calls. Our sleepovers happened less often. Then she stopped speaking to me altogether. On the phone. On the bus. At school. Nothing. Confused and hurt, I passed her notes begging her to tell me what I had done.

I was supposed to get off the bus at the church where my Girl Scout meetings were held, instead I rode all the way out to Lake Crystal Trailer Park where I got off and called to Jo-Jo, "I need to talk to you."

She looked around, watched the other kids heading toward their trailers, and nodded. "What do you want?"

"Why won't you talk to me?" I began to sob, "What have I done? I don't understand."

"You're embarrassing me," she said. "Calm down."

Okay. I could do that. I took a breath and hushed my voice, "Please tell me what's going on, Jo-Jo. I need to know."

Again, she glanced around. "Some of the guys are saying that we're lesbians."

"What's that?"

"It's girls who like girls."

"So. I like girls. What the heck are you talking about?"

"I mean girls who like girls *that way*."

I still didn't understand. "I love you." I sobbed, "I don't understand what is wrong with that. I love you." Her face shut down. She said nothing more but turned and walked to her trailer. Our friendship was over.

Crying, I walked the four miles home in my now hopelessly wrinkled Girl Scout uniform, lugging a ton of books, deliberately scuffing my shoes in the gravel that lined the side of the road. I didn't know what I had done. I only knew that I had lost something important. And that I loved her.

At fourteen, the Viet Nam war played out a world away. My father missed deployment with his unit by months and Mr. Busbee ambled into our eighth grade science classroom with his slew-footed gate and rocked our world. He cut a swath in his baggy corduroy pants and rumpled white shirts, sleeves rolled up to his elbows. When his unruly curls slid across his forehead he flipped them out of his eyes with unconscious practice. He must have been in his early twenties, just out of college, and was the object of many an adolescent crush, including mine. He taught us about evolution and talked to us about the war. The most important thing I learned in his class was to question everything.

I had never questioned the goodness or authority of our government, so when Mr. Busbee asked if we thought the United Stated should be in Viet Nam I was taken aback. I got angry, cornered by the idea that we might be wrong, that we might be perpetrators of evil instead of doers of good. Who did he think he was? Being an army brat, his question socked a hard punch to the solar plexus of my psyche. Reluctantly, I began what became a life-long commitment to asking difficult questions. If my beliefs couldn't stand up to questioning there was a problem. I scrutinized everything that I considered to be sacred even though my heart pounded in terror. I began the slow, clumsy rise to consciousness.

I questioned the things that gave me meaning and did not die. My beliefs needed to stand up to all the scrutiny I could muster. If they were right or true they could withstand questioning, I reasoned. If not, I would force myself to let them go, even the ones that gave me comfort.

Active questioning comes with an implied imperative to change when you encounter false reasoning, false facts, or incomplete understandings. I gained an unexpected insight: saying what you believe and living what you believe are two *very* different things. And so began a war with my father. We both lived out of our integrity: his formed, considered, and tested by a lifetime; mine, newly minted, passionate with the arrogance of youth, and untried. We did not declare a truce until well after the Vietnam War ended.

Early in the fall of the next year I got off the bus with my heart pounding in my throat. A girl from my neighborhood taunted me from the moment I climbed on the bus after school all the way to my stop. She wanted to fight. I thought I could avoid her because she didn't usually get off at my stop. Now, being a pacifist, I didn't believe in fighting. Here was my first chance to live out my new beliefs with integrity.

It was a warm day, the temperature rising from a cool morning to sweltering afternoon. My wool skirt, white cotton blouse, and light cardigan started out comfortable but by the afternoon stuck to my skin by a thin layer of sweat. A circle gathered around us when we got off the bus. The girl shoved me and the kids began to shout.

"Fight! Fight!"

I didn't move.

"Put down your books and fight, Connie," the girl menaced.

"I don't believe in fighting." I said, shaking visibly.

"You chicken shit."

"I'm not chicken. I don't believe in fighting. If I were chicken I would run away."

"Then fight!"

She was going to whale on me. I set my books on the ground and stood up.

"Listen, if you want to beat me up, go ahead. I don't know what it will prove, but I'm not running away. I'm not afraid. I just don't believe violence solves anything." That was a lie. I was terrified. I wanted to be brave and strong and right, but I really didn't want to have the crap beat out of me.

For a few moments the kids gaped. Then the girl backed off and the circle broke up. It wouldn't be fun to watch a one sided fight. My opponent shook her head.

"Shit," she spat, "you're crazy."

My high school was brand new. The kids who attended were not only the kids in the immediate and upper middle class neighborhood but also those from the outlying middle and lower middle class neighborhoods. I had a larger pool from which to select friends. They were still all white but it was about to get better.

Columbus, Georgia was on the soul circuit. Black performers booked into the Columbus auditorium regularly. My friend Gary, also an army brat and a drummer in a high school garage band, took me to every show that blew through town: James Brown (eight times!), Otis Redding, Wilson Picket, Aretha Franklin, Gorgeous George, Carla Thomas, Jackie Wilson. We considered ourselves soul music aficionados. We listened to the soul stations, knew the words to all the songs, and cheered when a favorite song would crossover to the white rock station. We were the only white kids in a crowd of seven to ten thousand people –and we both felt right at home. I danced in my seat with everyone, drowning in the ecstatic beat.

At my first show I went to the restroom and stood in line with thirty or so women. A large bottle of vodka made its way down the line, each person stopping to take a pull. It got to me. I was clearly underage. And white. I grinned. I didn't want to drink but I wanted to be a part of the camaraderie. A fraction of a moment passed. I took a swallow and tried not to cough as we all laughed: they at me, I at myself.

If my presence was resented, I never felt it. I was fifteen; later sixteen, and everyone could tell I was there for the music. No one acted like I shouldn't be there. After so many shows, people would wave or I would wave, acknowledging that we had been here together before, recognized each other, and maybe had even shared a slug in the bathroom.

I met my first black friend in Columbus when I left Hardaway High School and briefly attended a private school. Her name was Angel Crittenden and she was about my age. Her family owned the black funeral home in town. She was hanging out at my house when my mom mentioned, off the cuff, that she loved to have her hair combed.

"I like to comb hair." Angel said. "How about if I give you an Afro."

"Fine," Mom replied, "I'll try anything once."

After that, we decided I would look great in a 'fro, too. She worked for hours on my waist-length hair. Her idea was to tease it into submission. What did I know? She was the expert. I didn't think about the fact that her hair had been straightened.

Imagine if you will a Brill-o pad extending a foot from the roots of my hair shooting out over a foot in every direction. It was very unlike my mom's do. But I was proud. We went to Shoney's for strawberry pie and I strutted my do. Jimmy Hendrix- look out!

It took an entire bottle of conditioner and many tears to comb the rats out of my hair. I finally admitted it looked nothing like the Angela Davis Afro of my dreams.

When Dad retired, Mom joined the Methodist Church. I dutifully went to Sunday school and church with her. I was bored out of my mind. Nothing we talked about lined up with my experience of God. I became a slightly belligerent jerk.

"Why aren't we doing anything to integrate our church?"

"Why aren't we taking a stand against the war?"

"Why does everyone assume we need to be alike?"

One Sunday a friend and I went to the adult Sunday school class. I wore my favorite miniskirt and painted grapevines up my legs. We played two songs to the class. First we played *Give Me That Old Time Religion* to smiles and nods:

> Now give me that old time religion
>
> Give me that old time religion
>
> Give me that old time religion
>
> It was good enough for Mamma
>
> And it's good enough for me

And then Bob Dylan rasped out *The Times They Are A Changin'* challenging my parent's generation to not criticize what they couldn't understand and (the best part), to stop trying to control us.

I shared passionately how my faith in Jesus was connected to all the things I care about in the world. They talked to me about the survival of my immortal soul. We couldn't find common ground. We were all so busy being "right" that we couldn't find each other. And never did. They had the power and there was no room for me if I didn't move to their side. At least that's how I saw it.

Around the same time I got a niggling sensation that had something to do with God. I stared out my window into the night sky and felt threads tying me to stars and clouds and treetops. To the bats circling the streetlight, to the wind brushing leaves against the side of the house. The universe expanded and then expanded some more. Glory and fear jumbled up together. I yearned for something I could not identify. I yearned and yearned. *What do you want, God?* My yearning morphed into determination. I would to be a nun. I was never Catholic but I figured if God was calling this hard it must be to something fulltime.

In seminary I learned that many women experiencing call often wanted to be nuns or missionaries because those were our only models of women in ministry. I read everything I could get my hands on about nuns. I read *The Song of Bernadette* and I read a book, whose name I no longer remember, about a young girl who entered a convent right before the Nazi takeover of France. As a novitiate she was to fall silently to her knees when approached by the Mother Superior and kiss her ring of office. Okay. I could do that. I practiced, one might say, religiously, falling silently to my knees. I got rather good at it, but my knees began to swell. All for the service of God, I thought. I'm really getting the hang of this, I thought.

My mom took me to the doctor at Ft. Benning when my knees ballooned to triple their size. The doctor shook his head, "Do you play football?" he asked.

"No," I replied, " but I fall silently to my knees a lot."

I have traumatic arthritis in my knees to this day. And still I am not Catholic. Or a nun.

As a young child I asked my mom the difference between a Roman Catholic and a Protestant. She said, "Catholics have Jesus still on the cross, Protestants don't."

"Why?" I asked. This was interesting.

"Because the focus when Jesus is on the cross is his sacrifice for us. Protestants have an empty cross because we focus on the resurrected Jesus who conquered evil."

Maybe she said it that way and maybe not. Maybe it's how my grown up self remembers, but the essence is there: our differences are of focus. Some might say doctrine, especially those in power in both the Roman Catholic and Protestant traditions, but I say focus. I say focus because, as my Religion professor, Dr. Kwai Chang, said, "Religions (and denominations) are like fingers pointing to the moon: if you focus on the finger, you will miss the moon."

I skittered through my early adolescence on the brink of otherness. I was not black, not Southern, not a civilian, not rooted. I made merry leaps of connection into frays about which I had little understanding. Evil was visceral. Living with the disconnect of being both tightly woven into the fabric of life yet unraveled from my immediate community created a tension that fuels my passion even today. My experiences gave me the insight and intensified my call to proclaim the Gospel in which there are no "others."

. . . have patience with everything unresolved in your heart
and to try to love the questions themselves
as if they were locked rooms or books written
in a very foreign language.
Don't search for the answers,
which could not be given to you now,
because you would not be able to live them.
And the point is, to live everything.
Live the questions now.

—Rainer Maria Rilke

# Chapter 7   *Living Into the Question of Me*

MARTIN LUTHER KING, JR. was assassinated in April of my sophomore year.
I cried through the announcements in homeroom and dragged myself from
class to class. Once again what I believed in and hoped for was challenged.
At sixteen, I was isolated from the Civil Rights movement by geography
and age but I wanted to be a part of it. Even though Dr. King's church was
a mere hundred miles away in Atlanta, it wasn't a drive I was allowed to
make. I swore to myself that I would speak up against racism in history
class, in English class, even in my anatomy-physiology class, to talk back
to classmates who spit racist hatred with impunity. I hunched over my seat
with an ache in my chest and burning in my guts.

About a week after Dr. King's death, I asked if I could change the bulletin board in my anatomy class. I made the background solid black construction paper. In the center I put a picture of Martin Luther King, Jr., taken
from the cover of Time magazine, with his dates: January 15, 1929 – April
4, 1968. Beneath that I cut white letters out of construction paper to read:
"Martin Luther King, Jr.—A great man in the science of humanity." I could
do so little to further the cause except express my grief and admiration. By
the end of the day, though, it had been ripped down by one or more of my
fellow classmates. I was a foreigner in my own country, alone and sad, with

49

no one to share my grief. This much became clear: living a life of faith meant living a life of justice.

I wanted to be like Martin Luther King, Jr. I wanted to live like that, to stand for justice like that, to serve something more important than me like that. I desperately wanted a to be called to some great task. Then God began to nudge me. But once nudged I resisted. So there you have it. Only later did I discover that my call was not to any great work but to a million daily small tasks.

It was a time of upheaval in my life as well as in the world. Some months after Dr. King's death, Jerry Taylor and I attempted to date. It didn't work for me because every time we kissed, he giggled. Jerry's family was a bit odd. They were okay with us smoking pot at their house and Jerry told me his folks were swingers. I knew what that meant. It turned me off, but I acted like it was cool.

It turned out that Jerry was gay. Like most gay folk in the sixties he didn't talk about it but struggled in isolated silence. We stopped trying to date and had settled into a friendship when he was arrested in Weracoba Park for sitting naked in a tree. When the police brought him down he just giggled. He was high on LSD.

I went to my pastor and asked him to visit Jerry in jail and make sure he was okay. The church occupied a triangle of land on the edge of our middle class neighborhood, a modern building whose beauty was unassuming. The parking lot was empty when I arrived early in the afternoon. I made my way up the white concrete sidewalk, so new it had yet to weather to gray, and let myself in the side door. The hall was cool and I stopped for my eyes to adjust to interior light before I walked to his office door and tapped lightly.

"Reverend Hazen . . . "

"Come in," he called. I pushed the door open a crack and stuck my head in. Bookshelves crowded against two walls filled with, what seemed to me, mysterious tomes. Papers lay scattered across his desk, an old black rotary phone crouched by his right hand as if he had just hung up from a call, and the yellow legal pad in front of him was covered with notes and doodles.

"Hi, Connie, what can I do for you today?" He motioned to a brown leather captain's chair in front of his desk. I perched on the edge, feeling anxious.

"My friend was arrested yesterday. I wondered if you would go to the jail and see if he's okay." I hurried on, "I'm worried that they may not be treating him very well."

Reverend Hazen watched me carefully and said, "Tell me what happened from the beginning."

I spilled out the story as much as I knew. Naked. LSD. Arrested. "The police won't let me talk to him when I call—they wouldn't even admit he was there." I held back tears as I recited the story, consumed with worry.

"I don't think this is any of my business," he responded when I had finished.

"But he's alone and scared and maybe still high. I'm afraid they might do something bad to him. He doesn't have anyone!" My voice raised a decibel level. "Please." I begged.

"Give me his full name," he responded, jotting it down on his legal pad, "I'll see what I can do.

I had done what I could. I *assumed* that my pastor was the one I should seek out. After all, wasn't that the pastor's role? You know: feed the hungry, clothe the naked, *visit those in prison*?

Later, he told me he had gone to the jail and Jerry wasn't there. I still don't know if I believe him. What I *do* know is I was disappointed with the church for not being what it said it was.

That same year I was arrested for the possession of marijuana. I wanted to experience everything. I was wide open to different ways of exploring "the meaning of life." I wanted to expand my consciousness and smoking pot seemed like it might open the door to spiritual experience even wider. I wanted to grab onto life and ride it to the edges. I wanted to be a hippie—to change the world for peace and love. I wanted to smoke pot—and that it was illegal only added to the excitement and intrigue.

My friend, Brian, told me about a girl who had been committed to a local, private mental institution against her will. I was outraged. How could this kind of thing happen in the United States of America? My heart went out to her.

"Can she have visitors?" I asked. "Can she make phone calls?"

"Yeah. I talk to her when she has phone time."

"Give her my number. I'd like to talk to her."

I wanted her to know I was in solidarity with her. She called.

"Hi, this is Mindy, Brian's friend."

"Hi, I'm so glad you called me!"

"They've got me in here. My folks. They just can't handle that I am not like them."

I commiserated with her, trusting without question the unfairness of her situation. I would be her advocate and savior! Together we would defy the system! We talked daily for a while and one day she asked me if I could bring her some pot. She would find a way to get it from me—maybe through a window.

"Sure," I told her and began to make plans. Mindy and I spoke furtively over the next several days. In my grandiosity I was afraid her phone might be tapped. Mindy encouraged both my paranoia and my excitement at the idea of getting one over on the people who had unfairly detained her. *This was a matter of justice.* They couldn't do this. I asked Brian to give me a ride. I got my matchbox of pot and waited for him to pick me up.

We pulled into a small parking lot dotted with shade trees. The facility was a diminutive one-story and, I later learned, an exclusive residential mental health treatment facility. My heart raced. I was meeting my friend in person for the first time. Adrenalin rushed through me as I began my clandestine mission. Pot for the pot-less. Though it wasn't really about marijuana for me, it was about the ideas that smoking a joint represented: free thought, free love, and just plain freedom.

I climbed out of Brian's Buick and walked down the path looking for an open window. All of a sudden a side door opened and a plumpish, strawberry blonde girl who appeared to be several years older than me motioned furtively.

"Connie?" She called in a hushed voice.

I nodded. She wasn't what I expected. She looked hard. Her makeup was thick and garish, her hair stringy. She glanced around. I was looking for a cohort, a comrade. She seemed hardened and sneaky.

"Do you have it?"

"Yeah," I said, "but how come they let you outside?"

" I found the door open—but I'd better get back. Did you bring it?"

"Yeah," I repeated as I rifled around in my purse for the matchbox.

In the background a car door slammed. Mindy glanced around and nodded toward the parking lot.

"Excuse me, miss. I'm detective Greene, hand me your pocketbook."

Dick Tracy had just walked up with a sidekick, complete with hat and open raincoat. He took my hand and pushed up my sleeve. "Just looking for tracks," he snorted.

*Tracks? Tracks? Oh,* tracks, *like needle marks. Really?* My stomach crawled into my throat. *Oh God. Oh God. Oh God. I am so in trouble.*

"Your pocketbook." He reached for it. I offered him my small, camel colored purse, with a shaking hand. He dug around, his hand as large as the entire cavity of my purse, and pulled out the matchbox. "Young lady, you are under arrest for the illegal possession of marijuana with the intent to sell."

He loaded me into the unmarked police car. I was terrified. My folks were going to kill me. We got to the station and he sent in a female officer to search me.

"Strip."

"Strip? You mean everything?" She meant everything. I flushed a deep red.

"Bend over and spread your cheeks."

*Oh my God! Are you kidding?*

"Stand here." She instructed and proceeded to run her fingers through my waist length hair.

"What are you doing?"

"Making sure you're not hiding drugs in there."

"In my *hair*?" This was getting ridiculous.

"Can I go to the bathroom?"

She followed me as I walked to the restroom and held the door while I sat on the toilet. "Why can't I close the door?" I asked.

"Because you might be hiding something up your . . . " She raised an eyebrow. I blushed again.

"Can I at least have some toilet tissue?"

She handed me four sheets that she tore from a roll. I dabbed and stood.

"Can I get dressed now?"

She handed me my panties and dress. My mind raced as I struggled back into my clothes. *What was going to happen to me now?*

She walked me outside and put me into the back of a police car, then got in and started the engine.

"Where are we going?"

"You'll see when we get there."

It was getting dark and the territory we drove through was unfamiliar. I couldn't place any landmarks. For a while we passed the lights of houses clustered in neighborhoods. Then a gas station, a Seven-Eleven, and finally a rickety liquor store. Eventually the streetlights ended, the house lights disappeared in the rear window, and only headlights illuminated a narrow ribbon of road. Trees loomed on either side like sinister shadows. *Where is she taking me?* I didn't ask again, though. We travelled in silence. I, frightened and curious; she, preoccupied and inattentive. After what seemed like a very long time, we turned into a driveway and pulled up to a stumpy brick building.

"Come on, get out."

Burglar bars obscured the windows and the plaque next to the entrance read "Muscogee County Juvenile Detention Center." She took my arm. Opening the door, she gave me a quick shove inside. Her blazer flopped open and I saw her shoulder holster. She carried a gun. I hated guns. I was afraid of guns. Actually, my Dad told me to never call it a gun.

"Always call this what it is," he said, when I was quite small and sat on his lap playing with the sharpshooter commendation that he wore over the pocket of his uniform. "It's a *weapon*. It's used to kill people."

"Okay, Daddy."

She carried a weapon. I felt the threat—though unlikely except in my imagination—and my anxiety skyrocketed. I respected the weapon too much to trust the woman carrying it.

I was taken to a cold cell: three walls of painted cinder blocks, one wall a barred door. My cellmate sat on the bottom bunk.

"The top one is mine. You can have this one"

She clamored up to the top bunk and I sat below.

"What are you in for?'

"I was arrested for possession of marijuana. What about you?"

I don't remember now what she said but we talked and talked and she told me things I had no idea about. Her father sexually abused her. She had an abortion. She wanted to know if I had ever kissed a girl.

"No, I haven't."

"Do you want to?"

I think I did want to. She was so sweet when she asked, but I was terrified. Not of the idea of a kiss, but of being in that place and not knowing what was going to happen to me. And I didn't know this girl. I like kissing people I know and like. People I think I love. Special people.

"Um, I don't think so."

"You won't tell will you?"

"No."

I arrived too late for dinner, but when the guard or matron came around for bed check I asked if my parents had brought my medication.

"No they haven't. What kind of medication do they need to bring?"

"Birth control pills." I had been put on birth control pills to regulate my menstrual cycle.

She laughed, "Well, honey, you're not going to need those in here!" She moved on, dismissing me without so much as a nod.

I went to the bars and called to her, "It's not like that. I have a problem with bleeding too much."

But I learned when people see you a certain way you are in a mold not of your own making. She was still chuckling as she made her way past the cells on this corridor.

"I'm telling the truth!" I screeched to no one and everyone.

Two things occurred while I was detained at the Muscogee County Juvenile Detention Center. First, I had a machine-gun rage fantasy in which I escaped and returned to liberate all the kids held hostage there. I had never experienced that kind of rage before.

Second, the pain of my roommate, the injustice of the institution, the ways we were dehumanized, and the overwhelming sense of powerlessness brought me to my knees. I lay in my bunk, staring at the metal pattern holding up the mattress above me, and prayed, eyes open, that I might make some kind of sense of what was going on. Then I prayed for courage. I didn't believe I had done anything wrong. This was civil disobedience. Then I prayed for God to be with me so I wouldn't feel so alone.

Somewhere in the midst of my prayer I realized I expected God to be there for me, experienced God's commitment to me, and sheepishly acknowledged to God that I had not made a commitment back. I was old enough to declare myself.

"I am yours, God." I made the formal statement in my prayer, like a contract, having no idea what it would mean. But it didn't matter. What mattered were the commitment I made and my pledge to keep it.

I stayed in juvenile detention for three days until I was released to my parents pending trial.

"I need you to get me a lawyer."

"No," Mom said.

"But they searched me without a warrant."

"You did something illegal and you need to take responsibility for it."

It was a lesson I would have to learn more than once. I pled guilty and got two years probation and a heightened sense of outrage.

Before my court appearance I told my mom I wanted to be baptized.

"Jailhouse conversion?" she asked.

I called our pastor and he agreed to baptize me.

He arranged an afternoon for me to come in on a weekday. I arrived with my mom and dad. I don't recall having much of a conversation with him about baptism. He went over the vows I would make and asked me if I affirmed them. I did, so we got down to business. He donned his robe and stole and we walked to the front of the sanctuary. Opening a small book he began the ritual of baptism.

"On behalf of the whole Church, I ask you: Do you renounce the spiritual forces of wickedness, reject the evil powers of this world, and repent of your sin?"

My voice shook. "I do." My understanding of sin was already different from that of many of my peers.

"Do you accept the freedom and power God gives you to resist evil, injustice, and oppression in whatever forms they present themselves?"

This is God's call. "*I do.*" Absolutely. In every way I can, damn the consequences!

"Do you confess Jesus Christ as your Savior, put your whole trust in his grace, and promise to serve him as your Lord, in union with the Church which Christ has opened to people of all ages, nations, and races?"

"I do." Yes. Yes. Yes. My answers weren't merely answers. They were not rote, they were the beginning place and grounding for understanding of the meaning of my life.

He removed the lid from the font and invited me to stand next to him as he swirled the water with his fingers. Three times he brought his hand out of the water and touched the crown of my head.

"Connie Lee Tuttle, I baptize you in the name of the Father, and of the Son, and of the Holy Spirit. Amen."

Only my mom and dad where there to welcome me into the body of Christ. They embraced me. Somehow what just happened seemed larger than the room we were standing in, larger than three people and me. Larger than the amount of time it took. Something felt unfinished. Later I came to understand baptism not only as the act and declaration by an individual but as one mediated by the community. Witnessed. Affirmed. Called into being. Supported. The vows I made that day were not casual vows. They were not about the salvation of my soul after death. They were and are a pledge to a way of being in the world and a way of relating to God. My vows rose up because I had been raised in a community of faith that gave me words and stories and concepts to understand my experiences of the Sacred.

Are you still listening? Then know my baptism defines me. But it's more than my baptism that makes me who I am. The fact that I am an army brat gives me the lens through which I view the world. And so does being a woman. And a lesbian. And a mom. And though it would be years later, so does the lens acquired when I became a Southerner.

I found pockets of home in the South. Many of my heroes were born here: Martin Luther King, Jr., Flannery O'Conner, Carson McCullers, Tennessee Williams, Alice Walker, Tallulah Bankhead, Helen Keller, Juliet Lowe, Moms Mabley, Hank Aaron, Alice Paul. I found a hidden underbelly of fierce gentleness. And the music of poor people: sacred harp, bluegrass, James Brown, gospel, rhythm and blues. I learned from their fight and guts, from the tenacity of a people who are tied to the land and its history, and grounded in stories. I learned from all the questions circumstance and history forced me to ask. I was forged here, pressed up against the jagged, hostile, and razor-sharp edges of intolerance.

But I am a Southerner. Like grits swimming in butter. Like ham and red-eye gravy. Like collards simmering in potlikker, sopped up with cornbread. Like tomato sandwiches on white bread with mayo. And ice cold sweet tea by the jug. I like to act like I grew up on that Southern tea, thrived on it, suckled on it before I could walk. But that is true only in my imagination. Like most of the places I look to catch a glimpse of myself, parts are obscured by myth and parts embellished by imagination. Or maybe myth and imagination make it true.

But I *am* a Southerner. So call me cracker. Call me peach. I am a biscuit slathered with sorghum syrup. I am earthy: peanuts pulled from red clay, fried pies, and salty sweat. Like my daddy before me, I am a storyteller. I am a Southerner: dishonest at times and frighteningly honest at others. I am a Southerner. Fearless and fearful, kind and cruel.

I am a Southerner even when I wish I weren't.

Nineteen sixty-eight was filled with trauma, both personal and political. How did we live through it? In March, the My Lai massacre, perpetrated by American soldiers in Viet Nam, assaulted our collective consciences. In April, Martin Luther King, Jr. was assassinated. In June, Bobby Kennedy. July, Hank Aaron hit his 500th home run in the midst of death threats. August, the Democratic National Convention in Chicago erupted in violence. September, the trial of the Chicago 8, a group of antiwar protesters charged with inciting the violent riots at the Democratic convention, began.

Somehow, most of us survived and limped into 1969. That July I made my way to the Atlanta International Pop Festival (it preceded Woodstock by weeks) and jammed to Chuck Berry, Blood, Sweat and Tears, Creedence Clearwater Revival, Dave Brubeck, Janis Joplin, Johnny Winter, and Led Zeppelin. Neal Armstrong walked on the moon. Lt. William Calley was charged in the My Lai massacre and put on trial at Ft. Benning, Georgia. The Chicago 8 trial opened. And I got pregnant.

*The Healing Time*

Finally on my way to yes
I bump into
all the places
where I said no
to my life
all the untended wounds
the red and purple scars
those hieroglyphs of pain
carved into my skin, my bones,
those coded messages
that send me down
the wrong street
again and again
where I find them
the old wounds
the old misdirections
and I lift them
one by one
close to my heart
and I say holy
holy.

—Pesha Gertler

# Chapter 8    *Hard Lessons*

I'VE LEARNED ALL KINDS of things about all kinds of love in my life. The love of my parents, as the saying goes, gave me deep roots and strong wings. But then there is all that other learning about love I had to do. Loving my husband, loving my daughter, loving other women, loving community, loving myself. Loving God. I'm pretty bad at love, though I *am* passionate and give it my all. And I've been known to come apart when love is lost.

The beginning was very sweet. David had a crush on me that made me feel wildly attractive and sexy. I hung out with Hollis, Brian, Otis, and David, riding around in Otis' 1955 Oldsmobile 88, affectionately dubbed the Status-Mobile. One day, David and I were sitting in the back seat and, on impulse; I leaned over and kissed him. He told me on the phone later that he had almost passed out he got so dizzy when we kissed. I thought the kiss was wonderful, too, but I didn't pass out or feel near passing out. I felt special. I reveled in the power of my sexuality and I wielded it like some punch-drunk boxer.

David's passion was acting. He took leading roles in his high school's productions, garnering a governor's honors fellowship in theatre. At the Springer Opera House, the local community theatre, he played the lead character, Collin Fenwick, in *The Grass Harp*, even receiving a telegram from Truman Capote on opening night.

I was seventeen and in love with David Ward. I wanted to experience life to the fullest. I wanted to have sex. I wanted to have orgasms. We just weren't competent in our birth control practices.

At some point the consequences caught up with us. In 1969 there were no home pregnancy tests and no HIPA act protecting my privacy. I couldn't go to the local clinic because my mom knew people who worked there. Instead, we opted for me to see David's pediatrician.

The doctor did a pelvic exam and declared I had an infection and was not pregnant. He prescribed warm Betadine douches three times a day. I faithfully did my part but still the "infection" that kept me from getting my period persisted. I rounded nicely under my breasts and afternoon naps became essential. Years later, in the first flush of feminist self-understanding, I discovered that a pregnant woman's cervix turns an unmistakable blue color. Douching is contraindicated during pregnancy as it increases the risk of losing the fetus. The doctor, in his arrogance, attempted to make a life choice for me without my knowledge or consent.

I was a little more than four months pregnant, barely showing, when I sat my folks down. "Mom, Dad, I'm pregnant."

I wish I could say that it was the first time they experienced receiving this kind of information. It was not. Mom was pregnant with my sister when my folks married. Sherry was pregnant when she married. Now me. The family tradition continued.

My dad, God love him, said, "There are several things we can do. You can keep the baby and not get married, you can keep the baby and get married, or you can give the baby up for adoption. If you're not too far along, you can get an abortion."

They left it up to me. No pressure in any direction. I went to David.

"I am keeping this baby. You do not have to marry me. *I do not want to marry you if it's an obligation*."

"I want to marry you," he said.

And he did, as much as any sixteen-year-old boy could have, not grasping how his decision would change the rest of his life. For myself, I never regretted the decision to have and keep my daughter. I know I am the most fortunate of women because so many women are not allowed to make choices or supported for those choices once made.

David and I shared a passion for two things: the theatre and the revolution. We believed that change was coming: power to the powerless and the end of war, racism, and sexism. At least I looked forward to the end of sexism. The whole world was poised on the verge of enormous change. Woodstock had unleashed the possibility of peace. We celebrated the first Earth Day hoping to ignite a planet-wide environmental movement. Neil Armstrong and Buzz Aldrin landed on the moon. But overshadowing the hope lurked the Viet Nam War, the death of Jack Kerouac, Hurricane Camille pummeling the Gulf Coast, and the impending reelection of President Nixon.

The world teetered on the precipice of change and so did I, intent on launching myself into adulthood, into experience, and into making my own mistakes. The accelerant splashed onto the fire of my stratospheric lift off was the fervor of sexual discovery and new love. *Life! Here I come!*

December 1, 1969 we married with our families in attendance in the same Methodist church I had been baptized in a year or so earlier. After the service we returned to my folks' house and celebrated with homemade cake and toasted with Mateus Rose`.

That night I waited in our hotel room, our honeymoon suite, on the main drag in downtown Columbus for David to get off work. His boss at the shoe store wouldn't give him time off from inventory. So I waited. Young. A little scared. Very pregnant. And miserable from the hives: large, angry red bumps covering my body from neck to knees.

The day before, Mom had taken me to the emergency room at Martin Army Hospital on Ft. Benning. It would be my last visit under the care of military doctors. I sat in the room, chilled in my paper gown, feet swinging off the side of the exam table. Mom sat quietly beside me.

The doctor strode in an efficient swagger, his crew cut sharp and white lab coat pristine. He looked me over and said, "You have hives. A bad case of hives, but nothing to worry about."

I let out a breath as he made notes on my records and began penning a prescription. "Know anything you're allergic to?"

I have had skin allergies since I was small, but never, never hives. I started listing, "Wool. Dust . . . "

"Okay." He held up a hand to stop me then finished writing the script. As he tore it from the pad he asked as an afterthought, "You're not pregnant are you?"

"Yes." I blushed, deepening the red of my disfigurement.

He crumpled up the script and began again, handing it to my Mom as he left.

I spent my wedding night alone and in a misery of itching. By the time David arrived I could only fake my enthusiasm, flinching when he ran his hand over the raised welts marching up and down my body.

David's mom raised three boys and catered to them as if each were a crowned prince. A product of her time and a woman who adored her boys, she cared for their every need before it had time to manifest as a thought. I was not of that mold. When I discovered she ironed their *tee shirts for God's sake* I showed David the iron and ironing board. It may have made me seem like a bad wife to some, but it also made me a proud woman.

Unlike my Dad, David was a stranger to the kitchen. On one of our first mornings as a married couple he decided to fix breakfast for me. *That's more like it.*

"Damn it!!" Metal crashed against metal. A cloud of burnt sulfur wafted to the bedroom. I charged down the hall to find David staring at a cast iron skillet whose contents were unidentifiable.

"What did you do?"

"I was fixing you breakfast." He said, his tone hovering between anxious and defensive.

I peered into the pan again. Sure enough, what first appeared as a lump of charcoal was really an egg. A black egg. A noxious, black egg crouching on the side of an iron skillet bereft of oil and stinking with shame. I laughed and took over preparing breakfast. It took me longer than I like to admit to learn that David's seeming ineptitude got him out of a lot of household chores. I think he might have gone with, "It takes less time for you to do it than it does for you to explain to me how to do it—or to clean up after my disastrous attempts."

At the beginning of our marriage Robert, my large black cat, left. Robert and I were bonded in an interspecies love affair. We spent most of our time in each other's company. Robert went on walks with me, sat with me in the evenings, and slept with me at night. The first night David crawled into bed next to me Robert hopped down and left the room. I let him outside that night, expecting his return as usual. I never saw him again. If I believed in signs, that would have been a good one.

Most of all what I hated about being married were the universal expectations that we would have *his* career. Everyone expected it but me. I hated being reduced to an appendage. I hated how insecure I felt in his affections. My life was now supposed to be focused on him. His needs. His career moves. His happiness. No one paid attention to mine. Not even me.

I didn't understand how my parents, the same parents who told me I could be anything I wanted to be, do anything I wanted to do, were now saying that my place was to support David. "Things have changed," they said.

David auditioned for the Alliance Theatre Company in Atlanta. He was cast in a production of *We Bombed in New Haven*. I joined him. We crashed in a wreck of an apartment across from the theatre with our new friend Eddie, who also had a small part in the show. We slept, spooning on our sides in a single bed, and ate lots of grits and eggs, cheese and butter that we got from government commodities. I went to Columbus for my checkups and would return loaded down with fresh fruit from my parents.

Nights, I hung out in the green room playing the card game Oh Hell with the cast.

"Come on, preggie chickie, whattaya got, whattaya got?" one of the lead actors prodded as he dealt the cards and called the game like an auctioneer.

"Hang on, hang on," I'd respond, "I'm gonna take you down this hand." I was happy to be close to creative people and in the middle of all that creative energy.

I played gin rummy with Eddie during the day, lassoing him into countless games with no conversation, just the intense slapping of cards on the rickety kitchen table.

It did not occur to me that I was also in an intensely creative process. When I felt the first stirrings of Tanya inside me like a small, fluttering bird I drew in my breathe and held the miracle in my heart until my heart filled my chest and silent prayers rose from my core. *May I be a good mother. May I love this child well. May I keep my baby safe.* Rocking on my side, David asleep, I prayed and prayed and prayed for this miracle in my body that was beyond my understanding.

"DON'T PUSH MY KNEES TO MY CHEST!"

The nurse jostled the hospital bed down the hall as she rolled me back from x-ray. With one hand she guided the bed and with the other she tried to force my knees to my chest to stop the baby from coming. *This is not good!* Twenty-four hours of labor, seven hundred and fifty thousand times of having my vagina poked, three shifts of nurses with differing degrees of compassion, and now this indignity. I was tired, angry, and beyond caring if I made a scene.

In 1970, the Medical Center in Columbus, Georgia was a squat, grey hospital on the edge of the cotton mill district that tended to the poor of the city. The poor were not supposed to have opinions about their care, just gratitude. I, however, a month into being eighteen, had strong opinions about how I wanted to have this baby. I wanted natural childbirth. I wanted to nurse. I wanted the bitch to leave my knees alone.

I pushed out my feet and flattened my legs into two rigid boards. She shook her head in disgust and rolled me back to my room. Momentarily, an orderly arrived to wheel me to the OR. Florescent lights flashed overhead as we rushed down the hall. Sweaty sheets tangled around my torso. I was exhausted, damp and limp, the contractions sharp.

*I'm not ready!*

The nurses and OR staff talked around me but no one spoke to me. The icy room reeked of disinfectant. The doctor, whose native language was Spanish, couldn't get the nurses to understand him. The nurses grumbled none too gently as they hoisted my feet into the stirrups and told me to scoot my behind to the end of the table.

"I want to do this natural." I told the anesthetist as he pushed the gas mask over my mouth and nose.

"Count backwards from ten."

"I want to do this natural," I repeated. He secured the mask, silencing me. I surrendered and breathed in the gas. *Seven, six, five.*

Waking in recovery, I reached down to feel my belly. It was not flat, but it was empty. I called for a nurse. "What did I have? Is my baby okay? Where is my baby?" No one came. I shivered under the thin sheet and tried, unsuccessfully, to wrap it around me. After a while I drifted back to sleep.

An hour or so later, I woke when they wheeled me to my room. David and my Mom were waiting for me.

"She's beautiful," they both tell me and I am sure that she is. *She. I have a girl!*

Mom fussed over me, helping me into a fresh hospital gown and brushing my hair.

*Where is my baby?* My arms are hungry. So am I. It's now been way over twenty four hours since I have eaten. The nurse arrives and informs me it's too late to order a meal, but she will bring the baby soon.

"I'm nursing," I said, "please don't feed her. I need her to be hungry."

I hoped I sounded authoritative. She looked at me in disbelief and shook her head.

What seemed like eons later, long after both David and Mom left, the nurse brought her to me.

"Count all her fingers and toes."

Not knowing the tradition, my heart dropped and I frantically un-wrapped the receiving blanket.

"Honey, I'm just kidding. She's all there."

She *was* beautiful. She was that rare newborn without wrinkles but with smooth peaches and cream skin, wide blue eyes and rosebud lips. Her tiny head was topped with a shock of black hair. I was so in love I ached. My breasts grew heavy. I held her warm little body close to me, breathing in new baby smell. *I'm your mommy.*

I didn't know the first thing about nursing. I read about it, believed it was the best choice, and hoped instinct would take over. I opened my gown and nudged those perfect rose bud lips to my nipple. She nuzzled like a new kitten, searching for my breast.

"Why you givin' that baby the tit?" The glory of the moment shattered. The nurse returned and I had not noticed. She reached for the baby,

"It's time to take her back."

"She hasn't eaten yet. I need for her to nurse."

"We give 'em sugar water, honey. That's all she needs right now."

"I need her to be hungry so she can learn to nurse!" I fought not to be shrill, not wanting to upset the little one snuggling against me. "Can't she stay with me?"

"You need your rest, missy, you'll have more time than you want with her when you get home."

"Please. I need you to bring her to me at feeding times."

*Why do I have to beg?* I was willing to beg. I would do anything for this little one. I was scared and didn't want to rely on the good intentions of others that might or might not have existed. I also did not want to get into a power struggle that I was pretty sure I would lose. I backed down a little. Bile rose in my throat.

"Please." I implored, as she took my baby.

The next time a nurse came in she brought a codeine pill. "For pain," she said, "You ring anytime you're feeling pain and I'll bring you another one."

I swallowed it with a gulp of water and pushed back into my pillow. I was tired but too excited to sleep. My life had just changed in every conceivable and inconceivable way possible. My body had done this amazing thing that, strangely, I had not consciously participated in. A new being emerged and was waiting for me to discover her. The pillow softened as I sank into a borderless netherworld. The sharp edges of my psyche and my uneasiness began to melt.

I dozed, woke, and pushed the button. I liked that codeine. Sure enough, they brought me more of the elixir of "I don't give a shit" every time I asked for it.

Tanya did learn to nurse. She was a natural, for which I am thankful, as the nursing staff was of the collective and derisive mind that breast-feeding a baby "wasn't done." It was 1970 and natural childbirth and breast-feeding were considered fringe behaviors. Women no longer had to participate in childbirth or nurse babies. I didn't care what they thought. I was going to do it my way.

"Why you insist on doin' something that's gone the way of the dinosaur? You should consider yourself lucky that you don't have to."

The staff did nothing to help me figure out how to nurse. But I was stubborn and had the good fortune that my baby latched easily. I was obstinate enough to insist they let me breastfeed the entire three days we were in the hospital. It didn't endear me to them, but I leaned into my beautiful stubbornness and learned to use it to claim my power.

Stubbornness or tenacity, call it what you will. I call it my super power. It is not the power to hold another under my will. More like it feels solid, like finding my footing in a rocky stream. I have learned to use my super power when I make difficult choices.

David auditioned to become a member of the newly formed apprentice company of the Alliance Theatre. He made the cut and apprenticed for two seasons after Tanya was born. Company members performed minor roles on the main stage and starred in original plays on the side stage. The workhorses and stagehands, they built and broke down the sets on main stage and learned the craft from the inside out. They willingly worked eighty hours a week for the extravagant stipend of a hundred dollars a month.

The apprentice company often spent twenty hours of any given day together. They became a small family. Sometimes dysfunctional—what with sixteen strong personalities each trying to assert their creative genius—but family nonetheless. Total immersion in theatre culture fostered intense relationships. Tanya and I arrived every day for lunch, welcomed, but peripheral.

David, Tanya, and I lived on his meager salary. That and money from the discarded coke bottles I collected when I walked Tanya in her stroller the three mile round trip to the theatre and home each day. I put found bottles in the back of her stroller and stopped at the Piggly-Wiggly to turn them in for ten cents apiece. The total for the day would be the amount I had to spend on groceries for dinner.

Our apartment was the second floor of an old Victorian on Piedmont Avenue. The elderly landlady and her maid lived downstairs. Upstairs were our bedroom, a living-dining area where Tanya's crib was set up, a galley kitchen that could accommodate one person—but only if they turned sideways, and a bathroom four times the size of our kitchen.

I washed Tanya's diapers in the gigantic claw footed tub. I ran the water as hot as it would come out, mixed it with Ivory laundry detergent and a little bleach. I put a two by ten board across it to sit on while I stirred the diapers with the handle of my broom. Then I would rinse and rinse them again in hot water stirring, until they came out soap free. The final stage was a quick blast of cold water to cool them enough for me to wring them out by hand. I was a modern pioneer. Diapers need to be washed? I got this!

The second season we moved to another apartment in another house that was too far for me to walk to the theatre, so I stayed home, further still from the creative energy I craved. I went to opening night, but no longer enjoyed the nightly or daily interactions that, in reality, were merely art by association. But still, it had fed my illusions.

Wendy was around my age. Her mom was an actress in main stage productions and her father a member of the symphony. She was enamored of David and I found myself marking my territory whenever she was around.

"I love you," I breathed, as I wrapped myself around David.

He shifted uncomfortably. I leaned in and kissed him, full on and open mouthed.

"We both love you. Tanya, give Daddy a kiss." I pressed my eight-month-old baby into her Dad's arms.

She squashed her mouth onto his cheek. "Mwaa," she smiled big. "Daddy!"

I hoped the point was made but didn't question why I felt the need to make a point.

After the close of the last show of the season, Wendy's mom, Adrienne, gave me a ride home. I had to get back to the sitter and couldn't stay for the cast party. David would return in the early morning hours.

I got out of the car then I turned back to Adrienne. "Thanks for the ride. Would you like to come in?" I wasn't ready to be alone. "I made a cake today—we could have that and some coffee."

Adrienne had been quiet and uneasy with me on the ride home.

"I'd love to," she said, swinging her legs out of the car and joining me on the sidewalk. It was cold and damp out. Patches of ice scattered the walkway from the curb to our door.

"Careful," I laughed and took her hand to steady us both.

I led her into the kitchen and put on the water to boil and then went to settle up with the sitter. Tanya was asleep in her crib with her "neat shoes" on—a pair of high top white shoes, attached to a bar, heels in, toes out. She wore them at night to correct her pigeon toes.

"Look, Tanya!" I exclaimed when she was fitted for them. "These are *neat* shoes! Not everyone gets a pair of neat shoes like these to wear at night!"

From then on, when I put her to bed at night she, would call, "Neat shoes, Mommy, neat shoes." She lay peacefully asleep in her warm jammies, head turned toward the window where snow had been falling earlier. I turned back to the kitchen.

"Here you go," I said, cutting a large slice of chocolate chip cake and putting it on Adrienne's plate. I cut myself a slice, poured the now boiling water to drip through the coffee grounds and sat down. I smiled.

"So tell me about you and David. When did you get married?" She shifted in her chair, unable to get comfortable.

I launched into my romanticized story of our relationship. That first kiss where David got dizzy. Falling in love. Commitment to art.

"Were you pregnant when you got married?"

"Well, yes, but I told David not to marry me if he felt he had to, only to marry me if he wanted to."

"What did your parents say when they found out you were pregnant?" *Why was she probing into this?*

"My parents told me I had three options, I could give the baby up for adoption, have an abortion, or keep it. I decided to have the baby and keep her. I would have done it with or without David."

She looked pensive. "Were they angry with you?"

"I don't think so. They may have been disappointed, but I think by the time I came to them it was past time to be angry."

"Are you happy?"

"I am happy. Today is our anniversary. I spent the day making this cake. It *is* hard when he works so much, but I support his choices."

She hesitated, as if she were deciding whether or not to say something. My heart started beating fast and hard. Something was not being said. I didn't know what it was, but I was getting scared. Uncharacteristically, I didn't *want* to know what she wasn't saying.

"I'm really tired. I think I need to go to bed soon. It's awfully late. Thanks for the ride." I hurried to retrieve her coat and scarf and wrap up a piece of cake for her to take.

After ushering her out, I collapsed on the bed, scared and not knowing why. Tanya let out a soft sigh. Her steady breathing filled the silence and calmed my fears. After what seemed like hours, I slept.

Two weeks later, we were packing to move to L.A. The next step in his career: take on Hollywood. He came home after striking the set. Tanya was napping. He sat down on the side of the bed and began shaking.

"What is it, David? Are you okay?"

"No." He couldn't hold back his tears.

"David." I knelt beside him and took his hand. "It's okay. Tell me. Whatever it is we'll figure it out together."

Sobs racked his body. He was inconsolable.

"Tell me." I gently encouraged. "Tell me."

A deluge of words washed over me. "I had an affair with Wendy. She got pregnant. She went to D.C. and had an abortion." He grabbed hold of me and held on, shuttering with sobs. "It was a boy."

I held him. What else could I do when someone I loved was in that much pain? I was being strong while my guts were ripped out. *You slept with Wendy? How could you? And you got her pregnant? There is no way she could tell it was a boy in under three months. She's manipulating you.* But I said nothing, just held and rocked him until there were no more tears in him. So this is why Adrienne was so uneasy with me. She must have wanted to tell me that night we sat so calmly eating cake.

Two days later we boarded a plane for L.A. I followed him three thousand miles in pursuit of his career, loaded down with the pain of his betrayal and the loss of my innocence. I could no longer live in denial. Once there, we lived with David's agent and two wonderful gay men, Gerry and Ricky, who offered me solace over coffee every morning.

Each day, after I put Tanya down for her morning nap, I turned the shower on full force and let the water beat down on my head in an effort to numb my tumbled, slicing emotions. When I couldn't stand up anymore, I sank to the tile floor, my head on my knees, hands clutched around my shins while the water tried to pound me into insensibility. Finally, I curled over into a ball letting the stream wash away my tears and snot until the water turned cold and stinging needles peppered my skin.

I began to bleed for no reason. I bled and bled and bled. I found a free clinic that would see me. The doctor gently examined me.

"Have you been under a lot of stress?" he asked.

I began to cry. "My husband had an affair."

"How old are you?"

"Twenty."

"You're kind of young to be married already and have a baby. If your husband has had an affair, I'm guessing that's enough stress to have triggered your abnormal bleeding. I'm going to put you on antibiotics. I can't do anything about your stress, but if it continues longer than another two or three weeks, come back in."

I took the script and the information and walked back onto the street. Stress. Well, there was nothing I could do about that. Within weeks the bleeding tapered off and after two months my menstrual cycle normalized.

A year later we returned to Atlanta. My intuition started clanging and the familiar knot in my chest began to ache again. I grieved the end of my marriage before I spoke the words, hoping against hope that I was lying to myself, that what I knew was merely fear, not fact. But I couldn't use denial as a coping skill any more. My fear yawned like a dark pit with no edges and David didn't deny it when confronted. He was seeing another woman.

The kindest and truest thing I can say about my marriage is that we were too young. I loved him passionately. I loved discovering sex with him. I loved the thought of being two artists pursuing life together. I believed we were soul mates and couldn't bear it when reality didn't match my illusions.

At the time we lived in Sandy Springs, an outlying suburb of Atlanta. I felt isolated from both the city and the theatre community. When we separated my first order of business was to move into an old Victorian house that had been carved up into three apartments in the middle of downtown. Its aging grandeur referred back to a gentler time when the area had been a neighborhood filled with families, each home distinctive in its gables and gingerbread moldings, front porches and landscaping. The house was the last hold out against encroaching businesses and parking garages. My neighbors to the left and right were concrete and brick, utilitarian structures that housed print shops and metal fabricators.

The exterior of my new home was an unassuming gunmetal grey paint that peeled randomly from the wood boards on the side facing afternoon sun. The original glass in the windows wavered in the sunlight and the tiny back yard was a field of violets in the spring. Bare trees in the winter revealed a lamppost reminiscent of the one in C.S. Lewis's book *The Lion, the Witch and the Wardrobe*. My second floor apartment was a maze of rooms cobbled together without rhyme or reason. But oh the wonders of a giant, claw-footed bathtub filled to the edge with warm water, a candle burning in the windowsill and a good book to restore my heart and soul after a long week of work! So what if the dull gray linoleum curled and buckled in the kitchen- it had twelve-foot ceilings with deep crown molding and windows that shimmered in the starlight. I loved my second story view of not much.

Early each morning I got up and dressed and fed Tanya—who was all of two and a half by now—and continued our ritual of singing about the things we would do in the coming day.

"First we eat breakfast and then we get dressed and then we walk to the bus stop, and then we ride on the bus all the way, and then I kiss you goodbye and we wave and wave and wave. And then you play and have a snack and then you play and eat your lunch and then you take a nap . . ." Off key and sing-song-y I made up our story.

She talked back and sometimes sang to me, "And then you wait for the bus and wave and wave and wave . . ."

Every day was either a little adventure or an overwhelming feat to be accomplished, depending mostly on how deeply I grieved at any given moment. We would make our way down the metal exterior stairs to the bus stop up the street. The first bus took us downtown to change busses to get to Tanya's daycare in Midtown. Another bus and another change of buses to take me to the end of Marietta Street and my temp job. At the end of the day the routine reversed. If our buses where all on time and our transfers went without a hitch, we arrived back at the apartment by 7:00. I had energy enough to fix a quick dinner, have bath, story, and bedtime for Tanya, and a quick bath for me before I fell into a stupored sleep.

David lived nearby and watched Tanya one night a week while I went to an acting class at Callanwolde. Callanwolde was an old mansion being transformed into an arts center, another long bus ride away. I used the bus time to practice my lines, peruse a new script, or jot notes to myself about direction or character content.

Callanwolde was an elegant old lady with great bones. At the time, she was also in much need of attention and care. But neither sagging floors nor yellowed, peeling wallpaper diminished her gracious welcome. Once through the door, the atmosphere buzzed with the energy of busily creating people. I loved it there but felt a little like an impostor. My acting skills were okay, my directing somewhat better. No one thought enough of either to encourage their development.

While I dreamed of being discovered or mentored by someone I admired, I was just happy to be in the middle of all that creative energy. Walking through the heavy wooden door into the friendly chaos of actors rehearsing, potters potting, artists drawing or painting or carving, I peeked into rooms as I walked past and caught snapshots of weavers rhythmically working their looms, musicians caressing their instruments in search of phrasing, singers trilling scales, and writers hunkered around a table doing a close read of an original manuscript.

Jan, a young lesbian poet, came to our acting class looking for readers for an original piece. She selected me for the performance piece! Jan intrigued me. She oozed electric, sexual energy as she gathered us around and shared her vision for the work. When she was in the room I couldn't stop focusing on her hands, the way her breasts pushed against her utilitarian tan shirt. I wanted more than anything for her to flash one of her charming smiles at *me*.

She was the first self-identified lesbian I had ever met and in my spectacular ignorance I was disappointed that she didn't flirt with me. Or ask me out. I assumed that she would be attracted to me. I was pretty sure that lesbians would pursue any available woman. And, if not, then I knew my sexual energy shone like a beacon to anyone I turned it on. Either way, I was disappointed. I didn't interpret my disappointment as openness to having a relationship with a woman. I didn't think about it at all.

Around that same time, I met Catherine, another actress at Callanwolde. She was younger than me, eighteen to my twenty and just out of high school. Catherine's dark, loose curls rested on her shoulders, her smile made *me* smile and made me feel all warm inside. Like me, she was bewitched by everything Callanwolde and excited to be a part of it. I invited her to my apartment. She met Tanya, drank tea on my rooftop patio (the overhang of the back porch we accessed through my kitchen window) and we talked and talked, pressing our thighs together, both seemingly unaware of the touch. We talked about theatre and music, about love and about God. We became close friends quickly and I lost her friendship just as quickly. She called one afternoon to say she'd told her mother about me, Tanya, and my impending divorce. Her mother thought I was too old or too experienced to be her friend. She was so sorry, but she could only see me at Callanwolde.

I didn't feel older than Catherine. I suppose being a mother and a woman soon to be divorced made me seem older than her by decades, but in my heart and even my naivete, I felt more like her than most people I knew.

Why didn't I see my attraction to Jan or my more romantic connection to Catherine? It wasn't denial. Maybe it was lack of experience. I had no idea what I was feeling or what it might mean. How hidden was I from myself? How could all those feelings bubble so close to the surface and me remain so spectacularly unaware? Looking back, I see threads so strong and thick I find it hard to imagine I overlooked them.

Tanya and I lived a frugal existence. I made only enough money to get by and to pay for acting classes. I succumbed to one other extravagance: a haircut. My hair was down to my waist and so thick I would sit and brush it for hours getting it to dry. *A haircut*, I thought, *just the thing*.

I didn't tell David. My plan included secrecy. Or not so much secrecy as independence. A visible act, a choice I made without consulting David.

"What did you do to your hair?" he asked when he saw me, my hair now dusting my shoulders in a gypsy cut, the absent weight bouncing it into soft waves.

"I cut it," I said. "I don't have to run things by you anymore."

I was the opposite of Samson. Cutting my hair *enhanced* my power. *I do as I please.* I took the first small risk of defining myself and I loved it.

I began to bleed again. I bled for weeks. One night, in desperation, I got on a bus with Tanya and headed to Crawford Long Hospital. A nurse prepped me, giving me a chance to slip off my jeans and panties and pull a paper shift over my bra and t-shirt.

"She can't stay in here while you're being examined."

"I've got no one to look after her. Please let her sit by my head and I'll talk with her while the doctor checks me out."

Having no other options, she left without argument. Tanya came and sat on a stool next to me. The doctor arrived, paused with a double take at Tanya, and began the process of getting my ass aligned with the table. Feet in stirrups. Slide your bottom down. More. More. Okay. I sighed as he draped me with a large sheet. *Please know what's wrong!* I turned to Tanya, "Let's sing," I smiled to encourage her.

"You are my sunshine, my only sunshine . . . " We whisper-sang to one another while the doctor inserted the speculum.

Moments later he stood. "You have cancer," he said in heavily accented English. "You need to see a gynecologist."

He referred me to a gynecologist to see the next day. I pulled on my panties and jeans and managed to get a foot into each shoe before I gathered up Tanya and my perennial backpack. We stood on the dark street waiting for the bus. I hoped the busses hadn't stopped running yet.

"Are you okay, Mommy?"

"Yeah, honey, I'm okay." *What if I'm not okay?* I kept my hands clinched so they wouldn't shake. *Don't scare Tanya.* My heart flapped erratically and I broke into a cold sweat. *Breathe. Breathe. God be with me. Hold me. Help me breathe. Help me get through this. Help me get home. Help me get Tanya to bed. Help me.*

The next day the gynecologist checked me out.

"My breasts are sore." I told him.

He opened my gown and cupped each breast in his hands. He began to massage them, stroking their undersides. He rolled the nipple of my right breast between his thumb and forefinger and winked at me.

"There's absolutely nothing wrong with your breasts." He grinned. "They are *very* fine."

Scared and shaking, I scrambled off the table and grabbed my clothes. "Don't bother to send me a bill, mister. You'll be lucky if I don't report you."

I lost so much blood that I was too weak to work. I called my Mom.

"Come get me. I'm sick."

*Tired of Speaking Sweetly*

Love wants to reach out and manhandle us,
Break all our teacup talk of God.

If you had the courage and
Could give the Beloved His choice, some nights,
He would just drag you around the room
By your hair,
Ripping from your grip all those toys in the world
That bring you no joy.

Love sometimes gets tired of speaking sweetly
And wants to rip to shreds
All your erroneous notions of truth

That make you fight within yourself, dear one,
And with others,

Causing the world to weep
On too many fine days.

God wants to manhandle us,
Lock us inside of a tiny room with Himself
And practice His dropkick.

The Beloved sometimes wants
To do us a great favor:

Hold us upside down
And shake all the nonsense out.

But when we hear
He is in such a "playful drunken mood"
Most everyone I know
Quickly packs their bags and hightails it
Out of town.

—Hafiz

# Chapter 9 *Coming Out to Myself on the Way to God*

I REALLY DIDN'T WANT to move back to Columbus, Georgia, but I could no longer work and had to give up my apartment. I didn't want to live with my parents but I needed to and was glad for the respite. When I arrived I had been bleeding for forty days. And forty nights. Oh the irony. I was exhausted. It pushed me to my limits caring for an energetic child.

The day after I arrived in Columbus I drove myself to the emergency room at the Medical Center, the same hospital in which I had given birth to Tanya. After a cursory exam from the on call physician I was referred to yet another gynecologist for an appointment the next day.

"I'm afraid you have an STD," he said when we were sitting in his office after the examination.

"I've only slept with my husband!" I started to cry.

"That doesn't mean he hasn't slept with other women." He focused on the pencil he bounced on the surface of his desk, not looking at me. I knew David had slept with other women. I just believed, in spite of everything, that he would have told me if my health were in danger.

The doctor shuffled through a pile of papers at the corner of his desk, pulled out an article that had been carefully clipped from the *National Enquirer* and handed it to me. "You could have got it from a toilet seat."

"I didn't think you could get STDs that way."

"Well, read it. It tells about it right there in black and white."

Alice in *Alice in Wonderland* couldn't have felt any stranger than I did at that moment. Nothing made sense. An article from that phony rag, the *National Enquirer*? I've been on enough antibiotics since my first hospital visit to kill any bug that might have made it's way into my system. Even if I did get something from David. Or a toilet seat.

The next day I called the hospital and spoke with a nurse. I relayed the whole, long, sordid tale. "Please help me. Something is wrong and no one is helping me."

She gave me the number of her gynecologist. "He's great, honey. But you call me back if it doesn't work out."

By the time the doctor stepped into the exam room I was a puddle of tears.

"... and then he said I might have gotten it from a toilet seat." I hiccoughed out my final sob.

The doctor paused, a smile sneaking around his mouth, "Waalll," he drawled, "you *can* get it from a toilet seat but I hear it's not a very comfortable position."

I giggled. Sanity. At last.

Seems I had an infection exacerbated by my IUD. The doctor removed it, renewed my prescription for antibiotics and told me to come back when I needed to discuss alternative methods of birth control.

I healed, but remained with my parents. David, on the other hand, moved to New York.

The Goetchius House, the swankiest restaurant in Columbus, Georgia, hired me as a waitress. Of course, women could only work in the downstairs part of the restaurant where it was more casual. Men waited tables in the formal dining rooms upstairs. And got larger tips. But I was making money again and enjoyed the food and wine. My palate for wine became more sophisticated and I enjoyed the satisfaction and elegance of giving good service.

That fall I auditioned at Columbus College for an upcoming play and got the lead in Edward Albee's *Tiny Alice*. I could make it in Columbus, anyway. I got into the theatre scene at the college. Between working and rehearsing the play, working and performing, and working and being a mom, I was once again exhausted. My high school girlfriend, Andi, invited me to spend a weekend at her place in the country. I was happy to take her up on it. Tanya stayed with Mom and Dad while I spent a few days walking, napping, and reading.

The long drive to Andi's took me away from town to gravel roads and dusty silence. Her house sat back from the road, no other house in view in any direction. It was an inviting, rustic old structure with low ceilings and rough wooden floors strewn with rag rugs. A wood-burning stove billowed heat from the corner of the living room. Andi and I drank wine and talked into the night. When she left for work the next day I perused her bookshelf—it was always fun to see what others were reading—and pulled out a copy of *Lesbian/Woman*, by Del Martin and Phyllis Lyon.

The next afternoon I pulled her aside, "have you read this book?"

"No."

"I think I'm a lesbian."

I don't believe Andi took me seriously since she didn't react one way or another.

I reacted all over the place. Nothing was what I thought. I was thrown off-balance by my own private paradigm shift. Merrill. Jo-Jo. Catherine. It all started to make sense. I had been in love with Jo-Jo. Okay, puppy love. Crush. But young love like any young animal. With Catherine my subconscious adult reached toward the intimacy of heart and soul. Now I could finally name the missing piece: sexual attraction.

I set out on a long walk, thinking, talking to myself, and laughing. The air sharpened. Colors were somehow more profound. Holy Cow! I just figured it out. It. Me. Wow.

Andi gave me free reign of her farmhouse and VW bug while she was at work. I drove back into town, straight to the college where my friends hung out. It was early December and people gathered to celebrate the holidays.

I zipped into the parking lot at Columbus College, hopped out in a single smooth move, and strode toward a group of my friends congregating outside the entrance to the theatre building.

"Hey!" I called as I got closer, "Merry Christmas!"

I joined the clump leaning together against the concrete retaining wall and we smoked and laughed and shared holiday plans.

"I'm staying with a friend out in the country for a few days. Anyone want to go with me?"

The one person I didn't know spoke up. "Yeah. I will."

She was taller than me, lanky, fresh-faced, open . . . and a little boyish. I can't or won't say "masculine" because that description would be too severe, too harsh, too confining. Rather, she was self-possessed, exuding an air of confidence and competence in her Levi's and flannel shirt.

My heart quivered. Electricity shot between my legs. *Who is she?*

Tony, a techie on the production said, "This is Skyler. She's a friend of mine. We've worked lights at the Springer together."

I smiled, "Ready?"

"Sure."

We climbed into the Bug. I started the car, slid the tall gear shifter into reverse and lifted the lever that cranked the heater. I was nervous. *Who is she?* I asked myself again. She was self-assurance with an edge of cockiness. *She turns me on,* I realized, with a surprised start. *I've felt this before and didn't know what it was.*

She began to talk and I talked and I don't remember the ride back to Andi's at all. *One day I realized I'm a lesbian and now I have one in the car with me!* We sat up all night, feeding sticks to the wood stove, drinking wine, smoking a little pot now and then, and talking. I told her about *Lesbian/Woman.* About my new self-understanding. About my dreams. My daughter. My life. She told me about her adventures in theatre, her work as an artist, traveling to Bogota. About her father, now dead, who had been a state senator. Her mother's flight from the Nazis during the war. We napped on and off, curled together on the floor in a puppy pile, waking again to continue the conversation.

At first light, we took a walk through the fields around the house, through a small grove of trees, and into the high, dew-covered growth in the fields beyond. The conversation ebbed as we meandered together and then I was meandering alone, but aware that she hadn't left. Everything swung into sharp focus. Every sound, each insect whistle or click, inserted itself into my awareness. A breeze clattered dried fronds together. As the sun rose, smells of earth and vegetation insinuated themselves. The crisp cool air met with the sun's heat on my back. Everything was clear, defined, intense. I gathered armfuls of late autumn blooms, breathed in and lifted my face to the sun. *I feel you here, God. Thank you for this amazing day.* Eventually, I called to Skyler and we met up again on the dirt track that led back to the farmhouse, finishing our walk in companionable silence.

It was time for me to go back to Columbus and check on Tanya, my brief respite over. Though I slept little I was wide-awake and full of energy. I dropped Skyler off and she promised to come by later and follow me back to Andi's to return the Bug.

That evening she pulled into my parent's driveway and introduced me to "Fred," her navy blue, 1970 MGB. Laughing, we sped through town and out the single-lane country roads, playing hopscotch—first she passed me, then I her—yelling nonsense into the wind through our lowered windows. We left Andi's car in the drive and I climbed into the MG. My legs stretched out at a straight right angle from my hips as I eased into the seat.

Skyler put the top down for the trip back.

"Isn't it a little cold to ride with the top down?"

"Never. I ride with the top down even when it snows."

She impressed me with her driving skills as she took Fred through his paces. She maneuvered onto a long strip of unlighted highway heading no-where. Our conversation tapered off as we watched the headlights eating up the road in front of us. Delighted to be in her company, my heart thudding in anticipation and a little—just a little—fear, I reveled in the heat blasting over my feet, the cold bruising my ears and hair lashing my face. The lights hypnotized me into silence as they cut a swath into the night.

Her hand, perched lazily on the smooth wooden gearshift knob before it dropped and slid toward my hand. Our fingers entwined. I glanced at her then stared at our hands. My heart flapped like a wild bird in my chest until the gentle stroking of her fingers gently soothed my fears. My whole world existed in our hands. Her softness against my softness, her strength calling to my strength, her tenderness slaying me while the miles flashed by beneath us and the night wrapped around us in a sheltering cocoon.

I came back to earth when she pulled into the parking lot of a Waffle House. I was famished. Wait. I hadn't eaten in forever. We laughed and ordered hamburgers and coffee and talked and talked until light seeped over the horizon. How many days did we go without sleep? How many short naps did we catch with our seats tilted back and our hands shyly touching? How often did we talk until dawn? I can't tell you. Time didn't have much meaning. By day I was a mom, by night a soul on an adventure that I would not name.

Weeks went by. "Where are you every night?" my parents wanted to know.

"With Skyler," I'd say, as if that was enough of an explanation.

The intensity of our conversations and the magic of our interlaced hands powered my body, replacing sleep. One night, one morning, it may have been one or two or three in the morning, as we nursed yet another cup of coffee at the Waffle House, I looked directly into her eyes, screwed up all my nerve and said, "I don't think we can go on this way forever. We either have to move forward or step away."

She gazed at me. "What do you mean?" She wasn't making it easy.

"We either go deeper or go back." My voice shook. I knew what I meant. *Please know what I mean.*

"Okay."

"Okay what?"

"Okay, I agree."

Happy and terrified, I grinned. Skyler smiled back. We touched hands and rose from our seats. Back in Fred, my heart began to tap dance again.

"I want to take you somewhere"

"Where?" I asked.

"To where I go to look at the stars."

We drove away from town, away from the ambient light of the city, and deep into the countryside. The sky was a soft, inky black. The stars' crisp light bent close to the earth. After a long while, she pulled onto a dirt road and maneuvered the low-slung sports car over a bumpy field.

"Come on," she said, "Get out." She pulled me to my feet and tucked my hand into hers. We walked into the middle of the field and she pulled off her ruana, a thick wool poncho, and spread it on the ground. We lay on our backs and gazed at the stars skittering across the night landscape. Moments. Hours. Years later, she leaned over and touched her lips to mine.

Gentle lips pressed my tender lips. Smooth cheek brushing smooth cheek. I drew in my breath. Awe washed over me, a gentle heat in the cool dark. Reverently, I returned her kiss. We breathed together, gasping in the realization that we had survived.

The next day we walked down the road in front of the college, holding hands, and swinging our arms like schoolgirls. I wanted the whole world to know how happy I was. Inside I was singing:

> *Praise God from whom all blessings flow!*
>
> *Praise God all creatures here below!!!*

My prayer was one of thanksgiving. Joyful, glad, amazed by the blessing. I collapsed to my metaphorical knees in gratitude. *Thank you, God, for helping me figure out who I am! Thank you for making me, me! Thank you! Thank you! Thank you, God!*

"In a world where language and **naming** are power, silence is oppression, is violence."

—Adrienne Rich

# Chapter 10 *Endings and Beginnings*

A YEAR AFTER WE separated, David and I divorced. Our marriage ended because David took other lovers. I don't know his story. Perhaps he took them to end the marriage. It was the one thing I could not tolerate. And I don't mean tolerate as in 'allow"—I mean tolerate as in "to stay would kill me." My heart shattered. I was a failure. I had given up everything that had been asked of me. I had given up my dreams and myself. And it wasn't enough. I was pretty sure I was going to die. The truth is neither of us understood that we were too young and unformed to make a lifetime commitment.

I had my suspicions before his confession. And maybe the hardest or the most harmful thing I did was to talk myself out of them. Not listening to my own gut made me feel really, really crazy.

During the brief time of our marriage and shortly thereafter my last name was Ward. I was seventeen when David and I married in December of 1969 and I spent much of my married life trying to figure out who Connie Ward was.

David and I divorced in 1973. It was the year hip-hop was born in the Bronx, abortion was legalized, Billy Jean King beat Bobby Riggs in "the battle of the sexes", and I turned twenty-one. We had been married a little more than three years, three years too many, but too young and too earnest to know it when we started.

Besides, during that year of separation, I learned many things about myself. Among them: I was a lesbian. While the realization did not end the marriage, it would have one day. Or perhaps I am bi-sexual. Or perhaps the issue is that both of us were on a journey of self-actualization and our paths veered off from one another. The ending of the marriage freed me up to possibilities I might not have allowed myself to discover otherwise. When I encountered myself without expectations of what I *should be* my journey of self-discovery became more authentic. The questions I wrestled with were never ones of morality—good or evil, right or wrong—instead they were question about how to be authentic rather than inauthentic, how to live with integrity. When I unearthed heretofore undiscovered truths about myself, I embraced them. With joy. Thanking God. Never for a moment considering the consequences.

The divorce court in Atlanta convened in a mammoth courtroom, with ceilings soaring so high you had to tip back your head back to see them. The judge's wooden bench emerged from the floor like a massive tree in a primeval forest. Far below we sat, scrunched amid a sea of petitioners, waiting our turn. Ceiling fans lazily slung the warm spring air around the room. Since we had filed our own paperwork and had no attorneys, the case should have been cut and dry. The judge called me forward,

"Little lady, don't you think you should ask this man for child support?"

"No, sir, I don't. He doesn't make much and I work, so I'll be just fine."

"Well, that is not acceptable to me." The judge said and then he turned to David. "Sir how much do you make?'

"Four hundred dollars a month."

"Well, sir, I order you to pay eighty dollars a month in child support. Ma'am, I see here you are petitioning to return to your maiden name. May I ask why?"

"Yes sir, since I will no longer be married to this man, I want to return to my own name. I don't want to be defined by him for the rest of my life."

"Well, ma'am, what's going to happen when your daughter goes to school and her momma has a different name? People will think she's illegitimate. Have you thought of that?'

"Well she's not, sir, it will be easy enough to explain."

"I cannot in good conscience allow you to change your name. The decree for the divorce is granted with the proviso of child support and the retention of married name."

The gavel cracked. We walked from the room not sure what had happened, trying to let it all sink in. I was shaken and angry. The doors closed behind us and we walked straight forward to stand before the bank of elevators. I burst into sobs.

"Don't cry, Connie, this doesn't mean things might not turn out for us in the future."

He touched my shoulder tentatively in an awkward attempt to comfort my spasmodic weeping. The doors slid open and we stepped in. As they slithered shut, David held himself in check when I wailed, "I want my name back!

My secret within is a heart that feels
like a sky full of
fireworks and
constellations dancing
with each breath I take.

My secret within
Is a universe

And everywhere feels like home.

—Alia

# Chapter 11  *Going Off Course, Getting Closer to Myself*

ONE OF THE DOWNSIDES of being an army brat is that I didn't have a concrete context in which to explore my experience of call. I was so young, so immature, and I didn't have a road map. I didn't put together "call" with church other than, maybe, entering a convent. I couldn't put what I was feeling together with *anything* tangible—except that I would be open to whatever it might mean. If I could just figure it out.

It might not have been a great idea to attend a weekend retreat with the Moonies in the mountains of north Georgia with my four-year-old daughter, but it didn't feel risky. I was not afraid of being indoctrinated but I *was* curious.

I met Oakley, a bona fide Moonie, that is a follower of Sun Myung Moon (founder of the Unification Church) and her spiritual enthusiasm excited me. I spotted her selling carnations on the street outside the Deep Purple Lounge, an underground gay bar in Columbus. Her open-faced grin was a welcomed contrast to the smirks of drunken barflies. Dressed in the requisite t-shirt and jeans, her massively curly hair sprang out of two braids.

"God grieves when we turn away from His intentions for us," she smiled, as she handed me the drooping flower.

*I made God sad? My actions affect God?* I'd only heard that God's actions affect me as in "The Lord giveth and the Lord taketh away." Never that God would grieve my unresponsiveness, my lack of a serious, intentional journey of faith. My heart ached with a newfound compassion for God—the God of the fields and streams of my childhood, for the God whose love embraced and comforted me when I was fearful. I wanted to make God feel better.

"Father says we must all work to restore the world with him because when we don't, we break the heart of God."

I was listening. The idea that we could live in a way that made a difference to God thrummed on my spine. I wanted to be who God wanted me to be not because I was afraid of breaking rules that would send me to hell, but because I could be a part of God's plan to heal the world.

"Really?" No sarcasm, the idea was stunning.

"Yes," she breathed, "Father has brought a new revelation. When he was a prisoner in communist North Korea he had a vision and wrote *The Divine Principle*. It's truly amazing. I've been a Christian all my life but never felt like I could live my faith. Now I have found Father and I live my whole life centered on God."

*I* wanted to live my life for God. The hunger in me that had never found an outlet salivated for the feast of possibilities she described. I was too unconventional to consider going into the ministry, but now I recognized a sister of my heart telling me that she lived every hour of every day in the service of God. She lived simply and lived in community.

I mindlessly twirled the carnation, forgetting that I had bought it for Skyler. Settling down onto my haunches, I waited to hear more. And more. Oakley enchanted me. Her laugh made me smile. Her passion for God seduced me.

"I believe in miracles," Hot Chocolate's disco beat wafted out of the bar's opened door, "You sexy thing—you sexy thing, you."

We talked about the meaning of life, our experiences of God, what mattered most in the world. All the while an innocent crush niggled its way into my consciousness. I invited her to our apartment for dinner and she accepted.

The next day she arrived early and climbed the steps to our apartment over an old wooden garage. It was a bohemian crash pad complete with white washed wooden walls, uneven planked floors, and a kitchen and bath cobbled together with throwaway cabinets and leftover fixtures. After a simple meal of pasta with marinara sauce and a bottle of beer, Oakley and I curled up on pillows in the living room, our dishes cluttering the floor.

We talked into the night. I asked her tons of questions. She told me Reverend Moon was Christ returned, that Jesus had not fulfilled the mission of the Christ and Reverend Moon had come to finish the job. The little girl in me who had prayed so hard to be here when Jesus came back lifted her holy little head, cocked it to one side, and told the adult me to listen up. So I did.

During the next weeks I got to know Oakley better, saw how she lived and met her "family"—the group of Moon followers who shared an apartment. The ragged band –they were both scruffy and intensely sincere—lived together in a community that looked a lot like Saint Paul's description of the early Christian church: shared finances, each one according to his or her need, and a loving, passionate commitment to God and one another. I wanted it. I wanted the world to look like this. I believed this is what God had in mind for us from the beginning.

When an exploratory weekend retreat was scheduled in the north Georgia mountains, I registered. *Let's see what this is all about.* That Friday, eight of us—three inquirers, Tanya, Oakley and three folks from the communal house—piled into an old dented van whose color was faded beyond recognition. All the way to the retreat center we laughed, told stories and sang songs, Tanya chiming in with her sweet, childish soprano. It was late spring as we drove through the north Georgia forests where leaves unfurled in every shade of green. The days were warm and the evenings cool, one of the nicest times of the year. As we curved around the mountain we faced first into the sun and then away, finally arriving at dusk, our van huffing the last leg up the steep drive into the campground.

The main building held the kitchen and meeting room. Bunkhouse cabins surrounded it on three sides. As soon as we claimed our bunks and stashed our few belongings a volunteer shepherded us into the large open room that also served as the dining hall and the lectures began. Tanya and I both squirmed in our seats. We had been sitting almost three hours without a break on the ride here and now we were sitting again.

Metal folding chairs, positioned in a semi-circle, faced a white board in the front of the room. Unlike the Moonies I befriended in Columbus, the lecturer was a neat, well-groomed man, at least twenty years older than the rest of us. He wore a dark gray suit, a patterned tie and highly polished black leather shoes. Oakley assured me that he was important in the hierarchy, closer to Reverend Moon than she, a mere follower, was. I leaned over and stared at the dull, putty-colored squares of scuffed vinyl that passed for a floor. Though interesting, the lecturer droned on until I stopped caring. Tanya leaned against my side.

"Mom," she whispered, "I'm *hungry.*"

I pulled her onto my lap and whispered back, "It won't be much longer."

But it was. It was 8:30 before we broke for a sparse supper of soup and sandwiches, enough for us each to have a cup of soup and half of a scrawny sandwich. And we couldn't eat that until a fervent young Moonie gave a ten-minute blessing. At the close of the meal I gathered my tired, well-behaved little girl and tried to slip out to put her to bed.

"We're not done." I was told as we headed for the door.

"She's about the go to sleep right here." I smiled.

"You can't leave yet."

"I sat back down and cradled Tanya in my lap. "Just go to sleep here, Tan. I'll tuck you in bed soon." It was after eleven before we made our way, stumbling through the dark, back to the cabin.

The wake up call came at 5:30 the next morning.

"We'll come to the next session," I mumbled when the volunteer wiggled my foot.

"You *have* to come." She cajoled. I cranked open one eye. She looked as tired as I felt, her limp, stringy hair hung close to her head. That reminded me—we hadn't had our shower yet—it was too late the night before when we could only fall into bed.

"Where's the bathroom? We need showers."

"You can't now, maybe later."

We dressed quickly. *Breakfast! Coffee . . . eggs . . . toast . . . milk—something to wake me up and fill my rumbling stomach.* Reality was pre-poured—it looked to be less than a cup—of cold cereal splashed with watery milk and half of a small glass of apple juice. Tanya finished and was still hungry.

"We don't have seconds," they told me when I took her bowl to the kitchen for seconds.

"But my daughter is still hungry."

The kitchen worker was not moved. I went back to my seat, gave her the little left in my bowl and asked my tablemates if they were going to finish their cereal.

I bristled on Tanya's behalf. *This is starting to feel more like an indoctrination camp than a retreat.*

We slept little and attended classes all day long and into the late hours of the evening. There were charts and graphs and scriptural proofs.

"Christianity has not fully understood who Jesus really was or what God's will is."

*What?*

"God worked for 2000 years to prepare a small Jewish nation to be the birthplace of the Second Adam. The first Adam failed and Jesus' task was to complete the work of the First Adam. Jesus discovered God's formula for restoring the world but because his family and his disciples did not accept and accomplish their missions, Jesus was unsuccessful."

*Jesus was a failure? And worse, he was a failure because his followers failed him?* This was disconcerting. I wasn't theologically sophisticated. I heard him out but I realized there was so much I didn't know. Sunday school had educated me on the basic stories but not so much on the interpretation of the stories.

"Jesus was a failure because he couldn't find his Eve. He never married and that meant he could not complete his mission to restore the work of Adam. Jesus *should* have been a wealthy man. He was the most precious person who ever lived. He wanted to save mankind from poverty. He came not to serve but *to be served*. Absolute power and wealth would never corrupt him."

*Jesus was about wealth and power? About being served? If he had wealth and power we would know he was the real thing? Should the Buddha have been wealthy and powerful?*

I shuddered. This was the opposite of everything I ever believed about Jesus.

The man in the suit put up a "divine" timeline on the white board.

"There are approximately 400 years between Noah and Abraham and 10 generations between Adam and Noah, a total of 1600 years."

*Okay. But aren't Adam and Eve a mythical story about creation? Can you really place that story in time?*

"Jacob loved God and loved mankind." He continued. "He succeeded in bringing unity with his brother, Esau and thereby restored the Cain/Abel relationship."

He fleshed out his timeline: from Jacob to Moses it was 400 years. From Moses to Saul: 400 years. The United Kingdom: 120 years. The Divided Kingdom: 400 years. Jewish captivity and return: 210 years.

"Then God began His preparation for 2nd Adam (the messiah) who was supposed to complete the work our original or "First" parents hadn't. That period of time was 400 years, spanning from Malachi to the birth of Jesus.

*Where was this going?*

"God has once again finished preparations for the coming of the 3rd Adam. From the time of Jesus until 392 A.D. (396 years- round up to 400) Christians were persecuted."

We were about to get another timeline. This one miraculously mirrored the first: the period of the patriarchs from 392 A.D. - 800 A.D. Theodosius to Charlemagne: 400 years. The United Kingdom, 800 A.D. -919 A.D. (Charlemagne, his sons and grandsons): 120 years. The Divided Kingdoms, 919-1309 A.D. (east and west): 400 years. Papal captivity *(!)* 1309-1517: 210

years. Preparation for the 3rd Adam, beginning with Luther: 1517-1917: 400 years. Culminating with the birth of Sun Myung Moon, 1917.

"That brings us to now," he paused and took a slow breath, "Reverend Moon is the result of all these preparations."

I jolted in my seat. *I need to check out these dates,* I thought to myself. *It's compelling but a little too neat.* I tamped down the doubts that began to creep in and continued to listen. His arguments made God seem really weird. And then there was the set up for the 3rd Adam (Moon) to be both obeyed and wealthy. *This doesn't feel right. Does this guy in his nice suit and expensive shoes really believe all the stuff he's saying? He looks like my dentist.*

"Sun Myung Moon and his wife Hak Ja Han restore the original trinity. You can be faithful in ways that Jesus' mother and followers failed. You can bring about the completion of God's work through the third Adam."

*The reason things went bad for Jesus was because his followers screwed up?* The choice of whether or not to accept Moon as the new messiah now seemed terrifyingly important. If Moon *was* God's next shot at redeeming humanity and I refused then I would be like the Jesus' disciples. I would fail God. I twisted in my metal chair, my tailbone ground into the unforgiving surface. I was too tired to think.

Tanya sidled over to me and twined her arms through mine.

"I'm bored," she whispered. "can I go out and play?"

I was bored and wanted to go out and play, too. The retreat planners had other ideas.

"Later," I whispered back, rifling around in my backpack for another book or game.

The lecture went on for another three hours. About half way through I took Tanya for a potty break. As we squeaked down the row of participants, excusing ourselves profusely, we were met with disapproving stares. *She has to go to the bathroom! Get real! And we're really hungry but you don't see me raiding the kitchen. I'm just taking her to the bathroom!* But I didn't say it out loud.

About eight p.m., we broke for another dinner of thin soup and a half a peanut butter sandwich. The after dinner lecture was about fasting as a spiritual discipline and continued until well past midnight.

"Fasting readies you to receive new knowledge. Fasting prepares you to be a follower of Sun Myung Moon. Fasting cleanses your physical and spiritual body to make room for the purity that will enter."

*Fasting also makes you vulnerable mentally, physically, and spiritually to all kinds of bullshit if you are not a strong person. Fast long enough and you begin to hallucinate.*

The lecturer tapped into my spiritual longing but I felt manipulated. The battle between my longing and my discomfort continued. For one thing, the Bible was never a neat and tidy document to me. I wasn't raised on proof texts but it can be seductive to look at the use of numbers in the text as definitive markers for truth. When I was seven and visiting downtown Tacoma, Washington with my mom I saw a man in white robes carrying a scripturally notated sign that predicted the end of the world.

"Don't be afraid," my mom told me, "people have been predicting the end of the world since the world first began." That man proved his beliefs using numbers from the Bible, too.

The circular thinking, the cleverness of it all, made me very uneasy. I looked over at Oakley, who smiled and nodded encouragingly. Trying to relax my skulking fears, I smiled back. She was sweet and kind and, in some ways, a saint. Loving, sincere, and non-judgmental. But the leader was controlling. No matter how benevolent he seemed something didn't feel right. My shit detector was going off.

*Where was the God I recognized, the One who tossed me into the glory of creation and the beauty of music? Where was my God of love in all these graphs and charts? Where was the Mystery?*

The last day, Sunday, brought more of the same: lectures interspersed with fervent singing and even more fervent praying. I wanted this to be the real thing, but alarm bells kept clanging in my head. I was ready to go home after breakfast (more cereal but this time chocolate milk). Since there was no way home except the way we came, I slogged through the remaining lectures. The day ground to a lengthy close at sunset and we crawled back into the van for the trip home.

"Wasn't it wonderful?" Oakley breathed. "Now that you know the truth, do you want to join us?" Like me, she was exhausted and looked like she'd been on a bender.

"What does "Father" believe about homosexuality?" I asked.

"Oh, it's a sin. All men and women are supposed to get married. But don't worry, Father will give you a husband that he chooses for you to be your spiritual guide."

"Yeah. Okay. Let me think about it."

I thought about it. Jesus hadn't come back.

When I tucked Tanya into her bed at home that night, I said something I would repeat many times over the course of her growing up, "Tan, if anyone tells you they have "the answer" run in the opposite direction."

"Night, Mom."

Success is stumbling from failure to failure with no loss of enthusiasm.

—Winston Churchill

# Chapter 12   *Long Way Around*

I WAS DISAPPOINTED THAT Jesus had not come back.

But with Skyler adventures percolated to a steady boil and I turned my attention to the next escapade and the next. Every month we hosted a peanut butter gorge, inviting our friends over and making peanut butter sandwiches on every kind of bread with every kind of filling: jellies, bananas, tomatoes, onions, cane syrup . . . We started with one filling at a time and by the end of the evening had tried every combination possible.

She took me to a bauxite mine outside Eufaula, Alabama, where we swam nude in the sparkling clear aqua water and squished the snow-white mud between our toes. We followed Joni Mitchell from Tuscaloosa, Alabama, to Athens, and Atlanta, Georgia, to see her perform in concert. We went to a midnight show of Frank Zappa and the Mothers of Invention at the Fox Theatre in Atlanta.

We moved to Athens, Georgia for Skyler to attend college and lived at the edge of town in an abandoned house that once graced the cover of *House Beautiful.* We lived off the land. I learned to make salads of dandelions, violets, wild onions and wild carrots. Tanya splashed naked in mud puddles and we gathered around a fire each night with others camping out on the land to cook and tell stories. We worked for the parks department, pulling weeds in the middle of traffic medians and splitting rails for fences in nearby parks. We listened to music, made love, played harmonicas, and got high. When the weather turned cold we dismantled walls of our house and used the studs as firewood. We raided cow patties in the fields behind our house for psilocybin mushrooms.

And when the end of the semester came we packed up and went on a bicycle trip. To New England. For the Bicentennial. For Skyler to take part in the U.S. Olympics bicycling trials.

Tanya flew to New York to spend the summer with her dad, so I was free to stretch my wings. Unfettered by responsibility for those few months,

I sought out "new worlds and new civilizations." It was 1976, the country was about to turn two hundred, and the Fourth of July would be the pinnacle of our nation's celebrations. Jimmy Carter was running for President against Gerald Ford, and Barbara Jordan, the dynamic and powerful U.S. Representative from Texas, was the first African-American to deliver a keynote speech at a national political convention (Democratic). She later would come out as lesbian. Thousands of black children protested apartheid in Soweto, a black township outside Johannesburg, and were met by police with tear gas and bullets. The United Kingdom and the United States imposed economic sanctions against South Africa in opposition to apartheid.

Right before we left, I took a trip to Planned Parenthood. For the second time in my life I had my IUD removed. The final act of letting go of my marriage.

"What kind of birth control do you want to change to?" The earnest young doctor asked.

"I don't need any. My lover can't get me pregnant."

He shook his head and gently admonished me. "Men don't always tell the truth."

*Don't I know it!* "It's okay," I reassured him, "when my lover tells me she can't get me pregnant, I believe her." I grinned.

He turned to the counter and began ruffling papers, finally grabbing a bag and putting a large box of condoms in it. "Here," he said, "in case you change your mind."

I left, swinging the white paper bag, as I strode into the sunshine. My life, my health, were no longer at the mercy of my need for birth control. Skipping to the car, I laughed as I slid into Fred and handed Skyler the box of condoms. "For you," I said, "from the doctor. Try not to get me pregnant, okay?"

Skyler and I loaded our backpacks with clean underwear, socks, a couple of flannel shirts, a Swiss Army knife, and instant grits, rolled up our sleeping bags and tied them to the bottom of our backpacks. We folded a recycled army tarp that would serve as our shelter and stashed it between our packs and our backs. And then we boarded a bus for Connecticut; our bikes dismantled and shoved into large black trash bags for the ride.

We got off the bus in New Haven. Sitting on the sidewalk, our gear bunched around us, we pulled out maps and plotted our route. It was almost impossible to get out of New Haven. Our maps didn't help. Only the kindness of strangers and unfathomably intricate directions got us to the outskirts of the city and onto Route One. It was near dusk when we pulled off the road about ten miles out of town, hoisted our bikes on our shoulders, and hiked in forty or fifty yards to set up camp in a wooded area next to fallow farmland. We built a fire and boiled water for grits, then banked it and crawled into our sleeping bags. I drifted into a dreamless sleep.

I woke up to the crash and crackle of underbrush. Male voices drifted through the trees. They were drunk and trying to set up their own camp. This was not good. I reached over and put my hand on Skyler's shoulder. She shook her head and motioned me to stay quiet. Breathing raggedly, I tried to slow my heartbeat. We stayed still and silent while the tramping came closer and closer. I squeezed my eyes shut and prayed. *Don't let them find us.*

We didn't go back to sleep. I remained in a state of high alert, muscles tensed and at the ready to jump up and abandon my bike and every other thing I owned to sprint for safety. I looked over at Skyler and saw that she held the same tension. We stared at one another in silence until the noise died away and the night became punctuated with snores. When dark turned to grey light we slipped out of our sleeping bags and gathered our belongings. Less than thirty feet away, six college-aged guys slept on the ground amid a pile of beer cans. We slipped onto the road and walked our bikes until sunrise.

Route One ran along the coast and was pleasantly flat. All day our tires spun effortlessly. The excitement of being on the road cancelled out our sleepless night. When we reached Clinton we made our way to the beach where we loaded up on quahogs, large, local clams that had been harvested earlier that day. Before the sun set we biked to a campground and set up for the night. Stuffed. Safe. And happy with ourselves and the world.

The next day we headed toward New London, making great time. *I can do this.* My fears about whether I could keep up melted each morning in the sunshine. In New London majestic tall ships strained against their moorings, trying to get back out to sea. We walked along the docks, wanting to hold hands but afraid to. I had spent that first night holding my breath, fearful of making the slightest sound. It brought home how tenuous our safety was. Women and lesbians are considered fair game. We meandered through town stopping for saltwater taffy and toward evening, draft beers.

Two days later we arrived in Westerly, Rhode Island. Somehow our earlier scare receded to a vague memory replaced by oceans, seafood, and uneventful but productive rides.

Westerly is an old sailors' town filled with old sailors telling tall, old sailor tales. We biked past marinas lined with fishing boats and pulled into the parking lot of a rickety neighborhood bar. A Miller High Life sign flashed in the window.

I dropped my pack to the floor and slid onto a barstool. Next to me hunched a leathered old man with a jaunty grin. His weathered and swollen hands clutched a long neck Pabst Blue Ribbon.

"Where you from?" he asked.

"Georgia."

"You hear that? These gals are from Georgia!"

"You from Plains, Georgia?" someone called out.

I grinned, "Nah. Plains only has three hundred people."

And then they started to buy us drinks. "Ever had a Harbor Light?"

"Nope."

"Give these girls a Harbor Light!"

A Harbor Light is tequila, Kahlua, and 151 rum, lit, blown out, and tossed back. After downing two I asked, "Why do you call it a Harbor Light?"

"Because if you drink too many you'll see harbor lights no matter where you are!"

I laughed and they passed me another.

By ten o'clock it was pitch dark and rain spattered against the window of the bar. We could barely keep from sliding off our barstools. Phil, the old sailor I met when I first walked in, turned to me. "Where are you staying tonight?"

"We have to find a campground."

"Come stay at my place. We have an old trailer in the back yard you two can stay in tonight. Don't need to try to set up camp in the rain." *Or when you're this drunk* he might have said, but didn't. "My wife will probably even fix you breakfast."

He loaded our bikes next to a pile of fishing gear in the back of his rusty pale blue pickup. We stumbled and swayed into the front seat. The cab smelled a little like my grampa's truck, only more of ocean and less of soil.

We stayed two nights before moving on, blessed by an old sailor and his wife, who had their own tales of adventure to share with us. *When I'm their age, I'll have stories, too, and this will be one of them.*

We biked on to Narragansett and walked over the bridge to the island of Jamestown. Tall ships racing across the Atlantic as part of the Bicentennial celebration were going to sail past Jamestown to their final destination of Boston. The small island, population 17,000, teetered on the brink of 100,000 as visitors flocked to get a bird's eye view of the race.

We biked around the island until we found a spot on the beach where we could set up camp. Then we made our way into town to look for work. A decommissioned Staten Island Ferry had been converted into a restaurant. One of only two restaurants on the island. And they did, indeed, need help. Skyler signed on as a dishwasher and I waited tables. The menu was easy:

lobster or steak, both served with salad and potato. Plus a well stocked bar and extensive wine list. I found a thrift shop, bought a white waitress uniform for three bucks and my two-week career took off. We turned tables every thirty minutes from 11 a.m. till 2 a.m.

The first night I didn't know if I could make it back to the campsite because my legs and feet ached so. I hadn't sat down in fifteen hours. But pedaling a bicycle uses an entirely different set of muscles and as we biked the five miles "home" the aches in my thighs and calves eased. In the mornings we picked wild blueberries growing nearby and made blueberry pancakes over the fire on my old Girl Scout mess kit. The massive tips I made—over five hundred dollars—financed the rest of our trip

The tall ships blew past in all their glory. It was an amazing sight to behold. I felt like I touched history, imagining ships arriving in Boston two hundred years and more ago. Far too soon, it was time for us to move on. We collected our final paychecks and pointed our wheels toward Hartford for the U.S. Olympic trials.

The roads became hilly as we got on Route 2 toward Norwich and on to Hartford. We began having spats. The trip was harder on us than we were willing to admit. Night after night, we slept on the ground, sustained mostly by instant grits and an occasional "grinder," often huddled beneath our tarp while rain dripped onto our sleeping bags. Skyler became distant. I couldn't do anything right. I watched her for clues to what she was feeling or thinking because she wasn't sharing those any more. *It's okay.* I told myself. *We just have to get past this rough spot.* And the next. And the next.

Half way to Hartford, Skyler went into a tailspin, shouting at me when we stopped on a deserted roadway to take a drink of water. She took off down the road while I was still trying to repack my backpack. I sat on the curb and began to shake. *Where the hell am I?* I stared down the empty road. My insides quivered and my breath became shallow. *Okay. I'll find a phone and call Dad to get a bus ticket and find the nearest place to take a bus.* My need to survive trumped grief. I had to come up with a plan that worked and a way to stay safe. This wasn't fun any more.

An hour or so later Skyler returned to find me in the same place still contemplating my options.

"Come on," she said.

I did.

Right before we arrived in Colchester, we met some kindred spirits, people our age who were living off the land.

"Come stay with us a while. We're building a log cabin and could use the help."

It sounded fun to me. We followed them up a dirt track that eventually opened onto cleared land. Chickens pecked in the front yard of a mostly built cabin. We stayed a week, doing hard labor during the day, bathing in the icy creek nearby and getting high around a campfire at night. I still felt a distance between Skyler and me. Something didn't feel right, but I wouldn't trust my intuition. It was too scary to contemplate being on the road alone, knowing no one. It was too scary to think about losing her.

We left our new friends with three days to get to Hartford for the Olympic trials. The hills turned to mountains slowing our progress.

"Good training for the trials," Skyler said. "It's part of my plan to build endurance."

I guess I built endurance, too, though I was on a three-speed Sears and she was on a ten-speed Raleigh. We pulled into town the day before the trials began. Hartford represented a milestone, an achievement. We made it. We made it physically and we made it together without me being stranded on the side of the road. It was time to celebrate. We took the money we made in Jamestown and rented a room in a swanky hotel downtown. The hotel was empty for the Fourth of July weekend and we were two of only a few guests. Rolling our bikes onto the elevator, we rode to the top floor. Our room had a wall of windows looking out over the city. We headed to the indoor pool, covered the surveillance camera with a towel, shucked down to our skin, and dove in for a long, slow swim. We indulged in Chateaubriand and a bottle of wine at the hotel restaurant before returning to our room, pulling open the curtains, and settling back to watch fireworks explode over the city. *It's going to be okay,* I comforted myself, watching Skyler watch the fireworks.

The park where the Olympic trials were being held rumbled with barely contained chaos. I stood back and watched while Skyler's bicycle passed inspection and she got her number. All the other riders were in sleek riding gear. Skyler wore cut-offs, a flannel shirt and hiking boots. I tried not to think disloyal thoughts as she lined up with the other riders. She stepped out of the race when it was clear she was behind by several laps. I clapped and hugged her. She shrugged and tried to smile.

The next day we shoved off for Northampton, Massachusetts. Days passed as we pushed on at an easy pace, but our conversations became choppy and terse. "You aren't keeping up." "You don't pay attention." "I don't want to kiss you." My solar plexus hurt, not from the uphill exertion but from gut fears. *This isn't supposed to be happening. It's supposed to be different.*

There should have been a billboard on the road to Northampton, Massachu-setts that read "Lesbian Mecca." There were lesbians everywhere. Lesbian music. Lesbian cafés, lesbian bars, lesbian student unions. *My tribe!* I had never seen so many visible and out lesbians in one place before. Commu-nity. I craved it like some crave chocolate or alcohol.

We met some women at a sandwich shop who offered us a place to stay. They were students at Amherst and had an apartment off campus.

"Amherst, Smith, U. Mass., Holyoke. All have huge lesbian popula-tions," Anita offered along with a joint. Anita was a redheaded Puerto Rican lesbian who lived in the apartment where we crashed. We hung out for three weeks, staying up late nights talking politics, apartheid, and feminism. We talked about our families and our dreams and what the world would be like if women were in charge. We dreamed a feminist university and all the courses we would teach. We put up posters for concerts that were fundrais-ers for anti-apartheid work. We listened to Holy Near and Meg Christian. We sang along with Gil Scott-Heron and greeted each other with "What's the word?"

Fist pump, "Johannesburg!"

We got high and made love on our hosts' living room floor when ev-eryone had gone to bed.

Our dream-like existence ended when we bundled our belongings and got back on the road. I swiveled on my bike seat, looking over my shoulder, trying to capture the place and the people in my memory. And then there was nothing left to see.

"I'm going to miss everyone."

Skyler didn't respond. I shared more of my thoughts and feelings with the women I just met, more passion about the things that mattered to me than I ever did with Skyler. *Traitorous thought!* With fierce concentration I focused on the road ahead, pushing down hard on one pedal while pulling up the other by the toe clip. My breath strained against the swelling tight-ness in my chest. *Why isn't this getting any easier?*

The Berkshire Mountains stole my breath in a different way. Struggling to make it up each hill, shifting into the bike's highest gear, heaving great chunks of breath, sweat leaking into the small of my back, thighs rigid, I scaled each summit as if it challenged my worth. When I peaked a hill the pitched angle of descent jolted me into breathless terror, as my bike raced at uncontrol-lable speeds past tall weeds and small trees growing close to shoulder of the road. Not quite fast enough to blur, but fast enough that a piece of gravel could throw my front wheel out of control. The momentum pulled me part way up the next hill only to begin again. Between the discomfort, fear, and hard won achievement were moments when the beauty of the mountains broke through.

Stockbridge, Massachusetts is forty-six miles from Northampton, a hard day's ride over the mountains for us. We coasted into town at dusk and pulled off the side of the road. Ahead, through the trees, we saw lights burning in a house. Our campsite secured, we fell into the sleep of sheer exhaustion.

In the morning we realized we were sleeping in the backyard of the house whose lights we had seen glittering through the trees. The lot was deceptively deep. Sure that no one would notice our campsite, we headed into town.

Stockbridge is an appealing town, nestled in the Berkshires. That it was home to Arlo Guthrie, Officer Obie, and Alice's Restaurant giddied my heart. The Berkshire Theatre Festival Summer Stock was in season. We kicked around Main Street, gawked at the Red Lion Inn—an old coaching inn still in business—and found ourselves in a hole in the wall eatery that was the original Alice's restaurant. The one that Arlo's twenty-minute song was about. *You can get anything you want at Alice's restaurant—exceptin' Alice.* I got introduced to Officer Obie. I couldn't stop humming the tune or wipe the smile off my face.

We stopped for a beer and struck up a conversation with some folks who were our age and apprenticing at the summer stock theatre.

"Where are you staying?"

"We're camped out on the edge of town." After a detailed description of how to get to our campsite, the guy let out a long whistle.

"You're camping in Mr. Rockwell's back yard! You probably ought to move from there. They're real protective of him around here."

*We were camped in Norman Rockwell's back yard!* We hurried back and gathered up our gear. *First Alice's restaurant, then Officer Obie, and now we find out we spent the night in Normal Rockwell's back yard! No one will ever believe me!*

Around three that afternoon we happened upon a little café a block or two off Main Street with a 'Help Wanted' sign in the window. It wasn't the new Alice's restaurant, which was a mega-diner on a hill several miles out of town; this was a funky café catering to the artsy crowd. Mrs. Hill hired us both—me to wait tables, Skyler to bus and wash dishes—and offered to let us camp behind the parking lot. Things seemed to be going well.

On our day off we rode out to Great Barrington to explore the old church the very same Alice lived in during the '60's. It was for sale. I wandered around the interior perimeter, dreamt of buying the place . . . and of something else I couldn't find words for. Nothing that took root in my mind, just nudges and yearnings that I didn't stop to explore. Skyler created echoes to amuse herself while I sat quietly and breathed in the light as it sifted dust motes around the sanctuary.

It freezes at night in August in Stockbridge, Massachusetts. Our summer sleeping bags helped little and frustrated more. Work became a chore and Skyler got antsy to push on. We fought on and off. She took to drinking Crown Royal, neat, to excess. Once I found her drink of choice charming. Now it was disturbing.

She decided she wanted a different job, so she quit. Then she didn't like it that I was unavailable to play. She got drunk or high every day. Trying to convince myself that everything was okay, I didn't confront her much less myself. What once seemed exciting and edgy now felt uncomfortable and dangerous. She fixed on the idea that it was time to leave.

"Let's go to the west coast," she prodded.

My grandma lives on the west coast. I'd love to visit my grandma, see the farm, and show Tanya all the places I loved when I was a kid. "Okay," I said before she put me on the bus to Burlington, Vermont where I would pick up a car we would drive to Miami changing there for one heading to the west coast.

The bus tires crunched over the gravel lot onto the access road to I-91 north. The night sky reflected my image back to me through the glass. *I can't give up hope. There must be something I can do to make things right.* I leaned my head against the cool window and stared into the dark. *Our Mother, who art in heaven.* It felt right. God is my mother. Tonight I need a mother. *Mother, mother, mother, hold me while I am on this journey. I am not sure about anything any more. I love her so much, but it shouldn't hurt like this. Mother, I need you. Wrap your arms around me and let me lean into your vastness.*

I felt a Funeral, in my Brain,
And Mourners to and fro
Kept treading—treading—till it seemed
That Sense was breaking through—

And when they all were seated,
A Service, like a Drum—
Kept beating—beating—till I thought
My mind was going numb—

—from *I Felt a Funeral, In my Brain,* Emily Dickinson

## Chapter 13    *Learning the Hard Way*

A TORRENT OF PEACE washed over me. Places I didn't know were cold, suddenly warmed. Breath I did not know I was holding, released. Tears I had not shed ran down my face in hot rivulets, quiet and welcomed. Through the long night I breathed into peace, finally sleeping—cheek pressed against window, hair cascading in a curtain that shielded me from my travelling companions.

It was first light when the bus pulled into the station in Burlington, Vermont. I stumbled down the steps into the chill air. A payphone stood at the corner. I pulled a dime out of my pocket and a crumpled sheet of paper with the number of the drive away agency from my backpack. A man on the other end directed me a short walk to the office for an even shorter interview before I was ushered to a brand new, 1977, sage green Cadillac Seville. I was responsible for gas and would be paid $75 when I got to my destination in Miami.

After I picked up Skyler, we drove first to the East Village in New York City to pick up Tanya from her summer sojourn with her dad, then headed straight down I-95 to Miami. We delivered the car to a mansion on the beach and picked up another Cadillac before we returned to Columbus and loaded Fred with all our belongings. Finally, we strapped our bikes to the trunk of the MG with leather belts. The plan: Skyler and I would caravan out west. Our summer of freedom was back on track and promised an autumn of freedom to follow in its wake.

After delivering the car in Boise, Tanya and I crammed ourselves into Fred for the final lap. Persephone, our beloved mutt, hunched under my feet and Tanya reclined in the ridiculously small back seat. I didn't realize how deeply I hungered for the land of my childhood until we crossed the invisible boundary between the deserts of eastern Oregon into the green cathedrals of western Oregon.

Grandma had aged. I tried to count the years it had been since I saw her last. I must have been fourteen or fifteen the last time Mom and Dad and I made a circuit around the country to visit the friends and family we collected in our travels over the years. Though older, Grandma was still agile and as brisk as I remembered. She opened the farm to us while we got our bearings, looked for work, and settled in.

Now *I* was sitting at the kitchen counter with a cup of coffee chatting with my grandmother instead of my mother. A soft, warm place expanded deep inside me. I inhaled all the way to my belly, savoring this kitchen, this land, this time. The gentle memories I was making. Grandma listed the names of flowers starting in the green house: lobelia, valerian, white and pink alyssum and I received them like an offering. We cooked together in a comfortable cadence while she told stories of my mom and sister.

Tanya and I roamed the farm, climbed trees and picked up apples in the orchard, gorging on the overripe fruit. We crowded into the apple house, a structure not much larger than a phone booth, and breathed in sixty years of the scent of apple permeating wood. We climbed the woodpile in the wood shed and then dutifully brought a load into the house. We explored the empty barn and imagined cows chewing their cuds, udders dripping as they waited to be milked. We ambled down the dirt road to the river bottom, gathered snail shells in the shallows, and watched small whirlpools form and disperse. We hung over the fences calling to the cattle that grandma pastured for the neighbors. The farm ignited my cells. My body thrummed all the way out to my edges. *These are the things that matter.*

Other things mattered, too. Feminism mattered, my freedom to be myself without restraint—that mattered. Freedom to attempt the hard stuff, things I had never done before, things I dreamed of doing, things outside the expected norm. All that mattered deeply to me. I was determined to live the life I wanted.

Justice mattered. I grieved the death of Steve Bikko, the anti-apartheid activist bludgeoned to death while in police custody in Pretoria, South Africa. Racism mattered. And I refused to feel powerless. I was angry and had a duty to speak up.

And somewhere in that time of wandering on the farm I remembered how much God mattered to me. I was close to the thin places where God broke through. When the wind kicked up a dust dervish I pierced its vortex, swirling in place and tasting the mystery. *I remember. I remember.*

Robert Frost once said, "home is the place, where when you go there, they have to take you in." The Farm is home. My grandmother from another family behaved exactly as if I belonged, however circuitously, to this land and this people. There are many places I belong that are a part of me. My truth only becomes fact when it is mutual. If only *I* recognize myself as a part of something, no matter how true, the experience of connectedness is incomplete without mutuality. I learn this lesson often.

Skyler could charm just about anyone, but my grandmother wasn't charmed. She was losing some of the gilt with me, too. Things I once perceived as challenging authority now seemed small, petty, and disrespectful. I walked into our room to find her furtively blowing smoke out of an open window. She smiled and motioned for me to shut the door.

"What are you doing? We're not supposed to smoke in the house!"

"She won't know." She shrugged her shoulders.

"That's not the point and you know it."

"Fine," she said as she tossed the butt out the window.

*As if that makes it a non-issue.* Incensed, I jerked the door open and went outside to find the butt and make sure it was out. Uncomfortably aware that I had behaved just like her on occasion, seeing it from this side revealed how silly and aggrandized I had been. She was being.

Skyler got a job as a wrangler on a dude ranch outside of Yamhill, Oregon. The ranch did double duty as a logging camp and I signed on to be the cook for the loggers. We moved into a tiny A-frame across the gravel road from the barn on the property of our employer, the Flying "M" Ranch. We tried to believe we were still on the adventure we began in the summer but winter was a bitter reminder that the fun ends and life takes over.

The first night in our little A-frame we startled awake to the screams of banshees. Sounds of a wailing, maniacally laughing horde circled our shelter. Even Persephone, my intrepid canine companion, showed no interest in investigating. Hunkering down before the wood stove, she did not challenge the chaos outside. I pulled Tanya into the loft with us and we huddled under our blankets while the tempest swirled outside our small cabin until an hour before dawn.

"I forgot to tell you about the ky-otes." The boss admitted. "Nothing to worry about."

Every morning I lurched out of bed at four-thirty and biked down the dark gravel path, lighted only by the flicker of my bike lamp, to the lodge where the loggers would arrive for their breakfasts and to pick up their lunches. Twelve hardy men, each demanding three hardy meals a day. Breakfast began with oatmeal and finished with eggs, home fries, bacon or ham, sausage, pancakes or toast and loads of strong black coffee. While they ate I packed twelve lunches, two sandwiches each, fruit, chips, and cookies that I made the day before. After they left I sprinted home to wake Tanya and get her fed and off to school. I then raced back to the lodge to clean the kitchen and make sure I had what was necessary to prepare the evening meal. I baked cookies for the next day and dessert for supper.

Three-thirty in the afternoon I waited for Tanya's bus and brought her to the lodge where she sat on a stool at the kitchen counter to do her homework while I cooked. There had to be some very large hunk of meat, potatoes served abundantly in any form, salad, and because I insisted, some kind of green vegetable. And don't forget the dessert. They washed all this down with cold beer and more hot coffee. Finally, I cleaned the tables, the dishes, and the kitchen before taking Tanya home for bath and bedtime.

Skyler's job was to take city folk on horseback rides through the mountains, usually on the week-ends. She mucked out the barn, met with the farrier or the vet, exercised the horses, and plotted new trails. We fell into bed each night exhausted. No time for harmonicas or fires or making love. No time for conversation.

The Flying "M" was miles from the nearest small town of Yamhill and even further from the farm. A bus labored its way up and down the gravel mountain roads each day taking Tanya to school and back. Our only neighbors were the owners of the ranch and the loggers who worked on it.

I wanted to be around other women, other lesbians, other feminists. I subscribed to the *Lesbian Connection*, a free lesbian forum that connected women around the country and whose stated purpose was to foster lesbian community. I devoured each issue, reading and rereading letters, articles, ads, and book reviews.

"Why are you interested in all that stuff?" Skyler asked.

"I want to be around other women. I want to figure out what it means for me in my life." I tried to put words to my desire. "I want to have friends and be a part of something bigger than myself. To be with other women who are trying to figure out the same things I am."

My clumsy explanation didn't quite get at the deeper truth I hadn't accessed: being a lesbian was about more than being with Skyler and more than who I made love with. I felt isolated and sad and there was nowhere to go and no one to turn to. No one to help me understand the distance between Skyler and me. No one to support any choices I might make that were different from Skyler's choices. No one to talk about all the things that mattered to me but not to Skyler.

I started from a stupored sleep to the urgent clanging of bells slicing through the soft night noises of insects and owls.

"Fire," Skyler mumbled as she pulled on her jeans and boots, slid down the ladder from our loft bed and dashed out the door.

We lived in the middle of the forest. A fire threatened more than the livelihood of the logging camp, it threatened the lives of all of us who lived on the mountain. I bundled Tanya up and made my way to the lodge to put on pots of coffee and make sandwiches. Word filtered back. Firebreaks were being dug. Bucket lines formed. I packed lunch bags and thermos after thermos of coffee sending them out with every new person who showed up on their way to the fire line. Tanya read books on a couch in the lodge, sometimes doing small tasks in the kitchen, like spreading peanut butter or putting cookies in baggies.

Men covered in soot drifted in to grab an hour or two of sleep before heading out again. On and on it went, through the day and into the night again before the fire was deemed over and a skeleton crew was left to keep watch should the smoldering remains burst into flames again. Skyler dragged in, grinning and filthy, another adventure under her belt.

Fred, fond of paved mountain roads, detested the pocked gravel lanes than ran down the mountain to town. I steered us toward the paved roads we loved. I needed to do a grocery run and driving Fred was a lovely pleasure. The feel of the smooth, wooden gearshift under my palm, the responsiveness of the steering mechanism, the way my body slid into place like a race driver, the pressure of the clutch when I pushed it in, the hum of his motor as we accelerated to driving speed was a sensuous feast. He was sleek and beautiful, a little dangerous and a lot seductive. Just like his owner.

I slowed to a near crawl, twenty-five miles an hour, taking my time and wringing out every ounce of my little pleasure. The air was brisk and chill but the sun shone and the color of evergreens roused from the winter gloom, glowed.

Taking a curve, I down-shifted and slowly released the clutch. A foot high wall of gravel angling across the road appeared around the next curve. The county had been grating the road leaving an abrupt stop. I didn't brake, knowing it could send me into a spin. My right front tire hit the gravel and, as if of its own accord, slid up the wall of rocks and slowly continued to rotate the car until it turned completely over, bashing the top of my head against the ground before coming to a complete stop.

I turned off the car and pulled the keys out of the ignition. I did a body check. Everything seemed to be working. *I have to get out of here!* Carefully pulling my legs from the driver's well, I contorted my body and positioned myself to climb out the side window. Adrenaline pumped liquid energy into my veins as I hauled myself out of the vehicle.

My heart raced and my body began to shake uncontrollably as I looked at Fred's crushed form. Everything I experienced him to be was dead. No longer a sleek and seductive toy friend, he was instead dangerous and uncaring. I sat on the side of the road and waited.

An hour or so later a truck with two young guys pulled up. "Jesus, what happened? Is there anybody in there?"

"Just me."

"How did you get out?"

I stared at Fred. There was no way I could have gotten out. The side window was crushed almost to the ground on both sides.

"I don't know." I said. And suddenly it occurred to me that Skyler would be furious. More furious about Fred's demise than fearful for my wellbeing. I began to cry.

Tanya and I moved down to Yamhill and I got a job cashiering at a local grocery store. We found an apartment in a duplex and began to live the "city" life, meaning paved roads on which I could bike to work and a library card. The slush of late winter snow didn't slow me down. Eventually Skyler moved in and commuted to the ranch for her job. But even the move to a more populated area didn't cure my deep feelings of isolation.

Our next-door neighbors were a couple in their early fifties. Sometimes she and I would coffee klatch after Tanya was off to school and before I set out for work.

"He beats me sometimes," she said, pointing to her bruised eye.

"He doesn't have the right!"

"Well, tell *him* that. It's been going on for years now. I try not to get him mad but when he's drinking, sometimes he starts punching me. Then I get scared."

"Leave him," I said, not realizing how hard that might be to do.

"I can't."

"Then come over here when he gets like that," I begged her. "Don't let him hit you."

Three days later I heard a howl coming from our neighbor's apartment. Seconds after that banging began on our front door.

"Let me in, let me in," she pleaded.

I flung open the door, pulled her inside, slammed it shut, and threw the bolt.

"What happened? Are you okay?"

"He came at me," She shuddered and began to cry. "I poured a pot of boiling water on him."

*Holy Shit.* He began hammering on our door.

"Give me my wife back you goddamned bull-dagger! You can't take a woman away from her husband!" He continued to bang and holler, his frustration escalating.

"Shhh." I motioned to her to come away from the door. "Stay here. I'm going for the police. I took Tanya, not wanting to leave her in the midst of potential violence, and crawled out the bedroom window. We raced to Main Street, a few blocks over, and into the police station.

"It's really none of our business," the officer said. "You need to stay out of it."

During the short while it took for me to get home, her husband had gone back inside and sat slumped over the kitchen table in a drunken coma, his scorched arms crossed under his head. She was hurrying around the room, righting the overturned garbage can and picking up the smelly, damp trash, returning it to its rightful place. "It'll be okay, don't worry. Thanks anyway. I shouldn't have bothered you."

*Why would anyone stay in a relationship like that?* I wondered. Why indeed.

My neighbor's husband was so mad I was afraid to walk out the door if he was home. He cursed and yelled at me through the walls. The drunker he got the more repetitive his chants. "Goddamn bull-dagger," he slurred over and over.

Afraid to leave my house, afraid for Tanya, and unhappy in ways I couldn't name, I packed up what I could and left in the pre-dawn morning on a bus to Atlanta. Skyler would follow me in Fred, who was once again drivable, though never the same.

It was a three-day trip. Three days and three long nights in a cramped bus with precious little cash to purchase our meals. The fruit we brought with us was confiscated—something about not spreading an insect problem to farmers further east. A snowstorm shifted the original route through Colorado and instead the bus pushed over the California mountains, turned left at New Mexico then straight through Arizona, Texas . . . through long stretches of desert arbitrarily divided from itself by invisible state lines.

Tanya was a trooper. She wanted to understand why our neighbor was so mean. "I don't know, honey. But it is never okay to hit another person."

"Why did he hate us?"

I paused. *How much to tell?* "Some people are afraid of girls who love other girls and boys who love other boys."

"That's stupid."

"Yeah," I agreed. *And stupid can be very scary.* But I didn't say that.

The desert turned out to be a gift of meditation. The sun stretched across the horizon as it rose each morning. Large. Red. Pink. Then dazzling yellow as it took to the sky. Thank you, God. Thank you for the world, for my life, for Tanya, for everything good and beautiful that let's me know it all matters. I failed to recognize that I wasn't missing Skyler at all.

We arrived at the Greyhound bus station in downtown Atlanta, late in the morning of the fourth day. The facility was gray and nondescript, the floors and chairs scuffed colorless. A laconic police officer lounged near the counter, behind which employees slumped, distracted and world-weary. I put down my backpack and took Tanya by the hand as we stretched and worked the kinks out of our joints. Shuffling around in the front pocket of my pack, I pulled out the latest copy of *The Lesbian Connection.* I took Tanya in one hand, pulled a quarter out of my pocket with the other, and cradling the payphone between my shoulder and ear, dialed the number.

"This is the Atlanta Lesbian Feminist Alliance. We are located on Mc-Clendon Avenue in Little Five Points. Please leave a message and someone will get back to you."

"I just got here from Oregon and I have no place to stay," I began.

"Hi," came a woman's voice on the other end. "How can I help you?"

I let out a sigh of relief. "Hi. I'm moving here from Oregon with my daughter. We are here at the Greyhound station and we don't have anywhere to stay."

"So let me tell you how to get here on MARTA. There's a meeting this evening and I'm sure someone will be here who can help out."

I had found my tribe.

Within three weeks I got a job at the new, community-owned Little Five Points Pub, found an apartment in a neighborhood duplex, registered Tanya at her new school, and found Charis Books and More—a real, live feminist bookstore run by real, live feminists, some of whom were also real, live lesbians. And Skyler arrived.

"I was wedded to all the stars of the sky. There was not a single star left, and I married every one of them with great spiritual pleasure. Then I married the moon."

—Ibn Arabi

## Chapter 14   *I'm Going to Keep Calling Until You Get It*

SKYLER AND I BROKE up in 1978. Or 77. Depends on who is telling the story. I didn't know we were broken up until way after the fact though in some ways we had not been a couple since we left Oregon. Actually, she told a lot of other people without ever bothering to mention it to me. Not at the dinner table, not in bed, not as we gardened together. Not as we fought or struggled. I guess it slipped her mind.

"Mom," I wailed, "Skyler broke up with me."

"It will be okay," she repeated until I stopped bawling, "you'll figure it out."

She was right. I found enough anger and righteous indignation to go home and tell Skyler that *I* would be staying in our apartment. *I* had the job. *I* paid the rent. *She* needed to leave. I was strong and weepy at the same time; strong as I needed to be to survive, weepy as only one who is a four on the ennegram[1] can aspire to be.

I threw myself on my bed, a mattress on the floor beneath the fourteen-foot ceilings of an old craftsman bungalow. In the dark, it seemed as if there was night sky above me. The ancient, uneven glass of the original windows undulated starlight that crept through the tree branches. I began to pray. Aching, I struggled against the pain of loss. Of rejection. Of somehow not being enough.

I hadn't prayed in a while and I couldn't find the words to form my own prayer so I started praying the Lord's Prayer. Over and over and over I prayed. The repetition of its rhythm gave me comfort. I could hold on to it.

1. The ennegram is based on the work of the 4th century Christian mystic, Evagrius. Later Oscar Ichazo was recognized as the source of the Ennegram of personality. Fours are deeply emotional and creative.

The prayer was a tangible thing. I prayed each word with intention. I prayed each word by rote. I prayed the memory of the prayer. I prayed without thinking. I prayed without meaning. I prayed with longing. I prayed without ceasing. I prayed and prayed until I was all prayed out. And then I began again.

Some time in the dark of the night, when clouds had passed over the stars and the branches of the cedar clacked against the house, my prayer changed.

"I want to know you, God," I implored.

"I want to know you."

"I want to know you."

"I want to know you."

Light shattered the room and I shattered with the light. I was incorporeal. I expanded beyond my body. I disintegrated, flying into a million pieces, flaring like a star into the void of space. I could not contain the knowledge of God. It was too big for me, for my finite body, mind, self.

"WAIT!" I shouted, terrified that I would fracture into non-existence.

"WAIT!" I scrambled back from my prayer, reaching out tentatively. "Wait," I said, "I don't need to know you, not really, not that way. Maybe what I really want is a relationship with you."

And then I slept.

I trudged through the next day and that night I began to pray again. Wordless prayer. The prayer St. Paul talks about: the groanings of the Spirit. I prayed and groaned, sleeping fitfully, waking again to pray.

And in the distance I saw a chasm in the universe. And I was standing at the edge of the chasm looking across to God. And God was looking to me and I reached out and my arm would only reach as far away from my body as the tips of my fingers. And I kept reaching, edging to the edge of the chasm and I could not reach across. And I looked to God with longing and saw the Light, and saw the Light watching my hand reaching. And my longing began dripping from my fingertips as I tried to reach across the unreachable chasm. And in my longing the Light reached back and I knew that I did not have to cross that chasm myself, that I only needed to reach out with my longing. I knew that all my reaching would never bridge the chasm. And I knew that God reached back and that God would always reach back and that God would do God's work and I would do mine.

Later that morning I woke up and said to myself, "I think I've been called to the ministry." Really? Me? A feminist? A lesbian? The single mother of a six year old? I haven't set foot in a church for nine years. I must be seriously mistaken. But the thought wouldn't let me go and then the thought became an urge.

The next Sunday, after getting off work at midnight from the Little Five Points Pub, I woke early and wrangled my child into something resembling her Sunday best. I put on my one good pair of slacks and a reasonable blouse, loaded my daughter on the back of my black Sears three speed and pedaled to the local Episcopal Church. It was a lovely brick building nestled behind a crowd of blooming dogwoods, across from the local fire station and catty-corner to the deli. I lifted my daughter down and parked my bike. As we walked in I tried to remember which army chaplain from my childhood had been Episcopalian and what worship was like. The particulars, other than a memory of incense, eluded me.

We scooted into a pew near the back and waited for the service to begin. The truth is, I didn't know what I was looking for. I barely knew why I was there. And the Episcopal Church was in a little bit of an internal fight right then. It seems there was this prayer book written in 1928. A new one had been written that was more inclusive. The underlying issue, it so happened, was the ordination of women. After an interesting service that included a lot of getting up, sitting down, kneeling, and more getting up that felt much like the Catholic masses at Grandma's, I surmised that this was a 1928 prayer book kind of place. Surprising, given the liberal neighborhood, but true nonetheless. I was not destined to be an Episcopalian.

The next Sunday was Easter and I decided to worship with the local Quaker meeting. It's probably a good thing I went on Easter because it was the one day I absolutely *must* sing. Sitting in the meeting, wishing for a rousing chorus of 'He Lives' or 'Jesus Christ is Risen Today!' I waited quietly for the Spirit. Finally, a gentleman rose and quoted the line from Joyce Kilmer's poem, "I never think that I shall see a poem as lovely as a tree."

Okay, I thought, that's it. No singing. No appearance of the Spirit. I wish I had been able to appreciate the service and the community more, for I am sure there was both substance and depth, but I was on a quest, an urgent one, and had just marked Quaker off my list.

Next were the Methodists. As luck would have it there was a United Methodist Church two blocks from where we lived. We walked. The service was familiar and there was some good singing to be had. "This might be it," I thought, not knowing what I was looking for. I filled out the visitor's card and indicated I would like a visit from the pastor.

It was early spring and even though I lived in a rental house, I had planted a small garden in the back yard. The broccoli was up, the tomato plants flowered and formed the first hint of tomatoes. Marigolds, planted as companion plants, were blooming their heads off. And tucked in the back was a discreet row of marijuana plants. Weeks earlier I had purchased a praying mantis egg. Every morning, after I got Tanya off to school, I took my coffee and sat beside the garden watching each delicate change, all the while keeping an eye on my egg.

This morning, after giving the garden a good soak, I took a second glance. Small, white, almost translucent praying manti were beginning to emerge from the egg. Each one was less than an inch long and hundreds seemed to be spilling out of the egg, like so many circus clowns out of a tiny car. I knelt beside the garden bed, entranced, falling in love with these amazing creatures. They would patrol the insects in the garden and give me hours of joy. In the bright morning sun, the first to emerge began to turn a fresh yellow-green. I sucked in my breath. "Oooh," I let it out in a hiss, "I love you!"

"Hel-lo," a man's voice hollered from around front.

"I'm out back." I returned, getting off my knees and sitting back on my chair.

The Methodist minister was paying a call.

"Good morning." he greeted me enthusiastically.

The good reverend's brown polyester suit strained over his stomach and his slicked back hair shone in the early morning sunshine. *Is this my new normal?*

"Hi," I replied, "come have a seat. Would you like some coffee?"

"No, no, just came to call on you. You are the one who filled out a visitation card, Miz Tuttle?"

"Yes," I reassured him, "I'm the one. Come on and join me." I gestured to the second chair. "Come see my baby praying manti."

I'm pretty sure he had never had an invitation like that before. He made his way to the garden and as he neared my precious babies, he tripped. On what, I am not sure. Maybe his shoe laces, maybe a stone, but down he went, splayed face first into the wet garden, murdering several tens of my babies on the way.

"I'm okay, I'm okay," he said, getting up slowly. "Don't worry." He patted the wet mud on his knees.

*Don't worry? I'm okay? You just decimated fifties of my baby praying manti!* We finished our visit while I silently grieved and seethed. Clearly, I was not destined to be a Methodist.

The next Sunday, unwell and running a fever of a hundred and one, I loaded Tanya and myself onto my bike and set out. I'm telling you this so that you can see how strong the urge was. I am the sort who will curl up in bed with hot cup of tea and a row of medications at the first sign of a sniffle. But I was driven by something I could not ignore. I had to figure this out. I was walking around with this powerful experience, this urgent sense of call, and no one seemed to be able to help me understand what had happened.

Our goal is to create a beloved community and this will require a qualitative change in our souls as well as a quantitative change in our lives.

—Dr. Martin Luther King Jr.

# Chapter 15    *Now What?*

CLIFTON PRESBYTERIAN CHURCH SAT on the corner of Connecticut and McClendon Avenues overlooking the Candler Park neighborhood. Candler Park and its associated shopping district, Little Five Points, were home to Atlanta's alternative community. Former hippies, ecologists, lesbians, lefties, and community builders were cobbling together a neighborhood out of an area abandoned during the white flight of the sixties. Little Five Points boasted a family pub, a feminist bookstore, a health food co-op, a vegetarian restaurant, two theatres that produced live plays and concerts, and a plethora of small, boutique like stores selling art, music, clothing, pot paraphernalia, and handmade jewelry. All nudged up to the obligatory library, post office, and pawnshop.

The unimposing, painted concrete block structure barely looked like a church at all. The only thing that suggested it might be one was a rickety cross atop a small steeple. Barely tamed grounds slacked to overgrown wildness at the outer edges. An uneven mosaic of asphalt shards made up a small parking lot. The only spot of color was the vivid red front doors. Red like a streetwalker's dress on Saturday night, red like the blood of the Lamb. That red.

I pushed open those red doors and walked into a sanctuary filled with folding chairs set in a semi-circle, a piano in the rear, a moveable pulpit and non-descript communion table at the front. Without the pulpit and the communion table it would have looked like the set up for an AA meeting. Twenty-five, maybe thirty, people milled about waiting for the service to begin. Old hymnals propped open clear glass windows inviting air into the sweltering house of worship.

Unlike the Methodist church whose population consisted of older folks who rode out the downturn of the neighborhood, Clifton Presbyterian was filled with the newcomers. All the men were shaggy-headed, all the women dressed down, all the children were wild. I felt at home. *This just might be my tribe.*

I sat through the service entranced. Here's what's true: it was 1977. President Carter had just pardoned Viet Nam era draft dodgers, Star Wars (the movie) was released, and Anwar el-Sadat went to Jerusalem to seek peace with Israel after decades of conflict. The world was changing, old wounds were healing, and the road ahead seemed to be paved with un-imaginable possibilities.

This incongruous mish-mash of folks who had worked to end the war and challenged racism and sexism in their daily lives were committed to creating viable community. The heart and soul of Clifton was a band of people basing their lives on a justice-loving Jesus and working to change the world. And the preacher used inclusive language. In 1977 it was unheard of.

"This is it." I thought, going with "I'll recognize it when I see it."

The way I went about choosing a church to provide a context for this damn almighty call might lead you to believe I have no spiritual depth. Maybe I don't. What I *do* have is an ongoing conversation with God and when I listen well, there is clarity. Nothing deep. The struggle isn't usually about hearing more often than not it's about the responding. That day I was wide open with listening and not sure how to ask the questions. I just knew I had to find a church, sooner rather than later, to help me figure this out. I couldn't sit on this, this overwhelming intrusion into my psyche . . . I urgently needed to understand and felt propelled toward God at an alarming pace.

I left right after the service, too sick to stop and chat with the friendly and the interested. This much I knew: I had found my place. Now I could crawl into bed and ride out my misery.

By Wednesday I recovered enough to make my next move. I walked to the church in the middle of the day, before Tanya got out of school and before my evening shift began. Apprehension and excitement had my gut in a knot and my chest twitching. I was going to talk to the ministers about this call thing. I tapped on the door.

"Come in!" a woman invited.

"Hi. I was here Sunday and wanted come by and ask a few questions."

"Have a seat. I'm Murphy Davis and this is my husband, Ed Loring. We're the co-pastors here."

"Hi." I was nervous. How do you talk about this stuff? I'd never heard anyone talk about experiences like mine.

They sat together at a table and made room for me to pull up a chair.

I blinked. Up close Ed looked a little like Rasputin with his long hair, thick mustache, and deep brown eyes that seemed lit from within. Murphy was his perfect counterpoint: blue eyes, straight, shoulder length, blonde bob, and an interested, opened gaze.

These guys were going to help me figure out what was happening. Help me understand if this insistent urge was a call to ministry. And if it was a call, I needed to know: what do I do now?

I sat down and they asked some of the usual questions. Where was I from? Was I looking for a church home? I couldn't bring up what had happened to me. It was too intimate, too private. Too overwhelming.

"I feel called to the ministry," I blurted. "What do I do?"

Was I imagining their stunned expressions?

"First, you go to college."

Check. That needed a little thinking and a little finagling, but check.

"Then you would need to come under the care of the session."

Big, blank stare.

"The session is like the committee in charge of running the church."

Okay. Deep breath. Got it.

"Then you have to go to seminary."

Check.

"You'll have to come under the care of the candidates committee." This list was getting kind of long.

Four years of college and three years of seminary. I was twenty-five now. In the best of all worlds (which I was not in, by the way) it meant I would be at least thirty-two before I'd begin. Begin something. Begin this nebulous idea of ministry. Did I have that right?

"I'm a lesbian."

An extended pause. "Can you keep it quiet?"

This was the first of many times I would be invited to silence.

How was I supposed to answer that? I didn't know what was happening to me and I didn't know how to talk about it or what God was asking me to do. I only had this experience and then this big, I don't know, urge, and what I want from you is some help in figuring out what God wants from me. Isn't that what you do? And if it's not what you do, then who *do* I need to talk to? Surely you know what it is like to have this kind of experience because you're ministers. You must know what I'm talking about. Isn't this what happens to everyone who feels called to ministry?

I thought Ed and Murphy would want to help me out with this, especially since they'd been through it themselves. Hadn't they? They gave me a pretty thorough checklist (which might have been discouraging if I hadn't had this damn urge) and the only question they asked me is if can I keep it under wraps that I'm a lesbian. They didn't ask me about my actual call. They didn't say anything about people having visions. Maybe it's not something people talk about. But what they did ask me is, "Can you keep secret who you are?"

*It doesn't sound like you, God. Is this what you want me to do?* But I would have said yes to almost anything. Yes, if you'll just tell me what the hell is going on. Yes, if you'll help me understand what's happening to me. Yes, because I don't want to be alone with the largeness of it all. Yes, because God has overwhelmed my life. Yes! Yes! Yes!

"Yes," I whispered.

The most potent weapon of the oppressor is the mind of the oppressed.

—Steven Biko

## Chapter 16  *Finding My Way and Losing My Way*

IN 1978 JIM JONES led hundreds of his followers in a mass murder-suicide at their commune in northwest Guyana. Those who refused to drink the cyanide-laced Kool-Aid were forced to do so at gunpoint or shot outright as they fled. Final death toll: 913, including 276 children.

Around the same time, when Tanya was eight, my relationship with Clifton deepened. We moved in with Ed and Murphy, the pastors of our small, liberal, Presbyterian Church so that we might live in intentional community. We shared space, meals, and finances. I turned over my paycheck at the end of each week and was doled out what I needed for personal expenses. The idea was that shared living expenses allowed more of our incomes to be used for justice work.

This was what I was looking for: a community that walked the talk. The week began on Sunday. I got up at 6:30 in the morning, walked the two blocks to the church and began cooking breakfast for the 30-60 children from the neighborhood housing project whom we mentored, and who would spill through the doors at 8:30. Still sleepy, I turned on the oven to preheat for the biscuits and began cracking dozens of eggs into an enormous stainless steel bowl. Slide the bowl to the end of the counter near the stove. Pull flour and Crisco out of the cabinet. Sift the flour and rising agents, cut in the Crisco, add ice water, and pat into four large balls. By the time I finished mixing up a batch I'd be coated in flour up to my earballs. Placing several large cookie sheets on the counter, I rolled out the dough and cut circles of soon-to-be biscuits with a water glass. Before the morning was out I would bake over six dozen biscuits and scramble almost as many eggs.

After breakfast was Sunday school—not as inspiring as I might have liked—I engaged the ideas and the text with questions mostly about how this information would help me walk a faithful walk, live a faithful life. I hungered for an intentional spiritual life since the days of preparing myself to be a nun. This was as close as I had ever gotten and I gave it my best.

Every Sunday Ed preached fiery sermons like the former Baptist he was, grounded in the intellectual rigor of the Presbyterian professor he had become. His constant theme: living authentically in Christ means we live justice centered lives. Murphy worked tirelessly against the death penalty and Clifton committed to be a part of that effort.

I volunteered to plan an anti-death penalty fundraiser, adding yet another task to my already full days and weeks. In a month I had musicians on board, space at the local pub donated, and the neighborhood plastered with posters. I coordinated volunteers, food and drink sales, and set up a cover charge. We raised almost a thousand dollars by the time the party closed down at midnight. I staggered into Ed's arms for the last dance, happy with our results and triumphant in a job well done.

Wednesdays we had the children again for a meal and time to help them with homework and build relationships. I cooked that night, too. I would arrive after a strenuous day at work where I did a little of everything, from sheetrock, to tiling, painting, minor plumbing, trim carpentry, installing doors, and clean up. I began exhausted but was fueled by the imperative to be faithful. Somehow all of this must have something to do with my call to ministry.

I raced into the kitchen to pull out cutting boards and knives, preheat the oven, and unload the refrigerator of its bounty. We only served vegetarian meals and finding a way to make sure the kids got enough protein was important to me. Often I made quiche. I lined up twelve premade piecrusts and chopped and assembled zucchini quiche, mushroom quiche, tomato and parsley quiche- whatever was in season I could make it into a quiche! To the main course I added a large salad filled with every fresh veggie that didn't make it into the quiche. Winters meant hearty soups instead of quiche and the salad was a little less robust. The kids loved it but they began asking for biscuits with their Wednesday meal, so I added that to my list of tasks. Often I was too drained to eat but sat with the kids until time to clean up.

Thursday was prayer group. The entire community gathered to share and pray—for one another and for the world. We drew together in a circle, arms around one another's waists, and prayed. I stretched my spirit to embrace the prayers and lift them with all the intention of my heart. *Thank you, God, for giving me the possibility to live the life you called me to!*

Lent was another experience all together. Following weeks of Lenten deprivation a near orgy, tinged with desperation, of food, coffee and alcohol commenced after the Easter service. In the back of my mind I began to allow uncomfortable thoughts to take root. The experience of self-deprivation and orgiastic celebration had not been cause for spiritual deepening. Theologically, I didn't know what questions begged to be asked. I only knew I had, without questioning, followed the pack. Had I put too much trust in people and not challenged my assumptions? Before this, I pushed away prickly nudges, accepting everything—lock, stock, and barrel—because of this drive to pursue the call that overwhelmed me.

Ed met me at the door when I arrived home from work late one spring evening. "Your *daughter* is in trouble at school. I sent her downstairs." He gritted, his voice rigid with anger.

What on earth could she have done? I pounded down the steps to our apartment to find Tanya sitting large eyed in one of our wicker chairs, tears sliding down her cheeks.

"Hey, baby."

She began sobbing preemptively. I sat down opposite her and motioned her into my lap.

"What's going on, Sweetie?" I asked as I gathered her to me.

She heaved a breath "Mr. Wilson accused Carolyn of cheating. It wasn't true. I tried to tell him, but he didn't believe me, so I said if he was going to send Carolyn to the office he needed to send me too." Her voice trailed off.

"Okay," I said, " It's a good thing to stand up for what you believe is right and it's good to speak up when you think something is unfair. I completely support you in that. Honey, you did the right thing. But why were you sent home from school?"

"I got sent home from school for vandalizing Mr. Wilson's car."

Mr. Wilson was her favorite teacher, the teacher of her Challenge class. This didn't make sense.

"Okay, Honey, start at the beginning."

She hesitated. "Well, I was so mad I didn't go to the office. I went out to the parking lot and got in his van and turned on the windshield wipers. I didn't know it would run his battery down. I did it every day this week."

Jeez. "Was that the honorable thing to do?" I asked.

"No."

"Maybe you can think of what might have been the honorable thing to do." I paused, "If you were choosing to be punished with Carolyn, you should have accepted the punishment—you know, gone to the office."

She lowered her chin. "Yeah."

"Tanya, you are not a bad person, but you did a bad thing. What started out as a good thing ended up not being good because of what you did."

"I know."

"Do you know you are going to have to earn the money from me to pay back Mr. Wilson for his battery."

"Yeah."

"You know you need to apologize to Mr. Wilson."

"Yeah."

I hugged her. "I'm proud of you for sticking up for your friend."

She leaned her head into my shoulder. We stayed like that for a long time, watching the patterned sunlight through the trees and listening to the whisper of wind in the tall grass. I wondered what she was thinking, but I didn't ask. I just held her.

Later Ed demanded to know how I punished her.

"She has to earn back the money to pay for Mr. Wilson's battery."

"Is that all?"

"Yeah, that's all," I said. It was enough. It was enough for lots of reasons. One, I knew Tanya and what motivated her. My Dad was an important figure in both of our lives and he taught us both to value honor.

"Duty, honor, country," my dad would intone, meaning every word.

During the Vietnam War I thought his statement was mindless, old school indoctrination but I came to realize that honor is a value I internalized.

Duty: fulfilling the obligations and commitments that you make.

Honor: having a keen sense of ethical conduct, integrity.

Country: supporting the principles on which this nation was founded: justice, freedom, equality.

I knew Tanya wanted to be a person of honor. She knew right from wrong, not only as a set of rules, but she possessed a personal sense of morality. Honor isn't taught much any more as a moral concept. The idea is treated as archaic in the twenty-first century, if it's considered at all. We don't talk about living honorably as a spiritual practice, at least not that I've heard, but I believe it could be. I can be a practitioner of honor in the midst of the frenetic activities of parenting, working, keeping house, and attending to relationships. Even when the practice of mindfulness seems unmanageable, it is possible for me to live honorably.

I never joined the service, which my sister did. I was a pacifist. I protested the Viet Nam war. I became a Democrat. I am different from my Dad in so many ways. I only hope I can be like him in the ways that count.

I once gave Ed a huge compliment. "You remind me of my dad," I said.

"I am *nothing* like your father," he spat. He didn't know my dad, had never met him. Ed only knew my dad was retired military. His bitter hostility surprised me. And hurt.

Today I would only shrug and say, "You're right, Ed. You are *nothing* like my father."

"I can't control the waves of the ocean, but I can learn how to navigate my ship."

—Debasish Mridha

# Chapter 17    *God, You've Clearly Made a Mistake*

"Ed," I began one night as we were sitting in the living room after dinner, "I miss being around other lesbians."

"I know exactly what you mean," he commiserated, "I get horny, too."

I think my head exploded. Do you think that when I say I miss my tribe that what I'm really saying is that I want sex? Good Lord! Do you have any idea what it's like to live in a world where you are hated, feared, oppressed, and need the strength of those who share your battle? Oh wait. You don't. You are a privileged white, educated, Southern male who doesn't have a clue. You might claim to be a feminist but there is more to it than adjusting your language.

"I'm not talking about being horny," I muttered, having no idea how to move the conversation forward. I'll go dancing this weekend. I'll go to Charis Books and More. I'll wander around Little Five Points for an afternoon. There's a difference between living an intentional life and a non-existent life, Ed. And it's not about whether I have someone to fuck or not. I wish I'd had the presence of mind to say that at the time. Instead it came to me that night as I lay sleepless.

At the dinner table a few days later, an innocuous conversation turned into an emotional tirade.

"These are great tomatoes, where did you get them?" I asked.

"From the vegetable man at the corner of Ponce and Clifton." Ed replied.

Tanya leaned over toward Ed, a playful gleam in her eye, "Vegetable *person.*" She corrected.

Ed's face mottled with unexpected fury. "He had balls and a penis," he spat, "it was a *man*."

Tanya pulled back, hurt and surprised. Inclusive language was something we were all working on together. She didn't understand his reaction and neither did I. Dinner was close enough to being over. I didn't have dish duty that night. Standing abruptly, I scooped up Tanya and we made our way downstairs to our apartment.

"Why was he so mad, Mommy? Did I do something wrong?"

"No, Baby, you didn't do anything wrong and I have no idea what got him so angry. But it's not you, Baby. It's not you."

I sat in the dark on my screened in porch that night and did a lot of thinking. A lot of excuse-making to the questions bubbling up into my consciousness. *Was Ed threatened by the fact that I was a lesbian?* Another power struggle began but I wasn't interested in being a part of it.

*Shalom House,* we named it. A house right around the corner from the church and large enough for our two families to have a modicum of privacy. We lived in Ed and Murphy's house, an early twenties craftsman. Their bedroom and Ed's children's bedrooms were on the main floor. Tanya and I lived in a small apartment in the built-out basement. We lived in intentional spiritual community. We shared communal meals, lived simply, and worked for justice. We prayed and hosted weekly Bible study. Our home was to be a place of Shalom, a place where our desire was for the fullness of God's intent for peace, justice, wholeness.

It was anything but. I wondered—if I stayed long enough—would my name ever been on the deed to the house I gave all my money to? Would I ever be accorded the power of mutuality. I wondered. But not much. I suspect that those who came after me left as exhausted and bereft as I did.

Ed had the magnetism of Svengali. He inspired us to work hard for justice. His ability to control and manipulate bright, young, mostly educated women and men was stunning. That there was enough good and sincerity to offset doubt and dissention worked to his advantage, but not to mine.

Shepherd came from North Carolina to visit Murphy sometime in the late fall. She and Murphy shared a dorm room at Mary Baldwin, a women's college in Virginia, and Shepherd was in the middle of a divorce.

"Move in here," Murphy urged.

I liked Shepherd and really liked the idea of another person in the mix.

Shortly after, we sheet rocked and mudded the basement room that would become hers, she drove up with her blue 1968, duck tailed Camero packed to the gills. While she stacked boxes and organized the best she could, I perched on her mattress and we shared confidences.

Shepherd was lean and tall and had the physique of a runner. Her short brown hair fell over her brows in a jaunty swoop of bangs. Her speaking cadence was slow, deliberate, and measured. Southern and cultured. You couldn't tell that she came from a wealthy family, had come out as a debutante or, as a physician's wife, was an active member of the Women's Medical Auxiliary.

There was nothing flashy about her. She was down to earth, not interested in accumulating wealth or status and, like me, she wanted to live an authentic life. We hung out in the evenings on my cozy screened porch, curled up in the large, cushioned wicker chairs, and whispered stories of our lives thus far.

"Don't take advantage of Shepherd," Ed warned, "she's just coming out of a divorce."

*Yeah. One she asked for. One she wanted. It's change, but it's not like her heart's broken.*

"I'm not."

We began to slip out after everyone went to sleep. Rolling my car down the hill and popping the clutch so the noise of the engine starting wouldn't wake our roomies. We giggled like schoolgirls on a lark driving, top down, to an all night restaurant and bar where we feasted on eggs Benedict and sipped Crown Royal, neat. I had taken the best of my time with Skyler with me. After we milked every ounce of conversation, we'd climb back in to the car and meander down city streets until the need for sleep overtook us and we headed home.

One morning Ed confronted me.

"Where did you go last night?"

"We went out for a drink." Ed could hardly object to this since he was a hard drinking beer man.

"When did you get in?"

"I don't know, late." This interrogation could go nowhere good. I couldn't believe he thought he had the right to be in charge of my comings and goings. Yeah, I didn't want him to know my business, and it wasn't his job to police it either. Underneath, we both assumed that he would.

Another power struggle added to the rising count.

One night, I stayed in her room.

She had never made love with a woman and I had not made love in a very long time. We spent hours exploring each other, stopping, talking before distracting ourselves again with the feel of gentle touch tracing spirals on tentative skin.

"Where did you sleep last night?"

"Ed, I really don't think that's any of your business."

He scowled. Maybe it was our soft smiles at breakfast. Maybe we weren't as quiet as we thought we were. Maybe he was jealous. Murphy didn't look up from her eggs. We finished our meal in silence and I left for work, leaving Shepherd to manage her way out of the hornets' nest.

Shalom House was never the same after that.

There was too much on my plate. I was falling in love. I worked a labor-intensive job rehabbing Title VIII housing with Andy Lipscomb, a former United Methodist minister who radically shifted career paths. I cooked twice a week for the children's program, in addition to shopping for groceries, a new duty added to my volunteer job description as the official food coordinator. It meant that, in addition to the planning and cooking of two meals a week for anywhere from forty to sixty people, I was supposed to organize and file the receipts, enter amounts in the checkbook, and balance said checking account.

If anyone had asked, I would have admitted that bookkeeping was never my strong suit, but I thought I could do anything I set my mind to. The problem was I never set my mind to it. In my over-worked, over- scheduled, unbalanced life, those tasks never made it to the top of my list. Actually, they never even made the list at all. I have only myself to blame for that choice.

Ed, too, blamed me for that choice. As life at the Shalom House continued to disintegrate, Ed made moves to have me removed from my position as food coordinator. It hurt that he never talked to me directly, nor had any member of the session talk with me, ask me questions. There was no intent to restore community or to work through our differences. Somehow and for reasons I will never know, Ed's sole purpose appeared to be removing me from Clifton like some diseased growth. I don't now believe it was because of my lousy bookkeeping. I've been in too many organizations since then to know that there are many, many ways of dealing with personnel issues that don't involve the tact he took *and* that allow for positive outcomes for all involved. I heard whispers about closed session meetings. Then there was a secret session meeting held at a member's home. I was removed from my post. And, although I was not directly asked to leave the Shalom House *or* Clifton, it was time to go.

I couldn't believe my good, dear friends had let this happen. I couldn't believe my brothers and sisters in Christ went along with it or that no one ever talked with me. In one swift stroke, I lost community, spiritual family, and close friends. And I didn't understand.

I couldn't stay at the Shalom House any more. It felt more like a war zone than a home. Tension seethed with every encounter. The only positive is that Tanya was with her dad for the summer and wasn't exposed to the worst of it. Shepherd was left squarely in the middle. Murphy was her long-time friend and I was . . . I was everything unknown, frightening and dangerous.

I found a home several blocks away. Shepherd helped me pack and load boxes into her car and mine and haul them to my new place. I vacillated between tears and anger, crying as I loaded up my belongings and carried them around the outside of the house, up the hill to the road. Cursing as I lugged them inside a strange empty house. We swept, cleaned, and unpacked until we both collapsed, exhausted, onto my unmade bed and she held me while I wept great, heaving, sobs.

My new home was a gorgeous old craftsman that had morphed into a hippie crash pad. Rooms were painted navy, burgundy, and brown with pink trim. High ceilings graced each room. A deep, claw-footed tub crouched in the bathroom. Windows paned with original glass, wavy and flawed, deep moldings outlining ceilings and floors, and hearths surrounded by ornately carved mantles all suggesting a more gracious time. Heart pine floors peeked through layers of linoleum hinting at an earlier splendor. Living alone for the second time in my life, my bare feet echoed as they slapped the worn flooring while I wandered from room to room, feeling lost.

What am I going to do now? Lying on my bed, I stared at the ceiling and gathered my thoughts like so many rangy cats. Keeping quiet didn't help me. I needed to be heard.

I pushed myself off the bed and rifled through boxes looking for paper and pencil. I pulled out a notebook, sat on the floor with my back to the wall, and wrote without lifting my hand. Five pages later I stopped.

"Dear Ed and Murphy," it began and I proceeded to say everything that had been left unsaid. How I felt betrayed. How I had lost not only their friendship, but my entire spiritual community. How unfair the process was. How angry and sad and hurt I was. I told them I wanted to find some sort of resolution. Some understanding. Some possible reconciliation in the future. And if not reconciliation, some clean ending.

I never heard back from them. Years later I asked Ed about it. He said it was an angry letter and he didn't read it. There are ways to be silenced even when you speak.

God had clearly made a huge mistake. I was a mess. I couldn't do it. Not physically. Not emotionally. Not spiritually. I was used to leaving communities of friends moving around the world as an army brat. I was not used to losing a community because of things I didn't understand. Looking back, I see how young and naïve I was. And how important it was for me to make that journey in my faith development. I do not regret my time at Clifton. I got and gave so much. I deepened. I learned. I gained spiritual wisdom that informs so much of how I do ministry today. But in that moment, I was sure God would realize what a big mistake God had made in calling me. Mostly I was just stubborn and tired and on the outs with God.

*Certainty*

Certainty undermines one's power, and turns happiness
into a long shot. Certainty confines.

Dears, there is nothing in your life that will
not change—especially your ideas of God.

Look what the insanity of righteous knowledge can do:
crusade and maim thousands
in wanting to convert that which
is already gold
into gold.

Certainty can become an illness
that creates hate and
greed.

God once said to Tuka,

"Even I am ever changing—
I am ever beyond
Myself,

what I may have once put my seal upon,
may no longer be
the greatest
Truth."

—Tukaram, 17th-century poet-saint of the
Bhakti movement in Maharashtra.

# Chapter 18    *Number Two on the List:*
## *Go to College*

AGNES SCOTT COLLEGE IS a Southern Belle. Her gothic buildings sit amid immaculate gardens and carefully groomed lawns. The structures bore signs of genteel poverty. Very genteel and not-too-impoverished. Azaleas and magnolia trees dotted the hundred-year-old campus. Twenty-five years before I arrived, young women wore white gloves whenever they left campus. Fourteen years before I arrived, students were arrested for demonstrating against segregation in downtown Atlanta.

Stepping onto the campus was like stepping onto an army base.

"It feels like I've come home," I told my dad.

The layout was cohesive, the greens impeccable, and if litter dared to show itself, it was whisked away before one could do a double take. There was a pride of place, pride in the turn of the century buildings with their stone arches and vaulted ceilings, pride in the history of educating women, pride in its rarified academic atmosphere. Above all, students and faculty shared expectations of honor and achievement.

Set apart from the surrounding neighborhood by manicured lawns and precise landscaping, the college snuggled down across the railroad tracks from the lively little town of Decatur, Georgia. This was not some cozy, backwater southern town. It was two MARTA (Metro Atlanta Rapid Transit Authority) stops down from where I lived in Candler Park. Small businesses, musicians, artists and families came together in this quirky little town. They also elected Democrats, which set them apart from most of the state.

At twenty-seven, I had a cornucopia of interesting and odd experiences, was the mother of a nine year old girl, had worked at a variety of jobs, but was absolutely ignorant of the workings of institutions of higher learning.

First on my list of things to do to pursue my call to ministry was to go to college. Early on, I decided I wanted to go to a women's college and it just so happened that Agnes Scott was right up the street. Ignorant of the college application process, I proceeded thusly:

1. figure out where I wanted to go (Agnes Scott)

2. apply

3. find out how much it costs

4. pray for a scholarship

It's a good thing I got into Agnes Scott because I couldn't afford another application fee and I had no concept of a back-up plan.

In 1979 Patty Hearst was released from prison, the Ayatollah Khomeini seized power in Iran, Anwar Sadat of Egypt and Menachem Begin of Israel signed a peace treaty at the White House, a serious nuclear accident occurred at *Three Mile Island,* Dan White murdered Harvey Milk and the mayor of San Francisco, the San Francisco Board of Supervisors passed a gay and lesbian civil rights bill, John Speckling was executed in Florida, the first use of the electric chair in America after the death penalty was reintroduced in 1976, and McDonald's introduced the Happy Meal. In the midst of it all, with trepidation and hope, focus and frivolity, Shepherd moved in with us and I began my college career.

The entire student population of Agnes Scott was seven hundred and fifty. That meant small classes, individual attention, and high expectations. I was one of three majors in the Bible and Religion department. I was also one of three taking Greek. If going to college was the first thing I needed to check off on my list, I was going to get every ounce of knowledge and experience I could. Learning became an addiction. I maxed out the number of hours I could take every quarter. Like a thirsty dog after a long run, I lapped up my class work as if I would never see water again.

My day began when I got Tanya up and dressed, packed her lunch, and walked with her the short mile to school. Next, I grabbed everything I thought I might need for the day, slung it into my backpack and raced the train to Agnes Scott. If I set out even a minute late I was sure to be stuck at the railroad crossing in front of the school. About fifty percent of the time I lost and would arrive at my 8:30 classes ten minutes late. Mary Boney Sheats and Kwai Chang (all the professors on campus dispensed with the 'Dr.' title to set a more egalitarian atmosphere) were the two professors that made up the Bible and Religion department, and Ms. Sheats had a penchant for early classes. I had the distinct misfortune (in terms of time of day) of taking an 8:30 a.m. class with her nearly every quarter.

Agnes Scott is a liberal arts college geared to making its students both culturally and academically literate. It places emphasis on teaching students how to find information, think critically, and write clearly. Bible was a required course. Not because they were intent or even interested in converting students, but because of the belief (which I still hold) that to be literate in our culture, literature and poetry, as well as politics, history, and current events, one needs some familiarity with the biblical texts. Both professors approached the text academically, exploring its origins, history, and theology. The course was offered either as a one-quarter course geared to those fulfilling the requirement or as a yearlong course taught in greater depth and required of majors.

I arrived on campus ignorant of college life and the social strata that existed among the students. But I had this impelling and powerful call. The first hint that there might be trouble ahead occurred when I discovered that there was an active student group called the Christian Council who prayed daily for our heretical professors. They believed that the peaceful, centered Mr. Chang and the intellectually rigorous Ms. Sheats were both heretical. Just to reiterate, heresy is defined as an opinion or doctrine that is at variance with the orthodox or accepted doctrine. In this case read, fundamentalist doctrine.

Mr. Chang and Ms. Sheats didn't believe the Bible to be the literal, inerrant word of God. Since I shared their belief and didn't believe that either homosexuality or divorce was a sin, another heretic was added to their prayer list.

One morning as I stepped onto an elevator heading for my early morning class, a student refused to get on with me. At first I thought it was a mistake.

"There's room if you're going up," I offered.

Stare. "No. Thank. You."

I was shocked. Not until I arrived at the third floor did I figure out what happened. *She didn't get on because I'm a lesbian?* Still, I didn't get it. Did she think I would try to jump her bones in the closed and confined space? Did she think she would catch lesbianism? That I would contaminate her? I wasn't so hurt as shocked. And angry. Or both. Not at her treatment of me, but at her ignorance and arrogance.

During a class in Reformation history, six of us were in the class: four were members of the Christian Council, and then there was Rachel Jones and myself. We met in a second floor classroom at a rectangular table just inside the door. The Christian Council girls clustered on one side of the table, Rachel and I on the other. Ms. Sheats sat at the head.

This particular day seemed ordinary enough. We all arrived about the same time and spent a few minutes divesting ourselves of backpacks and coats, setting out notebooks, texts, and Ms. Sheats' extensive and thorough syllabus. I turned to Rachel to chat before Ms. Sheats arrived. Rachel was from South Carolina, brilliant, and kind. She wore her red hair short and combed back, like a boy's cut from the fifties.

"Baby dyke," I thought with affection. When I asked her once, she firmly denied it, though I never left off thinking she might discover herself in the years to come. Maybe she was nice to me because she felt the kinship but most likely because, honestly, she was a nice person. I hate how milquetoast the word *nice* sounds. It doesn't capture its gentle strength. Rachel was good, decent, and kind. She was nice in the most elegant sense of that word. Years later I discovered that she took a lot of flack for befriending me.

So there we were, sitting opposite one another, two against four. This is only in retrospect. On the one side, I in my jeans, t-shirt and chukka boots, Rachel in her chinos, button down, and loafers, on the other side, four lovely young ladies turned out to perfection: hair curled, make up discreet, dressed well enough for a Junior League meeting. One young lady flashed a lovely, large, and shiny, new engagement ring. Ms. Sheats sat at the head of the table; her short, gray-white hair styled very much like Rachel's, her notes in a neat stack. She greeted us briefly and began the class.

She began covering the major points of Martin Luther's disagreements with the Roman Catholic Church.

"However," she said, "he did not disagree with all the teachings of the church. For example, though he married and believed that priests should be allowed to marry, he did not believe in divorce."

"Weren't there *any* circumstances where he would allow for divorce?" I asked.

"Divorce is a sin!" My classmate across the table raised her voice. "There is no acceptable reason for divorce!"

"But what if, heaven forbid," I challenged gently, "you married someone who later abused you physically or who sexually molested your children? Wouldn't divorce be acceptable then? Wouldn't it even be imperative?"

I was stunned when the girl with the engagement ring burst into sobs. Her friends patted her hands and glared at me. Ms. Sheats stoically waited for the tempest to subside. It didn't. My classmate's wails escalated. I squirmed. Chair legs screeched as she pushed back from the table, grabbed her things and ran from the room. One of the other girls followed.

"Now then," said Ms. Sheats "let's look at Luther's writing concerning the souls of children who are born mentally retarded. Luther believed that those born with severe developmental delays, particularly children with what we now call Down's syndrome, did not have souls and should be put to death."

It was my turn to be shocked and dismayed. I peppered her with questions. "Why? How could he make that kind of a pronouncement? Did his followers kill their own children? Did he ever change his mind?"

The girls across the table continued to glare at me. *Why wasn't this more upsetting than the idea of divorce?*

I muddled through the rest of the class thrown both by my interaction with the other students and by the material. I stopped Ms. Sheats as she left the room.

"I'm really sorry. I didn't mean to disrupt your class."

She gazed at me with no perceptible emotion. "They needed to hear it."

"I don't get why my questions are so threatening."

She sighed, "Connie, people tend to approach their religious lives in one of two ways. Either they subscribe to a set of rules and follow them, or they understand a life of faith to be a call to justice and follow *that* call. The one focuses on piety, the other on righteousness."

Wow. We were the same, only different. The reason I never was torn up about my sexuality, the reason I never saw my sexuality contrary to my relationship with God, was that I didn't equate piety with faithfulness. I sagged against the doorframe. Some internal lever slid into place as I began to reinterpret a myriad of experiences.

"There are perils attached to each," she continued. "The one lends itself to a rigidity that can eventually hamper spiritual growth. The other can veer off into *self-* righteousness, if one is not very careful."

"So how I learned to be in relationship to God is different from my classmates. I think I got the better deal."

"There are pitfalls to both paths."

"It makes me think about how I am raising Tanya."

"Well, *do* think about it. Do you want Tanya to be innocent or righteous?"

And with that she swept out of the room, leaving Rachel and me in her wake.

Because I lived for several years in an alternative neighborhood, attended an unorthodox church, had a global perspective, and a naive streak a mile wide, I had no idea that my presence would disturb more traditional students. I had no intention of causing trouble. I wasn't there to make a point, I was there to check off the next requirement on my list. I just happened to live all the way out to my edges while doing it. I asked questions because I am an infinitely curious person. But mostly, I was trying to follow this impelling, powerful call.

I made a point to schedule classes so I would be finished before Tanya's school let out and could walk to pick her up. Dinner, homework, bedtime, followed in that order. For three years, we lived with my partner, Shepherd. Between her income and my student loans, I had the freedom to go to school without having to hold down a job other than mother. When we broke up, it became all student loans all the time. Okay, not really. I picked up part time work here and there, but thank God I had those student loans and a scholarship for tuition.

Now here's the thing. I was an open lesbian at Agnes Scott. I was open everywhere in my life and saw no reason I shouldn't be there. Having been blessed with no sense of shame about my identity and being a pretty vocal feminist, it only seemed right that I live out loud. Lying or hiding didn't match up with my idea of living with integrity. I wasn't loud but I wasn't silent, either. I just went to classes, spoke up when I wanted, and asked lots of questions, oblivious to any impact I might be having on my fellow students. As far as I could see, there were no other lesbians on campus, at least among the students (a dean and a couple of PE teachers had me wondering), but I was not a traditional student. I didn't live on campus and I didn't hang out with my college-aged classmates. In the Hub, between classes, I hung out with the other RTCs (return to college students) who were my age and older.

A year later the school had a panel discussion about "homosexuality" with the biology, psychology and philosophy professors weighing in. Somehow, I ended up representing the Bible department. Whether it was too hot a topic or whether I was just given the opportunity because I was, well, you know, *homosexual,* I don't know.

The meeting was packed. Every seat was taken and students who arrived late crowded around the walls. The room was large and graceful with high ceilings and large mullioned windows looking out to the quad. The professors and I were seated at two cloth-covered tables. I wore a black and white dress with a red belt that doubled as my hostess garb when I worked at the local French restaurant in my neighborhood. I was excited, though a little intimidated, to be on a panel with professors, but I didn't doubt myself or my ability to represent. Nonetheless, my stomach quivered as I waited for the discussion to start.

"Homosexuality may be a genetic predisposition," the biology professor began. The psychology professor referenced the American Psychiatric Association (APA) declaration in 1973 that homosexuality was not a disease by changing the 81-word definition of sexual deviance in its own reference manual. The discussion meandered through a plethora of organic and inorganic possibilities.

When I finally rose to speak the tension in the room escalated. I made a 10-minute theological argument exploring the differences between activity and identity. And then it was question time.

"The Bible says that a man shall not lie with another man."

"The Bible says homosexuality is an abomination."

"The Bible says that homosexuals are like murderers and idol worshippers."

"The Bible says you are going to hell."

I took a deep breath. There were so many, many things I could say. I passed on the idea of saying we should be careful not to make the Bible an idol. I passed on the idea of parsing the Greek and exploring historical context and decided that Jesus was my trump card. "Jesus says that if we love God with all our hearts and souls and minds and strength and love our neighbor as ourselves that we have fulfilled the Law. We may have different personal tests for the truth of what we believe and how we behave, but that is mine."

By the time the moderator called the meeting to a close I was wrung out.

When I tell people I am both a feminist and a lesbian (they are not the same thing) they often assume I'm strident. I don't think I'm shrill or harsh, at least not usually, though I am intensely passionate. I figure that if I can listen I might also be heard. I find the notion of the dialogue of ideas seductive. And I'm pretty sure I'm not right all the time. I'm also pretty sure I *am* right about some things. Either way, I'll listen, because when the universe has exploded inside your head, you're a little more open to the idea that there are probably a lot of things you don't know.

Despite—or most likely because of—the vigorous intellectual debates I engaged in, college was as close to heaven as I could get. I was being trained to reason, think, and articulate information and ideas. My arguments needed to be backed by reason and facts and integrate disciplines from biology to theology to history and language. Intellectually challenged on a daily basis, I embraced the process like a suckling pig latching onto a teat. I was as happy as I was challenged. You can't get much happier than that.

"To learn which questions are unanswerable, and *not to answer them*: this skill is most needful in times of stress and darkness."

—Ursula K. LeGuin, <u>The Left Hand of Darkness</u>

## Chapter 19   *Lessons in Humility*

I EASED PEARL, MY Leyland white 1970 MGB, into the parking lot of the *Sport's Page*. Midterms were over, Tanya was visiting my folks, and I arrived at the bar early in the afternoon to celebrate the end of exams. Shepherd and I had split up on somewhat amicable terms, but it meant there was no one at home. I wasn't there to party to a dull dance beat pulsing non-stop with drunken strangers, or for dim lights and mindless noise. I wanted to be in a welcoming place where I didn't have to declare, "I am a lesbian." Or, didn't have to be somewhere everyone assumed I wasn't. I just wanted to let down after an intense week of studying and test taking, somewhere that if they didn't know my name, they at least knew something essential about me and found it to be good.

Bars look different in daylight. At night, light from disco balls fracture against dark walls while grinding music throbs relentlessly. Sound and light, fantasy characters, and seductive glances fan desires. In the light of day all bars look a little old and out of sorts. Dings on the tabletops, scratched floors, and dirty windows with dust motes climbing slanted rays of afternoon sun. They smell different in daylight, too. No collision of a hundred different colognes and a hundred sweating bodies to cover the sour smell of spilled beer seeping from the cracks between the floorboards.

I slipped into one of the booths that circled the parquet dance floor and ordered a beer. Glass clinked in the background while the bartender set up for the night, sliding wine glasses into their slots, stacking beer mugs in the freezer so that each customer would drink from a frosty mug.

I fingered my mug, tracing the moisture as it crept down the side of the glass, capturing it with my finger and licking the residue. The only other people in the bar happened to be my neighbors from across the street and a friend of theirs. They motioned for me to join them.

"We want you to meet Allison."

So that was the person with them.

"She went to Scott for a while but now she's at the Atlanta College of Art."

I pulled up a chair at the end of their booth. Allison was much younger than me, engaging, and full of energy. I caught up with my neighbors and shared my midterm victories. During a lull in our easy and inconsequential chatter, Allison leaned out of her side of the booth and grabbed my hand.

"Wanna dance?" she asked.

I wanted to dance. I always want to dance. To feel the base line and drumbeat tingle up my spine. To sway and pop. To feel my body catch rhythms and ride them like a tide. "Yeah," I said, "I want to dance."

The music was low but steady as we stepped onto the floor and slowly circled one another, trying to find where our pulses intersected. And then we accepted the invitation of our bodies. She stalked me around the dance floor. I retreated; then advanced. She pushed close to me, breathing on my neck. I tipped back my head and extended my throat to her warm sighs. And when the music stopped, we swayed in the silence until I began to laugh. And she laughed, and it all seemed so innocent and silly and yet the energy we generated was palpable.

After my friends left, Allison and I went out for coffee.

"You really want to be a minister?"

"I'm not sure it's what I want, but God has been pushing me in that direction for an awfully long time." I paused. It was so difficult to explain. "It's like I *have* to or I can't be who I'm supposed to be."

"Oh." She pushed her cup around in a wet circle on the tabletop. "I was raised Catholic and when I came out I figured I had two choices. I could choose to be myself and go to hell. Or not come out and die."

My stomach fell. I stared at her whitening knuckles as she gripped her coffee cup. *Oh my God! Be yourself and choose to be condemned to eternal damnation or choose what the church teaches and deny who you are. Some fucking choice.* We talked and I talked about maybe a different way of look-ing at it. We kissed. She came home with me and I held her into the night. *I can help her with this.*

We would pursue a relationship of our mismatched selves. Believing I was in love, I thought I found someone who could handle the risks I was taking and I believed I could heal her wounded spirit.

She wanted . . . I am not sure what she wanted. Sometimes love is not enough and wounds are too deep for healing. In any event, neither of us found what we were looking for and, perhaps more importantly, I came closer to understanding that I could save no one.

The secret to happiness is freedom . . . And the secret to freedom is courage.

—Thucydides

## Chapter 20 *Family Freedom*

I SPED BY THE scrub pines, kudzu, and orange clay that lined the highway from Atlanta to Columbus in my little pearl colored MGB. The sun was high and blared through the windshield. I turned down the visor, but the brightness slid around whatever relief it promised. I was going to see my folks. I was going to come out. They knew, and I knew they knew, but the right conversation had not taken place. Yet.

Small mirages shimmered up from the road while Joan Armatrading belted at the top of my car radio's volume, "I can walk under ladders." *Am I lucky?* But that wasn't the question, was it? Would my parent's disown me? That wasn't the question either. I was scared but not too scared. The conversation I was about to have with them would merely acknowledge unspoken information that I refused to confirm or deny when they first asked 10 years earlier. They knew. I knew they knew. It was time for me to turn the light on.

I was nervous and not nervous. Friends of mine had been disowned, rejected, prayed over, exorcized, even beaten but none of that was on my radar. The conversation might be uncomfortable. But it would be over and we could move on. *I believe. Help thou my unbelief.*

I believed my parents were who I thought they were. Believed it a lot more than I didn't believe it. But still. *Would this be the proverbial straw that broke the camel's back?*

Arrested for the possession of marijuana at 16, pregnant at 17, and not once did I doubt or want for their love and support. If the past is the best indicator of the future, then I was golden. But what if this were the thing they couldn't get past?

I turned onto the Macon Road exit, down shifting to third, then second, as I pulled back on the reigns of my 98 horsepower engine. The synchronized gears slid smoothly into place and I took pleasure controlling the power of my little sports car as we eased to a stop. I might as well enjoy it now, because I was walking into the land of no power and no control.

It was a short two miles from the exit to my parent's home. I turned on to their street. Their car was in the driveway. They were home. I hadn't let them know I was coming. It would only amp up the tension if I called ahead of time and said, "I need to talk to you about something. I'm coming home." They had a lot of history of my needing to talk to them. Why give them hours or days to ruminate?

I pressed in the clutch, switched off my engine, and coasted into the driveway. The house was a one-story brick ranch squatting on a half acre of sand. Columbus sits on what was the ocean floor a millennia or two ago. You could still find sharks teeth and shells in some places. Sand burrs flourished, but so did azaleas and crepe myrtles, zinnias, snapdragons and Shasta daisies. Two lonely scrub pines attempted to shade the back yard. Honeysuckle hung heavy and lush, pulling at the fence that divided the yard from the train tracks.

I grabbed my backpack, hopped out of the car, and walked to the kitchen door that opened from the carport.

"Hi! I'm home!"

I kissed them each in turn.

"What's going on?" Dad smiled. Mom looked a little leery.

They were sitting back from the kitchen table, having finished their evening meal, probably just getting ready to move to the living room. Now I would give my opening line.

"I need to talk to you about something and I didn't want to do it over the phone."

My heart started banging against my rib cage. I felt light-headed. The orange patterns on the kitchen floor tile started to dance. Now that I was here I wasn't sure how to begin. *Why hadn't I rehearsed this on my way here instead of grooving to my car, to the music blasting, the sun's seduction, and the wind whipping against my skin?*

I needed to trust myself, to trust God, and to trust my parents. But that wasn't all. I looked at them knowing in that moment the reason for my hesitation: I didn't want to hurt them. I knew I was okay. I knew I wasn't rejecting them—or more specifically, my dad. I read somewhere that men experienced their daughters' lesbianism as a personal rejection. I didn't want them to think I didn't love them or that they had done something wrong. I didn't want to leave them in pain. Like the time I found my mother sobbing in their bedroom after I was arrested for possessing a matchbox of pot.

I hesitated, not because I didn't know *what* to say, but I wanted to say it in a way that would reassure and comfort my parents. *I don't want to hurt you. I don't want you to be afraid for me.* They tensed in anticipation. *Don't drag this out, Connie. Get it over with. What they're afraid of is probably worse than what is.*

"Mom," I turned and looked at her, "Dad," I took his hand. "I think you already know this, but I wanted to say it out loud. I'm gay."

The world around us was galloping toward change. It was 1981 and the Church of England voted to allow women into holy orders, assassination attempts were made on President Reagan and Pope John Paul II, Sandra Day O'Connor became the first woman nominated to serve on the Supreme Court, and major league baseball, the one time constant in our lives, was out on strike from May to the end of July. Let's see what I could toss into the mix.

Words tripped out of my mouth with increasing speed. "If you have any questions, anything you want to ask me, I'll answer the best I can. But I need you to know I am the same person I have always been—good, bad, the works. I know you will always love me and I need you to know how much I love you."

My dad teared up as he gripped my hand. "How did it happen?"

"I fell in love with a woman, Dad." I paused, "You told me there was nothing I could ever do that you wouldn't love me."

Another pause. *Oh shit. Say something!*

"Honey, we'll always love you—but we worry about you," Mom said.

I nodded. I had given them plenty of reason. The earth tilted back into place. The patterns on the floor stopped doing a jig and settled into recognizable forms. My folks were struggling. I could tell. But they held onto me and did not let me go. And I would never let them go.

"I don't want to hurt you I just want to share *all* of my life with you. It's hard if there is this thing we don't talk about."

There didn't seem much to say after that. They didn't have a lot of questions. Thank God they never asked if I was a child molester. I really hate it when people do that. Had it come from my parents it would have broken my heart.

I pulled a copy of *Is the Homosexual My Neighbor,* by Letha Scanzoni and Virginia Mollencott from my backpack and set it on the table.

"Mom, I know you might wonder what the Bible says about it and I want you to read this. Then let's talk."

She fixed me a sandwich and I wolfed it down before I left. I wanted all of us to have time to think, to feel, to process. For them to say things to one another they might not want to say to me or to have a first reaction that would not be the same as their next reaction or the reaction after that. To figure out what questions they might have. I lobbed a volley into their courtand they needed time to see where it would land in their hearts.

After I kissed my mom, squeezed my Dad in a bear hug, and told them how much their love meant to me, I scooted out the same door I'd walked through hours earlier. The air was crisp and the night sky clear of clouds. I cranked my car and turned on the lights as I backed out of the driveway. The glimmer of a thousand stars scattered across the night sky.

I eased onto the entrance ramp to I-185 and roared through third and fourth gears to overdrive. My tires hummed down the new highway as I blasted the heater. It was a top down night, no matter how low the temperature dropped. I needed the feel of the sky against my skin and the whip of my hair in my face.

*I'm lucky, I'm lucky, I'm lucky. I can walk under ladders,* I bellowed along with Joan Armatrading into the night wind. My parents loved me. I could stand anywhere against anything. I was free.

No. I was free before.

Now I was powerful.

Some people come into your life as blessings. Others come into your life as lessons.

—Mother Teresa

# Chapter 21   *The Blessing of Ben*

I FIRST MET BEN Kline at Agnes Scott. He became my mentor and my friend and ultimately changed my life. At one time he had been a dean of the college and later the president of Columbia Theological Seminary (he stepped down after some years both for health reasons and because he preferred to teach) and he occasionally taught a class at Agnes Scott as a visiting professor. I signed up for his *Philosophy of Religion* class during my last term.

There is such a thing as grace.

The class of five, which included a seminary student who cross-registered to pick up a needed course (the only male student I had in a class for the entire four years), met in a small room around a large square table. It was spring of my senior year, warm enough for the windows to be open and almost too warm to not have on air conditioning. Ben Kline embodied my idea of what a professor should look like: silver hair, a slightly off-kilter smile, a sweater vest and a dashing bow tie. That he was a professor at the seminary I wanted to attend made him the object of my fascination and delight. I was in a class being taught by a seminary professor! I pulled the text and a notebook from my backpack, draped the pack across my chair, and sat up expectantly.

"Philosophy of religion looks at the big questions: the nature and existence of God, religious experience, the analysis of religious language and texts, the relationship between religion and science, and the nature of evil. We are going to look at the nature of religion as a whole, not merely within the Christian tradition."

I loved this class. No. Really. I *loved* it. He taught in such a way that I actually felt my brain creaking as it stretched. After every class I went home, struggled with the texts, the assignments, the *ideas,* and came back with questions.

"What is God?" He posed the question and waited expectantly.

Every week he began the class by asking the next questions that emerged as I wrestled with the questions we explored the week before.

"Do we have any reason to think that God exists or doesn't exist?"

"If God exists, what, then, does the existence of evil mean?"

These were the questions that plagued me when I woke in the middle of the night and this man brought them alive—not with answers, but with the next question and the next. He was a genius. If all my classes in seminary were going to be like this I wasn't sure I could stand it. It would be like drinking too much whiskey or making too much love. He had me. He had me with the questions. He had me when he didn't give me the answers. He had me when I saw that the questions were large enough to hold my experiences and big enough for me to grow.

I loved Ben Kline.

Toward the end of the semester I went to his office at the seminary. The buildings at Columbia resembled those of Agnes Scott, though its gothic stone architecture was more modest. His office was in the main building on the third floor.

I knocked lightly at his door and he invited me in. The wood paneled room was surrounded by bookshelves rising to the ceiling and crammed with books. His desk sat in the dormer window, facing out so that the light was behind him. Stacks of papers huddled so close to the edge of his desk that the slightest movement might topple them to the floor. He rose and motioned me to a round table flanked by a couple of captain's chairs. We exchanged a few pleasantries, his expression both curious and piercing.

"I feel called to the ministry, and I want to apply to Columbia, " I paused, "and I'm a lesbian."

He looked at me a long moment, "Do you plan to volunteer this information on the application?"

"Is there a box to check?" I asked. I wrestled with a ferocious desire to bulldoze any obstacle that challenged this impelling drive to pursue my call with integrity. I wanted to get in, but at what cost? Realism waged war with idealism. How I started mattered. *If* I started mattered more.

He laughed. "Let's just get you in. Then we'll work on keeping you in.

Do not depend on the hope of results. When you are doing the sort of work you have taken on, you may have to face the fact that your work will be apparently worthless and even achieve no worth at all, if not perhaps, results opposite of what you expect. As you get used to this idea, you will start more and more, to concentrate not on the results but on the value, the rightness, the truth of the work itself.

—Thomas Merton, *Letter to a Young Activist*

## Chapter 22  *Jumping in the Deep End*

I GRADUATED FROM AGNES Scott College in the spring of 1983. That fall I began classes at Columbia. Nazi war criminal, Klaus Barbie was arrested in Bolivia, to be tried later in Israel. A special commission of Congress released a report criticizing  the practice of Japanese internment during World War II. The Space Shuttle Challenger carried Guion S. Bluford, the first African-American, and Sally Ride, the first American woman, into space. Pope John Paul II visited his would-be assasin, Mehmet Ali Agca in prison to forgive him. And I became the first open lesbian to matriculate at Columbia Theological Seminary in Decatur, Georgia. The world was changing and I felt like a part of that inevitable change. It was a hopeful time.

The elegant, circular drive swept in front of the main building, past the tennis courts, and back to Columbia Drive. But I took the insiders' route, turning into the parking lot on the side of the building. I slid my MG into a space close to the bookstore and dining hall. The bumper sticker on my rear bumper read, "If you love Jesus, do justice. Any damn fool can honk."

I was in. I was going to be a minister. I was here in the temple of learning and spiritual questing.

I made my way to the first plenary session for entering students. For four years I worked toward this day. It held all the promise and mystery of my life to come. I bounced down the hall then sidled into the large basement room. It was foreign to be in a class with a majority of men—all of whom seemed to be at ease. I took a seat toward the back and pulled out my notebook and pens, twitching just a little. Fluorescent lights hummed overhead casting us in a ghastly glow while cold air whispered out of ceiling registers circulating the faint scents of freshly washed students and chalk dust. Our desks, shared rectangular tables, were angled toward a freestanding blackboard. In the front, Wade Huey waited for us to take our seats. Dr. Huey's shock of thick white hair offset a gentlemanly deportment reminiscent of Colonel Sanders.

"Welcome to your first 'Formation of Ministry class, " he began, "otherwise known as P one eleven."

I leaned forward, anxious to catch each pearl of wisdom that would soon drip from his obviously refined mouth. The rebel in me snickered. A P*11* is an army issue can opener.

"I want to begin by telling you what, as ministers, you must guard against."

Silent and attentive, we held our collective breath.

"The following is true of these major professions: physicians have drug problems, attorneys have problems with alcohol and," he paused for effect, piercing us with his gaze, "ministers have zipper problems."

Shocked, I looked around. Zipper problems? Two things bothered me about this statement. One: there were enough women in the room for him to have come up with a different euphemism. Or did this just refer to *male* clergy? And two: *WHAT?* You mean to tell me that the people who are supposed to model the highest standards of ethics are no more than clay-footed mongrels panting after any woman in heat? You mean women coming in distress, in their most vulnerable times, are at risk from the very person they should be able trust?

He continued, "You will, by the nature of your job, be thrust into intimate situations. You will be closer to some people than their husbands or wives. You will learn things about people that have never been shared with another soul. Stay aware of your role in a person's life and do not cross those boundaries."

The lecture meandered then ended by going over the syllabus and general information about our next three years. I looked around the room to identify any promising prospects for friends. I was shocked to see Monica Wilson, a former cop who stood me up for a date years earlier. What was she doing here? I was torn between hurt and humiliation because I had been stood up and the excitement of discovering another lesbian on campus.

She still looked like a cop. More cop than minister, but what did I know? I didn't know many ministers and only a few more cops. Compact and clearly in shape, she wore her hair closely cropped and curly. She had a cocky confidence you don't find in most women. Or people in general. Some something that said: cop. Authority maybe, or swagger. But definitely an attitude I recognized. After all, Tanya's dad was now a cop.

I had two hurdles to get over with Monica. The first was our failed date that, it turned out, she didn't even remember. But I did. Boy, did I. It was the first and only time I had ever been stood up. Second, I was planning on being open about my identity, but was she? Open, that is. And if not, how should I approach her and let her know her secret would be safe with me? Did she know I was out? Of all the issues I anticipated the need to navigate, this was *not* one of them. It never once occurred to me there would be other gay or lesbian people here.

I smiled at her as I gathered my papers and shoved them into my backpack. She returned a noncommittal nod, her eyes empty of recognition. She didn't remember me? Talk about adding insult to injury. Or was she signaling for me to keep quiet, to not acknowledge her or that I knew she was a lesbian? *Or*, had she had some sort of religious conversion that involved change or celibacy and didn't want to be tempted by me? I'm pretty sure the last one was just my imagination trying to soothe my ego from our previous interaction, but I liked it and decided to go with it until otherwise enlightened.

I returned her noncommittal nod with one of my own and made my way to the ground floor to check my mailbox. This is where Columbia reminded me of Agnes Scott the most. The polished marble floor, rows of brass mailboxes, rich wood moldings, and the hushed Southern politeness of the receptionist seemed to have been transposed from one institution to the next. I waited for the crowd around the mailboxes to dwindle before reaching inside my box to remove a folded sheet of paper. I flipped it open and read "please come to the dean's office tomorrow morning, 10 a.m."

I turned to the guy next to me. "Did you get a summons to the dean's office?"

He shook his head.

So there it was. I wasn't going to take a poll but I was pretty sure the jig was up. I was an imposter. They figured out that I shouldn't be here. They were going to revoke my scholarship. There was something wrong with my paperwork, a technicality . . .

I mulled it over all afternoon. I called a friend who told me to wait and see.

"You wait and see," I wanted to shout. "You live with this fear and anxiety. You wait for the next nineteen hours not knowing what someone or someones want to do with your life! *You* mother-fuckin' wait and see."

But I didn't say that. I would wait and see not because I wanted to but because I didn't have any alternative. I sucked it up. I couldn't eat dinner. I couldn't sleep. I couldn't talk myself out of the anxiety that wrapped itself around me like a ball of rubber bands. I couldn't pray my way out of the fear. I pulled out my well-thumbed copy of Howard Thurman's *Jesus and the Disinherited* and began reading the familiar text. I carried this book with me for years, read and reread it, and found comfort and courage in his words. He brought Jesus to life, describing a context I understood and identified with. I reread the chapter titled "Fear" and centered as best I could. I fell asleep half way through the chapter "Love," hoping to find ways to be faithful in the work of loving my enemies. I began to think of the administration as my enemy.

The next morning I woke, showered, packed up for a day of classes, and trudged to my car. I felt ready, but in no way eager, for the meeting to come.

The hall of the administration building didn't seem as familiar and welcoming as it had the day before. I asked the receptionist where the dean's office was.

"Which dean?" she asked.

I didn't know. I rifled around in my backpack until I found the sheet I was looking for. "The Dean of Admissions."

"Okay, honey, you go down this hall and it's the next to the last door on the right."

The hall telescoped as I walked its length. I couldn't seem to get to the end. I glanced into each open door trying to sort out the jumble of feelings spinning around in my gut. *Am I afraid? Yeah. Angry? Not really. Can I be brave? What does that feel like? My dad said that being brave didn't mean you weren't afraid.*

*Breathe*, I reminded myself as I poked my head into an office. "Is this the dean of admissions office?"

"No, you want to go another two doors down."

I stepped back, squared my shoulders and uttered a prayer under my breath. *Just let me get through this with a little dignity.*

Two doors down a small plaque announced "Dr. Lee Carroll, Dean of Admissions." I walked in. There sat, not only the Dean of Admissions, but Paige McRight, a representative of the Atlanta Presbytery, and Pete Carruthers, the Dean of Students.

I swallowed and squeaked out, "Good morning."

"Good Morning. Come on in and sit down." This from Dean Carroll.

I sat.

The once spacious room had been partitioned into three small offices. We sat in what appeared to be the secretary's space, scrunched into chairs that put us nearly knee to knee. I took a shallow breath. Then another. The sterile walls started closing in. I shut my eyes, took a deep breath, and prayed as I exhaled. *God give me strength.* I opened my eyes as the room lurched back into place.

"Connie, I don't know how to say this, but it's been brought to our attention that you may be a homosexual. We'd like to give you the opportunity to answer that."

My utter exasperation at the question generated the strength I had asked for. *I hate that word!* Not only is it a mis-amalgamation of Latin and Greek, but its meaning is both obtuse and clinical. *I'm a lesbian! I love a woman! Is that word so hard to say?*

"I am a lesbian."

"Were you intending on letting us know?"

*Breathe. Listen. Breathe.*

I thought they might be asking an honest question and I wanted to give an honest answer. "I thought I'd give myself a week or so, just to get oriented, to get the lay of the land. I mean I wasn't planning to wear a sign. I figured it would just come up on its own, in context."

*Who tattled?* I wondered. *Who was it that wouldn't give me the opportunity to get my feet wet, to get situated, to make a way for myself? Who had I threatened, however unknowingy? Who wanted to cause trouble for me?*

Later I discovered it was a dean at Agnes Scott. A Presbyterian dean. A Presbyterian dean deeply concerned with the purity of the church. A Presbyterian dean whom I don't remember meeting except in passing, but who must have been frightened or offended by the very me-ness of me.

"You know the Presbyterian Church doesn't ordain homosexuals."

"Yes, I do know that." *Is it stuffy in here? I know it's September but they need to turn on the air.* A bead of sweat slid between my shoulder blades.

The trio sat in silence waiting for me to continue. They seemed a little confused that I agreed with their statement.

"Well, the Presbyterian Church is a series of courts, right?" I asked. "I think it's time for this issue to be brought to the courts. I can appeal up through presbytery, Synod and all the way to the General Assembly if I need to." I said it just like I had a plan. Just like I knew what I was talking about. Just like the premise had the merit I believed it to have. Just like I knew this was the first, though unexpected, appeal I would make.

I was severely outgunned in both power and information and I was not a seasoned political dissembler. I began to dither. "And we're supposed to always be open to more light from the Holy Spirit, right? I've been called to the ministry by the Spirit so I think that might be some more light." *Right? Right?*

They weren't going to agree with my assessment so there wasn't much else to say. They didn't have any more questions. Just needed me to confirm or deny the information. Done and done.

The dean opened the door that led into the hall. "Thank you for being so forthcoming, Ms. Tuttle."

It was over. Short and sweet. They weren't kicking me out. So far. They weren't revoking my scholarship. So far. The meeting planted an amorphous fear that became quite familiar over the next three years though at the time I didn't recognize it. A breeze played in the hall as a student opened a door to the outside. I exhaled and walked briskly down the corridor to my next class.

The opening salvo had been fired. The battlefield advantage was theirs. And the chief casualty of that first skirmish was my peace of mind.

Ah. I smiled. I'm not really here to keep you from freaking out. I'm here to be with you while you freak out, or grieve or laugh or suffer or sing. It is a ministry of presence. It is showing up with a loving heart.

—Kate Braestrup, Here If You Need Me: A True Story

# Chapter 23   *Learning Presence*

THE WORLD WAS CHANGING but not fast enough. Ronald Reagan was president. The United States invaded Grenada and, though the conflict was brief, it moved our country from a defensive military to first strike nation. My dad looked away, unwilling to acknowledge the shift. He was proud, as a career military man, that we were not a first strike nation. On the other hand, Bishop Desmond Tutu received the Nobel Peace Prize for his opposition to apartheid. I was changing in ways I was not aware. And Columbia was coping with the ramifications of having admitted its first openly lesbian student.

I carried a full academic load the entire three years of the MDiv program. Tanya entered high school and was involved in the National Honor Society, flag core, theatre, and Young Life. Our evenings were spent facing one another across the dining room table, churning out our respective homework. Occasionally I would grunt a "listen to this." or Tanya would try out an oral argument for her AP (Advanced Placement) history class. During exam times we focused with quiet intensity

I left for work between ten and eleven at night, about the same time Tanya was getting ready for bed, and spent my nights sitting with ill or dying patients. Working for a personal care agency meant that I provided their clients with company, support, minor housekeeping, and meal preparation. Mostly it was the work of presence, time, and attentiveness. I gave respite to family members who spent hours care-giving during the day or was part of a patchwork of employees caring for those who had money but no family.

I walked through the world holding a perpetual ache for people I came to care for. The loneliness of the journey through illness and death. The thousand small indignities. The struggle to find meaning.

"Why is God punishing me?" Mrs. Coldwell pleaded with me for an answer.

Propped up on several soft pillows, she languished on the couch in her lovely urban home and gazed unseeingly out the large plate glass window. The rolling vista of a beautifully landscaped and manicured lawn put on a show for her unfocused eyes. The pink turban encasing her bald head seemed exotic rather than a nod to vanity.

Mrs. Coldwell and her husband were upstanding and important members of Mt. Paran Church of God, a local mega-church. Now, with the cancer diagnosis, they were trying to make sense of what they had been taught to believe. Everything they were experiencing brought their faith into question. Circular arguments continued during our time together each evening.

"If I have been faithful, God would bless me. I have done everything I was told believers should do. I accept Jesus Christ as my lord and savior. I tithe to the church. I believe the doctrines of the church. I have been baptized and raised my children to be Christian. I have obeyed my husband and followed the Ten Commandments. Why hasn't God healed me? Why is this happening? Do I not believe enough?"

"Pray with me." She implored when the questions had been asked a hundred times.

I took her fragile hand, gently placing it onto my upturned palm. "Miz Coldwell," I began, "I'm not sure I know what to pray for you."

"Pray for my healing. I know if I can truly believe, God will heal me."

I bowed my head and tears threatened. My heart beat erratically. *Whatever made me think I was called to be a minister? I don't know what to say or what comfort to offer. I don't even know how to pray like she wants me to.*

"Miz Coldwell, I don't believe God is punishing you. I think he's right here with you, hurting when you hurt, holding you when you feel alone." I tried to use words and language that she could accept. "Everything I know about you tells me you have lived a faithful life. God is with you, he hasn't abandoned you. This is just a different part of your journey. It's not so much about what you believe or do, but just letting yourself lean into God." I said words about trusting God, words we both needed to hear in those fractured moments.

But I prayed like she asked me, using words and sounds that felt familiar to her, remembering that I wasn't her minister. I was a woman, unlike the ministers who visited from her church, who were all men and on whom she conferred absolute authority. Mine was the voice of the other. *What did they teach her in the name of God?* Anger closed my throat. Any word I might offer contrary to what she believed would be suspect. Her fear was palpable as her hand trembled on my palm. I took a slow, calming breath and began to pray.

"Gracious and Loving God, we ask that you hold Miz Coldwell in your loving arms. Open her to feel your love and your touch in her life. Comfort her fears. Ease her pain. Let her rest in the sureness of your care for her and feel you with her in all times and all places. We ask this in the name and the nature and the spirit of Jesus Christ. Amen."

She dropped her hand, opened her eyes, and gazed at me silently.

What did I, a thirty-two year old, think I could tell her about facing death? Or give any semblance of an answer to the questions plaguing her? Was there any comfort I could offer that she would be willing to accept?

"Our problems stem from our acceptance of this filthy, rotten system."

—Anonymous

## Chapter 24  *How Do You Solve a Problem Like Connie?*

AND THEN THERE WERE the committee meetings. An inordinate number of committee meetings at which my presence was required. I think a committee was formed just to handle the 'Connie' question. I would received notice by campus mail and traipse up the two floors to Ben's office.

"What do I do now?"

Ben always knew the political implications of whatever issue was at hand and helped me prepare my response. If necessary, he accompanied me. At one meeting I was informed that the president of the seminary wanted to meet with me on a weekly basis. I wasn't told the purpose for those weekly meetings so I gathered myself for the first one with trepidation.

I arrived a few minutes early and slipped into the restroom. *Is my shirt on straight? My hair okay? Everything in place?* The immaculate women's room still did not manage a tampon or sanitary napkin machine, the implication being that women didn't bleed monthly—some throwback to the idea the menstruating women are unclean. Even the lavatories were discreetly separate from the "retiring' room"—a spacious room appointed with a couch, two side chairs, a coffee table, and a slim side table over which hung a large, gilt frame mirror. I shrugged on my backpack and headed to the president's office.

"He's ready for you," his secretary said when I walked through the door. I wasn't sure I was ready for him.

Dr. Phillips leaned back in his deep leather chair and beckoned with one hand for me to take a seat. I slid my backpack to the floor and took the chair opposite his substantial, high gloss, wooden desk. The cushioned seat was lower than I anticipated and put me at a disadvantage. *I do not like feeling powerless.* I had no idea what was to come and was afraid I couldn't imagine the wost. My stomach plummeted into my gut. I clenched my jaw and fists in concentration. *I will not cry.* The clenching stiffened my spine. I let out my breath and waited.

Dr. Philips pulled in his chair, solemnly folded his hands, and placed them carefully before him on his uncluttered desk. I raised my dry eyes to meet his gaze. "Connie, I believe the Bible is clear about its stance on homo-sexuality."

We remained still a moment, each looking intently at one other.

He shifted uncomfortably in his seat and continued, "There are moral standards to which we expect those preparing for the ministry to subscribe."

I got the idea that he thought our meeting would be an opportunity for him to change me somehow, to guide me to rejecting my sexuality. Maybe to pray me out of it. Or ask me to quit. There would be no praying me out of myself. No 'miraculous' conversion. I kept looking at him, wanting to say something eloquent, profound, irrefutable, but what burst out was, "What *exactly* do you think I do that is so horrible?"

Images of light kisses, feathered breath across collarbone, the touch of breast to breast filled my brain. He stared at me in silence. I gazed back, now imagining delicate pink of labial folds, the touch of tongue to exposed flesh. *Let me paint you a picture,* I thought, as we sat together, my reflections painting icons of sensuality in the space between us.

We continued to sit in silence. He tightened his lips and pressed them against his teeth in a small, impenetrable seam. There was nothing kind or generous in the rigid line between skin and teeth. I sat with it a second, "I mean what do *I* do that *you* don't do?"

Was he conjuring images in his mind of his own sexual experiences? Of mine? I stared at his inflexible mouth, a tight line pinched across the bottom of his face. A light dawned. *He doesn't worship at the liquid velvet shrine.*

My gaze crawled around the room, taking in the bookcases that stretched almost to the top of the fourteen-foot ceiling, the immaculate display of seldom-used books interspersed with flawless silk plants that had no occasion to either live or wilt. For a moment I focused on the tall windows that lined one wall whose deep sills were large enough to curl up on and take a nap if you had the imagination for it. I heard a desk drawer open and looked back at Dr. Philips as he pulled out an appointment calendar. He seemed like a nice man: about twice my age, graying hair, compact body tucked into a somber gray suit, and clearly no stranger to church suppers. I just couldn't like him. Fairly or unfairly, he represented all that was powerful, hurtful, unimaginative, and oppressive in the church.

"I feel like a single grain of sand stuck in the cog of a giant machine and all available forces are being rallied to remove me," I told Ben after my meeting.

Our next appointment didn't go much better.

"Connie," he said, "have you considered a MTS degree instead of the MDiv?

"What is that?"

"A Masters of Theological Studies."

"But I feel called to ministry. Is that a degree for ministry?"

"No, it's not."

*But it would get you off the hook with the presbytery and the denomination, wouldn't it? Why don't you care about this call God has saddled me with?*

"I want the degree that prepares me for ministry." I sounded truculent but didn't care.

Every subsequent encounter unraveled my naïveté a little further. I was as sad as I was angry. I discovered the leaders of the church could be as clay-footed and self-interested as the rest of us. *Why aren't you asking me about my experience of God? Why aren't you tackling issues of intellectual integrity on campus?*

"Dr. Philips, you know I graduated from Agnes Scott and we have an honor code that everyone subscribes to. Why isn't there one here at Columbia?"

"We don't believe those in the ministry need an honor code." His righteous indignation clanged between us, "It's assumed."

I wound up and tossed out the next pitch, "Then why have I seen more cheating here in one semester than I did in the four years I was at Agnes Scott?"

He picked up his phone and spoke to his secretary, "Do I still have that meeting at 10 today?" I had been dismissed.

I trudged out of his office. There were no rules for these conversations. Every time I hit a ball—even if it was a home run—the game ended. *A million women, men and children are starving in Ethiopia, racism is rampant in our country and abroad, women can't get equal pay for equal work, women and children are being beaten, raped, and sexually abused right here in this city and all around the world—and you're spending your time worrying about how one lesbian threatens your way of life? You want me to be pious? Well, I want to be righteous.*

I skulked down the hall toward my next class.

The Emperor Has No Clothes!

After she said it,
The crowd grabbed her roughly.
The emperor
Was spirited off
By Secret Service men
Disguised as angels.

"Wait a minute," she said,
"I just want to
think this through."
But they bound her wrists
With rope
And prodded her with irons.
"By whose authority?"
they demanded.
She couldn't answer,
Being bound and gagged,
So they invented for her
A man with horns
And supernatural cock,

Much bigger
And more talented than theirs.

She was still saying it
As priests approached
With notepads and pills.
"You're overwrought,"
one said gently
as he took her by the arm.
She tried to turn her head
Back toward the empty tomb
But men were putting neon signs
Around it.

—Kathleen Norris, published with permission of the author

# Chapter 25  *The Road to Hell*

"MAY I JOIN YOU?"

I looked up to see one of my classmates, a tall man in a dress shirt and khaki slacks, holding his lunch tray.

"Sure," I responded. I didn't know many folks yet and was glad for the company.

The legs of the chair rasped across the floor as he pulled it away from the table and sat down across from me. I smiled.

"How are you liking our New Testament class?" I began.

"Okay. But I wanted to talk to you about something else." He stopped and allowed for a significant pause. "Connie, it's been laid on my heart to tell you that you are going to hell."

I stiffened. *Really?* "And just who laid this on your heart?"

"God."

I couldn't tell if he was merely earnest or arrogant beyond belief.

"Wow," I paused, my heart beginning to thud. *Don't respond with anger. To be prophetic is to love the people enough to challenge them to change. I don't want to do what he is doing.* I took a breath. My ears started ringing and my bite of sandwich turned to sand in my mouth. "God has told me something very different."

"If you believe the Bible you have to know you are sinning."

"I believe the Bible but we must find different things to be important."

"It's *all* true," he insisted.

"It's a guidebook, not a play book." I managed a small smile. "And the Bible is not my God. That would make it an idol."

"I don't want to argue with you, I just want you to know that you are going to hell so you can be clear about the choice you are making." He moved to get up.

"I don't want to argue either, but if you are going to sit down and tell me I am going to hell then I think it is only polite to listen to my response." I felt my cheeks begin to flush. All around us conversations peaked and ebbed, papers rattled and dishes clanked against tables as students began making their way to classes.

Settling back into his seat, he pursed his lips and waited. *Not exactly looking open-minded.*

"There is a difference between activity and identity." I began "It isn't a choice I make like someone makes to steal or cheat or murder. The only choice I make is whether or not to be who God created me to be."

"God makes it clear in the book of Romans," he began, "first chapter, verses 24-28." He began to quote the passage

> Therefore God gave them over in the sinful desires of their hearts to sexual impurity for the degrading of their bodies with one another. They exchanged the truth about God for a lie, and worshiped and served created things rather than the Creator—who is forever praised. Amen. Because of this, God gave them over to shameful lusts. Even their women exchanged natural sexual relations for unnatural ones. In the same way the men also abandoned natural relations with women and were inflamed with lust for one another. Men committed shameful acts with other men, and received in themselves the due penalty for their error. Furthermore, just as they did not think it worthwhile to retain the knowledge of God, so God gave them over to a depraved mind, so that they do what ought not to be done." (NRSV)

I was impressed. I couldn't quote scripture like that.

"The Bible also says to love your neighbor as yourself," I responded.

"I'm telling you this because I love you and I don't want you to go to hell."

Two more students pulled up chairs beside him. My sandwich sat untouched on the tray in front of me. I wasn't afraid. Not for my eternal soul. Not for my safety. I considered the best approach to take, one that might allow for some real dialogue. It was tricky.

"Jesus said if we love God with all our heart and soul and mind and love our neighbor as ourselves then we have fulfilled all the laws and the prophets."

"Homosexuality isn't love. It's a perverse act, an abomination before God."

"But," I gently refuted, "the word abomination, if you study the Greek, is a word referring to specific acts of idolatry done in the worship of other gods."

"If we start saying homosexuality is okay, then what about sex with children or beast-i-al-i-ty?" he challenged.

"I guess I would say that neither of those activities are loving of God or neighbor. Children and animals can't give consent. In both cases it would be the powerful abusing the powerless." I stopped and gazed at the men across from me. We were the last ones in the dining hall and our conversation echoed in the now empty, cavernous room. Glasses and silverware tinkled in the background as the kitchen crew loaded the dishwasher and reset for the next meal. "In neither case would it be a question of identity"

"You can choose whether or not you act on your attraction. You can be celibate."

"Didn't Calvin say people are called to celibacy for a period of time, with specific intent, but not for a lifetime?" These guys were Presbyterians and presumably Calvinists as they matriculated at a Presbyterian seminary. "But when it comes to gay people, do you assume that if someone is gay they are automatically called to celibacy? I can guarantee *I* have not been called to celibacy."

A clock ticking on the back wall clattered in the silence. We were at an impasse and it was time for class. "Gentlemen, thank you for sharing your concern for my spiritual well-being," I pushed back my chair and picked up my tray. "I pray for the day you will value not who I love, but that I love." My legs were a little shaky as I made my way to return my tray to the kitchen. *How many conversations like this will I have in the next three years?* I wondered, breathing in slowly and slowly letting it out. *God, help me to speak with love to their fear.*

My new friends were gone when I turned around. I walked to class alone.

However sugarcoated and ambiguous, every form of authoritarianism must start with a belief in some group's greater right to power, whether that right is justified by sex, race, religion, or all three.

—Gloria Steinem

# Chapter 26 *The Fray*

THE ADMINISTRATION RESOLVED TO wage war against me. Not me as a person, a unique individual. Not me as someone trying to figure out this call thing. Not me as a complex conundrum trying to be faithful. But me, "The Lesbian". And they had every tactical advantage. They had the personnel and financial resources to engage in a multi-fronted battle that included trying to change my orientation, asking the presbytery (as representative of the institutional church) to block my candidacy for ministry, gumming up my schedule with meetings that that required psychological and emotional preparation, and refusing to allow me to take certain courses required for the degree.

I had this vision of peaceful engagement. I wanted to hold the prophetic and the pastoral in dynamic tension. A prophet rises up from the community, stands outside its borders, and calls the people they love to repentance. Contemporary Christian prophets say hard things that need to be said while challenging the Church to be the radical community Christ called into being. I also wanted to be pastoral, to walk with those who were afraid to enter the uncharted territory of God's grace.

Sort of like Peter when God challenged his culturally bound prejudices. He was praying when he had this mystical experience and heard a voice telling him to do something totally contrary to what he believed was necessary for him to be a good and sinless man. He refused. But God kept coming back, insisting that Peter let go assumptions about what God finds acceptable. "What God has made clean, you must not call profane," the voice persisted another three times. (Acts 10:15 NRSV)

I wanted to walk a pastoral walk, but I forgot how pissed off people get when they feel threatened. Especially when they are the ones in power. I really believed it would be different in this holy place.

And there was another disadvantage. I was not a "cradle Presbyterian" and as an adoptee I had less standing than someone born into and raised in their church. Fear that my presence would plunge the seminary into poverty when donors discovered that Columbia had admitted an open lesbian only increased tensions with the administration.

I shed my jeans, t-shirt and sneakers, slid into the armor of my all-purpose purple polyester dress, hose, and heels. Pulling into a parking space in front of the administration building, I climbed out of my car and up the concrete steps to the main door. I pulled open the heavy wooden door and strutted down to hall to Oscar Hussel's office. I was used to these meetings now. No less afraid and certainly no more confident, but at least now I didn't tremble visibly. I would stiffen my back into a profile of self-assurance even as my intestines quivered.

I was the last to arrive. Dean Hussel's spacious office contrasted Dr. Philip's orderly, almost sterile one. A bank of windows framed a shifting tapestry of greens: emerald grass, bushes tinted olive and lime, and jade hued trees nodding in a soft breeze. Inside, heaps of jacketless books crouched on the floor beside his desk, on his desk, and were stacked double deep on dusty shelves lining the walls. Stale air rested across a solitary streak of sunlight in listless layers of dust motes.

Ben made way for me to join them at the round table across the room. I inched past Will Ormond, a New Testament professor and Dean of Faculty, catching a sour whiff of alcohol as he tapped his dirty, Manchurian-like fingernails on the table before him. Oscar Hussel flashed an empty grin. Dr. Philips hunched over his own boxy torso and shot a wary glance in my direction. Dean Caruthers, fairly new to his post, teetered on the edge of his chair like an adolescent boy in a roomful of men. And Ben. Ben's dashing, cherry red bowtie winked at me as a smile crinkled his eyes. I smiled back and sat down.

"We've asked you here to talk about the issue of having a lesbian attending Columbia with the intention of being ordained in the Presbyterian Church," began Dr. Philips.

I nodded.

"The Church expects those preparing for Christian ministry to subscribe to the highest moral standards."

I nodded.

"I can't believe that *who* I am is immoral," I interjected. "You seem to be talking about some activity called homosexuality. My sexuality is a matter of identity. It's not what I do, it's who I am as an expression of God's infinite, amazing, and diverse creation." Ben looked down, a whisper of a smile playing at the edges of his mouth.

"I *do* believe in the morality of relationships," I continued with all the idealistic passion of the prophet I wanted to be. "I want my relationships to be loving, to have integrity, to be trustworthy, and most of all to be Christ-like—whether it is with my partner, my parents, my friends, or my world."

Looking around the table, capturing each one's gaze I silently implored, *Look at me. Listen to me. Argue with me if you need to—but please don't silence me by not engaging.*

We sat in silence. A chair scraped as someone shifted to get comfortable, one trousered leg sliding across the other. A quiet cough. I waited, hoping for a vigorous conversation, a discussion, real dialogue. What seemed like many minutes passed. I sat a little straighter in my chair and crossed my legs too, nylon hissing over nylon, the feminine sound as loud as a mortar round. The pulse in my neck pounded against my throat. I swallowed.

"And if we want to talk about morality," I quietly persisted, "then let's be honest about what your real concern is." *This is what speaking truth to power looks like so stop shaking.* "I think your real concern is economics. If you let me stay here, graduate from here, you are afraid that financial giving to this institution will suffer. I know a retired alum has threatened to picket. He is well respected and would have a lot of influence. So I don't think you care that much about whether my sexuality or relationships are moral as much as you care about the finances of this institution."

Our collective discomfort was palpable. I waited for a response. Closing my eyes, I took slow breaths and waited. *What now?* Someone was saying something about scheduling our next meeting. Chairs grated as they were pushed back from the table. Ben touched my elbow as he leaned down and whispered, "Come on, Connie."

I rose as gracefully as I could, smiled, and made my way out of Dean Hussel's office. I would ask Ben later what had happened and what it meant. For now, I needed to exit with as much dignity as I could muster. My knees rattled against each other as I walked, straight-backed, down the hall and out into the world.

That's the strangest thing about this life, about being in the ministry. People change the subject when they see you coming. And then sometimes those very same people come into your study and tell you the most remarkable things. There's a lot under the surface of life, everyone knows that. A lot of malice and dread and guilt, and so much loneliness, where you wouldn't really expect to find it, either.

—Marilynne Robinson, Gilead

# Chapter 27   *Learning Ministry*

THREE OF US PACKED into John's decrepit Toyota Corolla, and set out for Grady Hospital to begin our semester long stint as chaplains. My compatriots, John and Jim, watched the road. I wondered if they were some of the men at school who disagreed with women becoming pastors or if they knew I was gay and didn't like it or if they were just thoughtful and introverted.

I was upbeat and excited. Real hands-on ministry! Comforting the sick and dying. I had a lot to learn and eagerly anticipated both ministering and being seen as a minister. And I was scared. This wasn't really about me and yet it was. I would be learning a ministry of presence. We read the theory—Martin Buber, Parker Palmer, Henry Nouwen—and discussed it in class. To *be* with others, deeply aware of them, open to their stories. Even more—to accept and confirm "the other" without agenda. To be empathetic, to understand or *stand under with*. And we would be graded on it.

Grady Hospital is an urban Atlanta hospital on the outskirts of downtown that sprawls over several blocks and serves many of the city's poor. We parked in the parking garage across the street and clattered down five floors of metal stairs before stepping onto the sidewalk that ran in front of the hospital. Patients arrived on foot or in taxis, pushing their way through the large glass doors that exhaled a breath of heat with each influx. Recently released patients huddled at the bus stop, clutching plastic bags of hospital accoutrement. In the background, car horns blasted, buses rumbled over potholes, and a cacophony of hollered conversations competed.

We wended our way through the crowd and shoved open the heavy glass entrance door. A gust of heat welcomed us with the sour odor of unwashed bodies, urine, and antiseptic as a security officer at the information desk directed us to the chaplains' office where our supervising chaplain waited.

"Welcome to SM211," he boomed. "I'm Steve and I will be your supervisor for this part of your clinical pastoral education."

Steve was a red guy. Thinning strawberry blonde hair bordered his ruddy face and sprouted wildly from his speckled forearms. He gestured for us to follow him into a conference room.

"We will be meeting here once a week during the semester for three hours. The rest of the time you will be on the floor, visiting patients and the families of patients."

The shabbily furnished conference room was filled with a couple armchairs, a small, threadbare loveseat, and a rickety coffee table that had seen better days. Even though there were no windows, the room was cozy rather than claustrophobic. I flopped into a chair.

"Each of you will be assigned to a medical floor. The patients will be going through diagnostic tests or being treated for their ailment. You won't be assigned to oncology, transplant, psychiatric or emergency." He picked up some papers from the coffee table and began passing them out. "Here is a copy of the syllabus but let's start by introducing ourselves and state briefly what you hope to gain from this experience. We'll go over the syllabus after introductions. I'll start. I am a military chaplain originally from New Jersey. I have been married twenty years and have three children, two in college and one in high school. I am studying to become a certified supervisor."

I smiled. *This is great! Someone from my tribe!*

"I'm John and I'm from Alabama. I've been married twelve years and we have a two-year old girl. I am trying to decide between parish ministry and hospital chaplaincy." John was a big guy who had to stuff himself behind the wheel of his Corolla.

"I'm Jim. I'm from Mississippi. My wife and I have been married five years and we don't have any children yet. I'm taking this as part of my required coursework, but I'm not really interested in chaplaincy as a vocation."

"I'm Connie and I'm an army brat so I'm from all over. I have a fifteen-year old daughter. I hope to learn how to better be present with those who are suffering. Oh, and I'm a lesbian." Jap Keith, the supervising professor at Columbia, had encouraged me to be up front with my group.

Silence. *This is never a good sign.*

After some several beats Steve resumed his patter. "Grab your ID badge off the table before you leave the room. Please wear it at all times when you are in the hospital. Now, if you'll look at your syllabus you will see that you are expected to work a certain number of hours on the floor. You are expected to write and present a verbatim to the group each week. Note the guidelines: give a full description of the room and the patient and a word for word transcript of the conversation. Then write a theological reflection and any theological or pastoral questions that arise for you. Make four copies and bring them to our Friday meeting. Each week you will present a verbatim and we will discuss it as a group. Any questions?"

Steve answered our questions and sent us on our rounds. I was to work a third floor medical wing. *Will anyone accept me as a chaplain? Will I know what to say?*

The original hospital was completed in 1892. There had been expansions and updates over the years, but it retained the air of an elderly veteran who had seen countless people come and go over more days than most of us could count. My ward was turned out in putty: putty colored floors, putty colored walls and putty colored doors. A strong odor of disinfectant with a faint undertone of urine saturated the air.

I introduced myself to the nurses at the desk and walked skittishly down the hall. *Come on, Connie—you gotta start somewhere.* I prodded myself as I paced back and forth. *No way out but through*, I thought as I entered the room of the first patient I was to visit as God's representative.

The first several days on the floor were all about me. I'm ashamed to say it but those days were filled with self-doubt and anxiety. I entered each room, introduced myself, asked if they wanted prayer (*oh my God! What if they want me to pray?*), and quickly took my leave. Like a small girl tripping around in her mother's heels I pretended to be grown, pretended to be a minister, pretended to pray. Desperate for some kind of grounding, I tottered through my days wondering if anyone really believed I was who I postured to be or if they all saw that my shoes were way too large and would, no doubt, eventually be my downfall.

But days passed and the floor became a known entity. I recognized the staff. I knew my way around the ward. I learned to read charts. The unfamiliar grew familiar. At last I took a deep breath, put on my own shoes, and walked my own walk.

Entering an east-facing room at the end of the hall I encountered a prim and elegant lady who sat propped in her bed reading an oft-used and tattered Bible. She looked up as I entered the sun-drenched room and smiled. The name on the door was Johnson.

"Good morning, Miz Johnson." I glanced at her chart. She was admitted for tests. "I'm Connie Tuttle and I'm the chaplain on this floor."

"Good morning. I'm so glad you dropped by," She replied in a soft, southern lilt. The sun burnished her caramel colored skin and glinted off her well-groomed, straightened black hair. I walked to the side of her bed and pulled up a chair, not wanting to loom over her.

"I've never had a woman preacher before."

"Oh, what church do you attend?"

"Church of God in Christ—and we don't believe in women ministers."

"Will that be a problem for you? That I'm a woman pastor?" I asked. "Because I can get one of my colleagues if you would be more comfortable."

"No, no, I'd like you to stay. Tell me where do you go that they let women preach?"

"I'm in the Presbyterian Church, but we've only had women preachers since the 1970s."

"You go to school for that?"

"Yes, and actually, I'm in school right now."

"What kind of things do they teach you there?"

"You know, the basics: Bible, ethics, theology, church polity, pastoral care and the hard stuff like Greek and Hebrew."

"So you know a lot about the Bible."

I grinned. "There's a whole lot I don't know, too. We all study all of our lives, don't we?" I nodded toward the book resting in her lap.

"Are you saved? Have you ever spoken in tongues?"

"I've never spoken in tongues, but I have felt the Spirit down to the bottom of my soul and I know I'm saved." One thing I learned quickly was to use the theological/religious language that people were most comfortable with. While I might not think of salvation as being saved from the burning pit of hell, I had experienced redemption many times in my life.

A serious look crept over her face. "I've never received the Spirit," her voice cracked as she whispered her confession.

"What do you mean?"

"I've never spoken in tongues. If you don't receive the gift of tongues then you haven't received the Spirit. You aren't saved because to be saved you have to receive the Spirit." A fat tear rolled down her cheek. She grabbed my hand and squeezed, her fear tangible.

I closed my eyes, ideas and information circling. How could I challenge her understanding in ways that would be healing without being disrespectful of her tradition? Even more, how could I not challenge it and leave her in distress?

"There are lots of ways the Spirit manifests," I began. "Jesus said he would send the Spirit as a Comforter. Paul tells us there are many gifts of the Spirit and that no one gift is better than the other."

"Can you show me where it says that?"

We spent the morning gleaning the text and chewing over the possibilities. We laughed and told stories until the orderly came to take her for her next test.

"Miz Johnson," I said, "I have experienced the Spirit through you today, so please don't say you don't have any gifts of the Spirit."

She granted me a soft smile. "Next time we'll have to pray together."

"Yes we will," I replied. "And I will be praying for you until we can pray together."

"I will pray for you, too, Pastor Connie."

In the chaotic spring of 1985 an earthquake killed over 10,000 in Mexico City; 45 American recording stars including Cyndi Lauper, Huey Lewis, Kenny Rogers, Willie Nelson, Smokey Robinson, Tina Turner, Paul Simon, Stevie Wonder, Ray Charles and Bob Dylan released "We are the World" for USA for Africa; Live Aid, a 16 hour super-concert in London, was televised worldwide to raise money for Africa relief; the iconic USA Route 66 was decommissioned, and Rock Hudson died of AIDS.

I wrestled on the green paper surgical gown and contorted to tie up the back. My chest tightened with fear. *This is my sister. I need to go in there. It doesn't matter if I am terrified.* After pulling the elastic bands of the mask around my ears and donning a paper cap that looked like what my mom wore at night to protect her hairdo, I snapped on latex gloves and slowly pushed open the door.

My patient had AIDS. In 1985 we were all afraid of AIDS. Doctors lacked medical knowledge about both the disease and its treatments. We weren't sure how it was transmitted. Fear and loathing. Fear of the disease and fear of those who suffered from the disease. Fear of gay people. Fear of catching it. Fear because no one understood it. The religious right called the disease God's judgment against gays. And some afflicted with AIDS thought it might be. Not until two years later was AZT, the first antiviral drug, available for use in the treatment of the syndrome.

She was lovely. Her blonde hair shimmered in the sunlight. Her makeup was tasteful; her long, manicured nails dripped pink against the sheet. Only her Adam's apple betrayed her previous gender. She glanced in my direction, at my stiff, mummy-wrapped self; then rolled away from me toward the window.

"Hello. I'm Connie, the chaplain on this floor."

"I don't need a chaplain."

*Was she afraid I would condemn her?* I stayed on the far side of the room, too anxious to get closer. I wanted to tell her I was a lesbian and didn't condemn her but I couldn't figure out how to say it. And I didn't want to get close to her. I stood across the room saturated in dread. Every fear I had galloped to the forefront. I was afraid of being sick. I was afraid of dying. I was terrified of getting AIDS and not only dying, but also dying a horrible death. And I couldn't imagine what hope I could offer. She was going to die.

I stood there, frightened and troubled, isolating her even more than the fortress of the room and the fortification of my attire by my inability to *just be* with her, one human with another. I frantically searched for words that would not be meaningless. None came. My surgical get up screamed "unclean." Rather than being the precaution to protect her compromised immune system from infection, it re-enforced the barrier between us.

"I don't feel like talking. Will you please go?"

"Yes," I mumbled. "I'm sorry." I reached behind me, pulled open the door, and eased myself out. I was trembling. *What kind of chaplain are you? What kind of person are you? What hope did you offer?* I snatched off the cap, mask and gown and pushed them into the trash. Self-hatred washed over me like hot vomit. I rolled back the gloves and tossed them on top of the discarded paper. What hope, indeed. I better figure that out if I was ever going to be a minister. *If you are like this, Connie, what will other people be like? If you can't reach out to her, who will?*

Three doctors huddled in an impromptu conference outside the door discussing her case punctuated with snickers and disparaging remarks. Listening to their unedited scorn intensified my self-loathing. I was heartsick. Sick that I could not make myself be in that room with her. Sick to my core that she faced uncertainty and death alone. And sick with disgust that I was so glad to be out of that room.

When I returned the next week, determined to confront my fears, she had been discharged.

The room was cold and though it was a shared room, only the bed closest to the door was occupied. A beautiful young black man, stripped to the waist with a sheet casually thrown over his lower torso lay back against two pillows. A large gold medallion hung from a heavy gold chain and rested on his muscled chest. His Afro needed to be picked and his eyes were jaundiced. He kept his hands folded over his lap to cover an erection. Quiet hung in the room against the noise of hospital business outside the door.

"Hello. I'm Connie and I'm the chaplain today. I stopped by to see if you wanted to talk."

"I'm Chop. You a pastor for real?"

"Yes, I am." *Fake it till you make it, Connie.*

"I got the sickle cell."

"How are you feeling?"

"I've got bad pain," he winced. I knew something about the disease. It is genetic and affects people of African descent. I knew it was extremely painful and that blood cells morphed into sickle shapes that interrupted blood flow. His erection, likely caused by the sickle cell crisis he was in, was extremely painful as well as embarrassing for him. I smiled to put him at ease. I wasn't uncomfortable and didn't want him to worry about something over which he had no control.

"I need to ask you something," he whispered, his eyes boring into mine. I met his gaze.

"Okay," I said. "Ask away. I'll answer if I can."

He kept looking at me, searching for something in my demeanor, in my eyes. Not sure if he found it, but having nothing more to lose, he risked asking the questions that tormented him. "Why is God punishing me? Why does God hate black people?"

My chest ached. I didn't break our gaze. I willed him to see himself as a child of God. I poured love and acceptance through my eyes into his. *This is my truth, friend. May it bring some comfort,* I prayed. "I don't think God is punishing you. You have a genetic disease."

"Yeah, that only black people get."

"There are diseases only Jews get, and that only Mediterranean people get . . ." I paused, then continued quietly, "Chop, God doesn't hate anyone."

"Then why? Why I got this pain? What'd I do?"

"We've all done stuff we shouldn't have done."

"Even you?"

I grinned, "Especially me. But God doesn't work that way."

"Then why?"

"We all want to know why, I guess it's just part of who we are as human beings. But let me ask you a question." I caught a whiff of patchouli. My favorite.

"Okay, shoot."

"Can you feel God here with you?"

"What do you mean?"

"Well, Jesus came that we might know God is with us in all places and times, in every struggle and every hard place. So can you imagine, can you let yourself feel the presence of God with you?" A blast of cold air raised goose bumps on my arms. "Chop, God is right here with you sharing your pain and your fear and giving you strength."

"I don't feel him."

I watched him for a moment. He was trying to be present for this conversation in the midst of acute pain. I sat in metal chair beside his bed, leaned against the cold side bar and spoke slowly and quietly. "God feels your pain with you and is walking with you through this. God doesn't hate you. God loves you. God is *right here.*" *How,* I wondered, *do you distill centuries of wisdom and years of study into something relevant for one being in one specific time of life? The mystery, the majesty, the complexity—how do you talk about it all when one simple word or idea is what offers hope. It is enough. It is enough. I pray it is enough.*

"Is that really true?"

"I believe it with my whole heart." I wanted to challenge his belief that God is a vengeful, hateful God. I wanted to erase it. "Try to let go of this idea you have that God hates you or is punishing you so you can feel God's love and draw on God's strength."

He leaned back into the pillows and closed his eyes, eventually sliding into a light slumber. He looked to be in his early twenties. I was pretty sure this one conversation wouldn't change years of teaching and conviction. I only hoped I had planted a seed. Sitting beside him while he slept, I leaned against the bed frame and prayed until my shift ended.

"Religion has the capacity to silence critical thinking and create blindness in entire groups of people."

—Darrel Ray, *Sex & God: How Religion Distorts Sexuality*

# Chapter 28    *She's One of Those*

I PRESENTED A VERBATIM about my visit with Chop.

"Why is it so important that he was undressed?" the interrogation began.

"Our instructions are to note all those things in our verbatim."

"If you were uncomfortable with his nakedness, you should have called someone else to come."

"I wasn't uncomfortable!"

"Maybe you shouldn't even be here," Jim's voice tightened and pitched a little higher. "What makes you think that you can provide pastoral care to a heterosexual black man?" Everything they had wanted to say to me from day one came spewing out.

"Why do you ask that? What does his being straight have to do with anything?"

"You make everything about you and not about your patient!"

"I do not! You're the ones doing that!"

They peppered me with offensive questions and comments about my ability, my call, and even my very being. They launched unfettered hostility couched in opinions and commentary. Nowhere felt safe. I had assumed that as we grew to know one another in this context, sharing the intimacy of this learning experience, we would become friends. Instead, they saw me through some yawning Lesbian-shaped lens that distorted everything I said or did.

"Who do you think you are? You are hurting people more than helping them." John lobbed the final grenade. "There is no place for you in Christian ministry."

I wasn't going to let them see me cry. Not waiting to be dismissed, I picked up my backpack and made my way from the room. "I'll find my own way home."

I walked down the hall, holding up the wall as I slid along its smooth surface. I came to the restroom, shoved the door open and, finally, began to weep. Pushing my back against the cold tiles, I slid to the floor and pulled my knees to my chest. Moans gagged me as I strangled on my tears. *Would it ever get easier? Did anyone see me?* Sometime later, having cried until there were no more tears, I made my way to Steve's office.

As soon as I tapped on the door I began to cry again. He motioned me to take the chair on the other side of the heavy, wooden, hulk of a desk that stretched the length of a city block between us. His office was crowded with barely enough room for his massive desk and the chair in which I sat sobbing. He leaned back and watched as I retched out sob after sob.

"I don't understand," I gulped. I didn't understand how they could be so cruel and dismissive. I didn't understand why they couldn't see me as a minister. I didn't understand why they hated me. But all I could say was, "I don't understand."

Steve continued to watch me. Finally, he tossed a box of tissues across his desk. "Tell me about your relationship with your father."

*Tell you about my relationship with my father? I am in so much pain I can barely talk and you ask me about my relationship with my father? Is it more interesting for you to try to figure out why I'm a lesbian rather than tending to my pain? Glad I can help. Asshole.*

"I love my dad. We have a great relationship," I finally managed. In that precise moment I realized that he would not be the one to help me and that he was the adversary who allowed my classmates' ignorance free rein. *He's just as ignorant as they are.*

"I need to go."

My tangled thoughts chased after answers as I walked to the bus stop. I prayed I had enough change. The bus grumbled to a halt and waited for me to make my way on board before lurching off. I stared blankly, frozen by rage and pain. *What can I do to make this feel better? Who can I talk to?* As the bus ambled over rutted back streets I began to get angry. I would go to the professor who taught theory and oversaw our hospital placements.

Jap Keith's salt and pepper hair and trim beard lent him an air of authority. "Come in, Connie. What can I do for you?"

His airy office was set up like a therapist's. A desk snuggled against the back wall. Two nice area rugs delineated the use of space. In front of book-shelves were two upholstered wingback chairs, a low table between them. He motioned for me to sit with him. I took a breath trying to gather my thoughts. I couldn't get through the story without bawling.

"You are completely transparent," Jap observed.

"What does that mean?"

"It means you're not hiding anything. You're who you present yourself to be."

"Is that good?" I was trying so hard to understand.

He smiled. "*I* think it is."

I snuffled, holding back a tsunami of grief with a limp tissue.

"What is it," he asked softly, "that upsets you the most?"

Without thinking I wailed, "He's supposed to be my *teacher*." Never before had I articulated how sacred that relationship was to me. I'm not sure I was aware of it until that moment.

We talked until my tears emptied, my breathing calmed. "I think this is about more than today. It feels like I'm crying for every time someone said something ugly to me, every time I've had to defend myself, every time a road block has been thrown up in the two years I've been here."

"I think you may be right, Connie. And it won't be the last time you encounter something like this. Maybe even with the same people, because you have to finish this semester in this group and with this supervisor."

My heart did a nosedive. Somewhere deep down I wanted to be rescued. I was worn to a nub.

"You can learn a lot from him and from this experience." He leaned toward me and made eye contact. "Your life will be filled with people like him. You may not be able to trust him as the teacher you hoped he would be, but now that you know you can't trust him, learn what you *can* about dealing with people who aren't trustworthy."

Sometimes I get sick and tired of having "learning experiences." But he was right. A shift of perspectives can bring air back into a room and circulation back into my extremities. I am, as I said before, a four on the ennegram, a deep feeler who finds feelings to be addictive at times. In my resurrected self, as a reformed four, I hung on to Jap's words, hoping I wouldn't slide off the edge of the world.

You don't always win your battles, but it's good to know you fought.

—John Greenleaf Whittier

# Chapter 29   *Going Down Faithful*

THE FIRST SKIRMISH WITH the seminary administration focused on the assumption that I would want to change my orientation as much as they wanted me to. When it became clear that I did not share that interest or concern, my weekly meetings with President Phillips petered out. A minor scuffle ending in a draw.

The second engagement centered on the question of morality. I actually thought I won that one . . . "win" being a relative term. "Winning is always relative," or so said my dad.

At the same time these offensives were taking place, the Atlanta Presbytery Candidates Committee attacked my rear flank. No one would call me a strategist. Ever. My dad would say, "You have to be an idiot to wage a war on more than one front." And here I was, outgunned and outmanned. Fighting on two fronts and my only weapons of engagement were faithful presence, a fairly good mind, a compelling experience of grace, and this call that latched itself onto my soul and wouldn't let go. Left with the choice of fighting on multiple fronts or not fighting at all, I chose to fight.

The seminary could take the easy way out if the Presbytery did their dirty work for them. Should the Presbytery deny my application to become a candidate for ministry in the Presbyterian Church, Columbia could then deny me the opportunity to graduate with an MDiv with impunity because it would be the official stance of the church.

I found another missive in my mailbox at the beginning of my second (midler) year telling me I needed to apply for candidacy with the Atlanta Presbytery. Candidacy was required for the Professional Assessment (also required) at the end of senior year, a condition for the degree. *Great!* I thought, without sarcasm. *I will be as articulate as I can about this call thing I'm wrestling with. And there are only six people to convince.*

It was dusk in early winter. The campus hunched under a blanket of gray light as I trudged through the drizzle, circumventing rain pocked puddles, from the parking lot to the Richards Building for my first meeting. I was, by turns, excited and scared. I longed for some kind of movement in this stalemate. Again, I hoped I would be heard and armed myself with the flimsy weapons of intelligence, passion, and faith in the struggle for right over might. *David won, didn't he?* I said to myself, reasoning that David slew a giant with a whole lot of not much, as I climbed a flight of stairs to the second floor.

Paige McRight was waiting for me at the top of the steps. "Make yourself comfortable," she gestured to a row of folding chairs lining the hallway, "and I'll come get you when we're ready for you." She let herself into the room where the committee was meeting without waiting for my response.

I parked myself in the closest chair and sat as straight as a girl in charm school, holding the pose until my neck began to ache, then uncrossed my ankles and slouched, knees akimbo. The overhead lights washed out the walls and opposed the night gathering outside the mullioned windows running across the opposite wall. I gazed at my reflection in the black glass. Heat pored out of a hidden register so I sloughed off my coat. I stood and paced. *This is Connie, God; I really need you tonight. Please don't let their hearts be so hard they won't give me a fair hearing.* I pressed my nose to the glass and wiped off the oil with my fist. I paced some more humming *Onward Christian Soldiers* under my breath when the door creaked open and Paige motioned to me.

"We're ready for you now."

Paige and five very white men sat around a bulky rectangular table. I angled into the closest chair. It clacked against the wall as I pulled it out. Gazing briefly at each one I tried to guess where he stood. One, Ben told me, was rabidly anti-gay. Another was supportive. The rest were mostly neutral, but conventional. Paige, the only woman, might be an ally.

After introductions, the questions began. "Tell us about your sense of call," Paige invited.

*Okay! This is where I get to talk about this mind-blowing sense of call! These are the people who will help me understand. It's their job. They'll help me sort this out.* I poured out my story of call. The mystical experiences. Prayer that took flight. The drive to follow God's leading no matter where it took me.

I finished and looked around the table, not able to read their expressions.

"Let's take a short break," Paige said, as she gestured me to follow her into the hall.

Glad to get out of the stuffy room, I followed. "How do you think it's going?"

She paused a moment. "I think they're uncomfortable. Presbyterians don't like talking about mystical experiences." She smiled, considering. "When we go back in you need to talk about how your church experience has shown that you have gifts and skills for ministry. That is what they are looking for."

"But that's not my story." I was so disappointed. This wasn't going to be that place that could help me make sense of my profound experiences of God. "I can't just make something up."

When the meeting resumed, Paige lobbed the next question. "Why, if you feel so strongly called to ministry, did you disclose your sexuality?"

I took a breath. "Are you saying I should have lied about who I am to pursue my call? That doesn't make sense to me. How can I be in relationship with God if I don't have integrity?"

No one attempted to answer my questions.

"I'd like to share with you a paper I wrote about homosexuality and the Bible. Would y'all be willing to read it and let it be part of our conversation?"

"We'd be glad to."

I had come prepared. I opened my backpack and extracted copies of the paper. "I look forward to discussing this further next time," I said as I passed out the documents.

My part was over and we set a date for our next meeting. I would be ready.

But before the next meeting took place word filtered down to me that Bill Adams, the Presbytery Exec., had relayed to the Candidates Committee that they were *in no way* to put me under care and they were to let me know at the earliest possible moment. I wrestled with how to proceed. If I were denied candidacy then I could never reapply. If I withdrew, I could apply again at a later date. But it also meant that I couldn't have the Professional Assessment that was required to complete the MDiv. I wanted to be a minister so badly I opted to withdraw my request. I would have to figure the rest out later. Weeks later I received an official letter stating that the committee had complied with my request for withdrawal.

The constant barrage to my internal landscape left me desolate and miserable. I hunkered down and dug a few more trenches, each class a way through, if not a way forward. I might not win the war. Hell, I might not win the battle. But by God I would go down faithful.

Salvation

By what are you saved? And how?
Saved like a bit of string,
tucked away in a drawer?
Saved like a child rushed from
a burning building, already
singed and coughing smoke?
Or are you salvaged
like a car part—the one good door
when the rest is wrecked?

Do you believe me when I say
you are neither salvaged nor saved,
but salved, anointed by gentle hands
where you are most tender?
Haven't you seen
the way snow curls down
like a fresh sheet, how it
covers everything,
makes everything
beautiful, without exception?

—Lynn Ungar, "Blessing the Bread"

# Chapter 30  *Advancing*

THEIR NEXT OFFENSIVE WAS to refuse to let me complete the course-work required for the Masters of Divinity degree. Three supervised ministry placements were necessary: in a hospital, in a jail or prison, and in a parish. Near the end of my junior (first) year I stood in line to sign up for interviews for a parish internship. Churches would be on campus to interview students for our placements. I walked from the signup sheets to my mailbox only to find a note from Dean Hussel informing me that I would not be allowed to interview.

I was already tired and it was only the end of my first year. No St. Joan I. Only Connie. Out of my depth, out of sorts, out of energy, and out of my league. *What had I been thinking?* But thinking wasn't what brought me here. Nor belief. Nor a desire to make a statement. *Prayer brought me to this place and prayer would get me through. And by the way, thanks God, for sending me into combat without reinforcements. Why not get someone who understands all these machinations, all the politics—someone who was brought up Presbyterian and knows all these people and knows the way things work? Someone who's not the red-headed stepchild. Or is my sin of dehumanizing my adversaries and seeing them as cardboard characters my strength here? They're afraid of what they don't understand,* I told myself. *Walk with them through their fears,* I said to myself over and over. But to God I shoved my fist into the air and bellowed, "Damn it, what do you want from me now?" I always did have a dramatic bent.

A parish internship is necessary for the Masters of Divinity degree. Since I couldn't interview for a placement, I couldn't see a way around it, but I kept on keeping on. I went to my classes. I did my homework. I waited for God to make a way out of no way.

In my midler year (the three year program is delineated by junior, midler, and senior years), Dean Hussel took a yearlong sabbatical. New Testament professor Dr. Charlie Cousar was appointed interim dean. Early in that year I found another note in my campus mailbox. "Please make an appointment to see me at my office." It was signed, Charlie Cousar. By this point I hardly had the emotional energy to be anxious. I sauntered down to his office to make an appointment.

"If you have a minute now, I have some time," he offered.

"I don't have a class this period," I returned. He gestured me to a chair and closed the door.

"Connie, as you know you need to intern at a church as part of the requirement for an MDiv."

Yeah, I knew that. I nodded. *Where is this going?*

"I'm going to make a call here and give you permission find a supervised ministry placement."

"Are you kidding?"

"No," He grinned, "I'm not kidding."

"Thank you, Dr. Cousar!!! Thank you!" I grinned in reply and sat back in the chair, thoughts swirling. I tried to take in what he said but it felt surreal. Of all the things I might imagine this meeting would be about, this hadn't been anywhere on my radar. I felt a little dizzy. *Oh crap, I have to intern in a church!*

"The thing is, the seminary can't allow you to interview with the churches that come to campus. And we can't offer you the financial support that we usually offer interns."

"Okay." *So what? I get to intern in a church! I'm going to graduate with an MDiv. Okay! Okay! Okay!* I was ecstatic. "So, if I find a church that will take me, Columbia will accept the placement?"

"We will," he smiled again.

*Okay. So now I have to find a church somewhere that will take me and I have to find a way to make money while I'm interning and what if only someplace up north will take me and will I be able to pay rent in two places if I do find a placement and, and, and . . .*

"Great. Thank you so much, Dr. Cousar. Thank you. I really mean it. Thanks." I babbled while I grabbed my things and backed out the door. I had to get home and start calling churches.

I could say I won that battle, but really it wasn't my victory. So I'll say we won that one. Dr. Cousar, Ben and, perhaps, some quiet others working behind the scenes, pushing the line forward, making small miracles. An artillery company I didn't know I had saved the day.

I had two hills to climb. First, I needed to find a pastor who was willing to stick his or her neck out and second, I would need to submit my petition to the session (ruling body of the local church) and hope the session would agree with the minister.

I called my friend, John Storey, the same friend I worked construction with, who was then pastor at Clifton Presbyterian Church.

"I need to find a church that will let me intern. Before I start cold calling out of state, is there anyone in Atlanta you think might be open to it?"

"Try Steve Montgomery," John suggested. "He's at Northwoods Pres. I think he's someone who might be open."

I looked up the number and dialed.

"Northwoods Presbyterian Church, may I help you?"

"Is Steve Montgomery available?"

Moments later he picked up. I took a breath and let fly. "Hi, Steve. John Storey suggested that I call you. I'm an out lesbian and Columbia has finally given me permission to find an SM210 placement. They won't let me post or interview on campus. I have to find my own placement. They won't fund my placement but I'm willing to work for nothing."

Steve sat in silence on the other end of the phone taking it all in. I bombarded him with lots of information. We talked for a while before I realized he had been my one ally on the Candidates Committee. He asked a lot of questions and I answered in breathless, run-on sentences. Finally, he said, "I'm interested, but I have to talk with the session first. Let me see what I can do." On a church retreat that weekend he approached members of the session. That Monday he called me back. "Can you come in Tuesday and meet with the us?"

*Could I come in Tuesday? You bet I could come in Tuesday. Or Wednesday or any day you want, any time you want.* It didn't feel real. I expected another roadblock, another gully to traverse, another fight . . . but I was going to meet with the session on Tuesday! Of course they could still decide not to hire me. It might be too much of a risk. They might change their minds before I got there. They just plain may not like me. Hope fought hopelessness for supremacy.

I mapped my way to the church, turned up the volume on a Joan Armatrading cassette, and pulled on to 285, the perimeter highway. *What would it feel like if I were just a regular candidate interviewing?* First of all I'd be at Columbia. And then I would be interviewing with a number of churches hoping to find a good fit, but the basic procedures available to other students were privileges to which I had no access. Right now, it would be this, Northwoods Presbyterian Church, or nothing. Or finding something in another city or another state. Or nothing. And if I found something in another state or city then I would have to find a way to finance both the trip and the stay. I really hoped this would work out.

This amazing thing happened. Steve met at the door and reintroduced himself before bringing me into the room where the session was meeting. Sitting around tables pushed together into a friendly square, open faces greeted me. I was nervous but knew instinctively that this was not a battle. I didn't have to employ any strategies, I just had to be myself. And hope that it would be enough.

"What are your gifts and skills for ministry?"

I sat a minute then responded. "I can think and speak and sit with people who disagree with me." *Are those gifts or skills for ministry? I really hope so.*

"What are your interests? What kinds of things would you like to be involved with during your time as an intern?"

"Tell us about your sense of call."

They asked me questions like I was any seminarian interviewing to intern at their church. I could hardly believe it. There was no hidden agenda, no veiled anger or anxiety.

"Okay, Connie, we appreciate you time and we'll let you know our decision in the next couple of days."

The phone rang late that evening and Steve was on the other end. "The vote is unanimous. We would like to hire you as our summer intern."

Later, Steve told me, "You made the conservatives happy because we didn't have to pay you and the liberals happy because we're taking a step toward justice."

I was happy because I felt affirmed for the first time in a very long time.

The summer was filled with all kinds of ministerial tasks. I taught a course on the Bible and homosexuality to a pretty large class. The folks were open and had good questions. I provided pastoral care and found I loved being with the people in those important and intimate ways. And I got to preach.

I stood behind the pulpit feeling like a kid with her mom's bra draped over a flat chest, hoping that, one day, I would be able to fill it. The sanctuary's blond wooden beams and curving pews embraced both congregation and worship leaders, close enough to be intimate, large enough to cradle mystery. My heart thudded as I rose and went to the dais. I looked at the gathered community. They wanted me to succeed. They were willing to see me as a pastor. After all I had gone through to get to this place, I was humbled. Who was I to think I could speak for God? There is an awesome and terrible responsibility to speak to others with authority about the deepest things we can imagine: meaning, life, death, our relationship with God, our relationship with one another, our relationship with the world. Who did I think I was?

"Christ invites us to live into God's future that is already here and not yet here. In this time we are called to live 'as if,'" I concluded at the end of my first sermon, " . . . to live *as if* we were unafraid, *as if* we were free." I preached to myself and to my new church home. "To live *as if* the kingdom, God's dreaming of shalom, is now."

"You're not a one issue preacher." Steve told me. "You understand your context and care about the people without compromising yourself. You're challenging people in a way they can still hear." I soaked up his praise.

Steve treated me like a colleague. The church treated me like an associate minister. I worked hard and loved every minute. Steve's evaluation of me and my work confirmed the community's experience of my gifts and skills for ministry. Many years later I discovered that several professors from Columbia contributed money for me to receive some pay during my time at Northwoods: Ben Kline, Shirley Guthrie, Lucy Rose, Catherine Gonzalez, Lee Carroll, Charlie Cousar, and Erskine Clarke.

The summer-internship-that-almost-wasn't nurtured and affirmed me as minister. My heart, broken in so many places, received respite and healing during my summer at Northwoods Presbyterian Church.

Now is the time for the world to know
That every thought and action is sacred.

This is the time
For you to compute the impossibility
That there is anything
But Grace.

Now is the season to know
That everything you do
Is sacred.

—Hafiz


## Chapter 31    *"This Grace That Scorches Us"*


THE U.N. DESIGNATED 1986 as the International Year of Peace. In the Iran
Contra Affair, National Security Council member Oliver North and his
secretary, Fawn Hall, shredded documents that implicated them in selling weapons to Iran and channeling the proceeds to fund Contra rebels
in Nicaragua. Also, in 1986, the Space Shuttle *Challenger* disintegrated 73
seconds after launch, killing the crew of seven astronauts; Chernobyl, a
nuclear power plant in Pripyat, Ukraine, USSR blew up, killing at least 4056
people and forcing 350,000 to relocate due to radioactive fallout. *Hands
Across America* formed a human chain of at least five million people from
New York City to Long Beach, California, raising money to fight hunger
and homelessness. Desmond Tutu became the first black Anglican Church
bishop in South Africa.

Weariness crept into my bones. Each day became an exercise of will.
Tanya, now a sophomore in high school, was busy with homework, flag
core, track, and drama, while I struggled to get out of bed and through
the demands of the day. Academic, emotional, household, economic, and
parental demands competed for my flagging energy. Many tasks were half
done and some remained undone all together.

The last battle consisted of a series of skirmishes. A final requirement
for the degree was a professional assessment. It should have been fairly

straightforward, but as with all else, it was not. By the time of the assessment the student was supposed to have a working relationship with an "appropriate ecclesiastical body" in order to qualify for ordination. I had two problems here. One, I had withdrawn my application to be a candidate under my home presbytery which was my "appropriate ecclesiastical body." Two, the seminary had already determined that I did not qualify for ordination. I wrote the faculty and requested a waiver on both points. December 9, 1985 I received word that the waivers had been approved without exception. I assumed Ben had been advocating on my behalf with the faculty and had succeeded in getting a majority vote.

I waited with Ben for everyone to arrive for my professional assessment. Dr. Clark entered looking like the consummate academic with his graying tonsure and wire-rimmed spectacles. I was allowed two fellow students of my choosing to be part of the assessment. I chose Perky Daniel and Bob Reno. Perky, like me, was a graduate of Agnes Scott. She was a great favorite in the presbytery, being both musically and intellectually gifted. Most assumed she would go on to have a stellar career. Bob and I shared a passion for social justice, especially around the issues of hunger and poverty. He moved methodically, making his way across the room, his gentle expression set in a soft smile. Finally, Dr. Moessner, a New Testament scholar, lumbered in and took a seat. Ben opened the meeting with prayer.

I needed that prayer. I needed praying for. I would take whatever help God had to offer to get through this next requirement. I was wrung out. Anything could happen. Even if my committee sent a positive recommendation to the faculty, the faculty still had to vote. Would the administration strong-arm the faculty into the vote it wanted? I had to stop thinking about the what-ifs and stay in the moment. I just had to just get through this day. This meeting. I looked over at Ben who nodded encouragingly. *Okay. Here goes.*

I was prepared. On the table were the required self-profile, an autobiographical statement of my personal, religious, and professional journey, along with personal statements about how I had changed and grown in both my theological understandings and spiritual life during my time at Columbia. In addition, I was required to make a statement about my understanding of Christian ministry: how I was responding to my call, and what I saw as my natural gifts and skills for ministry. Also on the table: my course transcripts, grades and supervised ministry evaluations. Finally, I made a formal written request for admission to degree candidacy. Ben had prepared reports about his role as my advisor and his responses to my academic record, my final evaluation from supervised ministry, and my self-profile.

I didn't have the energy to be nervous. Somewhere deep down I thought I ought to be, but this, like everything else, was out of my control.

Another lesson on letting go and trusting God. No matter what happens. *How many times do I have to learn this lesson?*

It was early May, warm and sunny, a light breeze ruffled the leaves in the tree outside the second floor window. Ben led us through the prescribed procedure.

"We will open with Connie making a statement about the reports and about anything she would like to add. There will be a time for us to respond and ask any questions, then Connie will be dismissed and I will move whether or not the assessment be sustained. We will vote until we reach consensus. Connie, if you'll wait outside, once the vote is taken we will invite you back in and report to you our vote before it is reported to the faculty. Any time you are ready."

I looked at the notes scribbled on a torn piece of scratch paper. No help there. I closed my yes and sent up a quick prayer. *God, please help me to say what needs to be said in a way that can be heard.* Peace flooded my chest and ran down my arms. I was ready.

"I have been following this insistent call to ministry for the last eight years. I don't always know what it means or where I will be led, but I do know I will respond as long as I am able or until I hear differently." The words began to come. "I know some people are frightened and some are angry and some are horrified by the idea of a lesbian in ministry. But I have also met many people who have children, siblings or friends who are gay and need to hear the Gospel of liberation, hope, love, and inclusiveness that is the heart of the Gospel."

"My gifts are that I can think and feel and speak," I repeated the mantra I had come to embrace about myself as minister. "I can speak for those who have no voice. My experiences of the world and of people are expansive. Within me, because of all I have seen and heard and done in my life, I carry the vision of Christ's dreaming for humanity. I want to care for people who have been deeply hurt, even damaged, by the church *and* for those who are fearful of difference and change. I want my life to be prophetic and my actions to be pastoral." I paused for a breath and remembered there were still many things I didn't know.

"I am still trying to figure out what that looks like. What the church has not realized is it belongs to everyone. The community of faith is mine as much as it is anyone's. For these last three years I have felt like I was pounding on the doors of the church, shouting "Let me in! This is my home, too!" If the Presbyterian Church won't have me, if we continue to reject our Reformation understanding that we are always open to more wisdom, more light, more understanding, then I will have to find another way." I waited a moment to see if more words needed to come. "For now, this is all I know."

The floor was opened for questions. I wish I could remember what they were and how I answered. I *do* remember that the questions were respectful and that I searched carefully inside to answer each one as truthfully as I could.

"Thank you, Connie," Ben brought the conversation to a close, "Thank you for your openness and willingness to engage with this committee. We are going to excuse you while we decide what our recommendation to the faculty will be."

"Thank you," my gaze swept the gathered circle. "Thank you, Ben. Thank you all for your time and willingness to listen."

I withdrew and meandered down the hall to examine postings on bulletin boards. Before too long, Ben poked his head out the door, "Come back in, Connie. We're ready for you."

Smiles glowed in the already sunlit room. I exhaled, not realizing I had been holding my breath.

"Connie," Ben's smile widened, "by unanimous vote we are recommending your admittance to degree candidacy to the faculty."

Perky and Bob hugged me. Dr. Clarke and Dr. Moessner stood and shook my hand. Ben squeezed me tight, murmuring in my ear, "You did it!"

I exited down the staircase and out to the side parking lot. My shoulders ached. My tongue felt foggy: I couldn't form words with any clarity. Fatigue smothered the glimmers of hope trying to make their way to my consciousness. I drove home and disrobed as soon as the door closed behind me. Crawling into my unmade bed, I slept until I felt Tanya gently rocking my shoulder, "What's for dinner, Mom?"

The rain shower slowed to a dribble and watery sunlight peeked around the clouds. Damp grass released its newly ripened perfume. Forswearing the elevator, I climbed three flights of stairs, stopping on each landing to shake water from my hair.

"The faculty has come to a decision," Ben began as soon as I entered his office. He sat at the table just inside, ungraded papers stacked about the perimeter in some order unintelligible to me. "As you know, we sent your professional assessment to the Faculty with the recommendation that you be admitted to candidacy for the MDiv. as an academic degree. Your professional assessment committee also strongly affirmed your gifts for ministry."

I felt warm and safe. Seen and heard. I closed my eyes, lowered my head and let Ben's words wash over me.

"The Faculty has been meeting all year trying to figure out how you are getting this degree."

"What do you mean?"

"Connie, a Masters of Divinity has always been considered a professional degree, something akin to a law degree, but we decided to award it to you as an academic degree."

"What does that mean?"

"It has to do with whether or not we award you the degree with a recommendation for ordination."

I wasn't getting this. It was one of those times I felt woefully inadequate. I was sure this meant something, but not sure what. Ben looked into my blank face.

"Traditionally when we grant a Masters of Divinity degree the faculty votes to award it with or without a recommendation for ordination." He paused. "You had that wonderful recommendation from your professional assessment committee."

"Okay."

"After a year of discussing your situation and upon the recommendation of your professional assessment committee, the faculty has agreed to award you the degree as an academic degree rather than as a professional degree with the caveat that "while we *may* not recommend you for ordination, we affirm your gifts and skills for ministry."

I listened hard. Warmth crept through me. Pins and needles ran down the backs of my thighs pressed against the wooden seat of the captain's chair. *They affirm my gifts and skills for ministry.*

He continued. "Our use of the term 'may not' is important theologically. It means that it was not in our power to make the choice to recommend you. If we had used the phrase "shall not" agency is implied."

Ben had my back in ways in which I was never aware, took flack on my behalf that he never shared. Always the theologian. Always attentive to the nuances of words. I appreciated the work he must have put into that seemingly simple statement.

"Connie Lee Tuttle, Masters of Divinity degree," boomed the announcer.

I climbed the steps and walked onto the stage. Dr. Philips and Bill Adams waited for my approach. The day was a scorcher and I was sweating beneath the black, academic robe. I was happy and sad and resolved to stay in every moment of this day, to take it in as deeply as I could.

Mom, Dad and Tanya were somewhere in the sanctuary, but I didn't look for them. Knowing they were there, witnessing this rite of passage, held me up. I concentrated on the next step and the next as I advanced toward the men who had done everything in their power to keep me from this moment.

I bent my head to receive my red, gold and purple trimmed master's hood. Bill Adams offered me his hand to shake. I stared into his eyes as I shook it and prayed to release my hurt and anger. Dr. Philips handed me the rolled diploma, also shaking my hand. *How does it feel to relinquish this document to me?* I smiled, but did not trust the stilted smiles they returned. Elated and trembling, I turned toward the sanctuary. A cheer went up from the balcony. I didn't know who was cheering or if it was for me. It did not matter.

I raised a triumphant fist in the air and marched off stage.

# Chapter 32    *What I Learned Along the Way*

I HAVE COME TO understand that everything is holy.

I learned to love Godde[1] with my body. Every taste, smell, touch, sound, sight is a holy moment. My task is to try to enter into each holy moment and savor the physical experience of it. Pain, heat, and cold become more bearable when I don't fight the sensations, but enter deeply into them. I learned that ecstasy is not limited to sexual delight.

I learned that the more room I make for the Divine, the larger my view of Godde becomes. I learned never to think about Godde in ways that are rigid and fixed and that while I practice a particular spiritual path, I travel with all my spiritual sisters and brothers on the planet.

I learned that for something to be spiritually healthy it must be mentally healthy. And I learned that neither the presence nor absence of mental health or intelligence is necessary for spiritual journeying.

I learned that I need community to live my faith authentically.

I learned that faith is not about how fervently I believe something but how deeply I am able to trust Godde. And that faithfulness does not guarantee results—though sometimes results are unexpected and greater than I could imagine. I learned that I am called to be faithful in a million small tasks each day.

I learned I may never see the impact of any act I perform or stand I take, whether faithful or unfaithful.

I learned that answers are not as important as questions and that there is beauty in paradox.

I learned that every place is home and everyone is a part of my tribe.

I learned the lesson of my mother's life: that love is the most important expression of faith. And to love one another, Godde, our planet, and our enemies is our only and highest call.

I learned that love is not a feeling but a way of being. I learned that without justice, there is no love.

I learned the lesson of my father's life: that standing for what you believe is right demands everything of you, that engagement is a messy,

---

1. I began using this spelling of Godde as an expression of the Sacred encompassing all gender expressions.

sometimes filthy, business that requires you to be your best self in the worst of circumstances. I learned that courage is not the same as being unafraid.

I learned that Love grants courage. Had I not been loved so well by my parents and by Godde I would not have had the audacity to walk this path.

I learned to stand in awe of Love.

. . .
this is the reason
we were made:
for this ache
that finally opens us

for this struggle,
this grace,
that scorches us
toward one another
and into
the blazing day.

—© Jan Richardson from "This Grace That Scorches Us" in *Circle of Grace: A Book of Blessings for the Seasons*. Used by permission. janrichardson.com

## Chapter 33 *Nine years after graduation: back to the Atlanta Presbytery Meeting*

"I CANNOT ACKNOWLEDGE ANYONE who is not an ordained or elected member of this meeting," the moderator admonished me.

I continued to stand. Didn't she think I knew it? I studied the *Book of Order*. I knew I wasn't ordained. I knew I wasn't a delegate of a local session.

I tried not to fidget. Tried to keep my knees from locking. Tried to keep up with the arguments made as each new person stepped up to the microphone placed in the aisle. Tried to find my righteous anger. My skin was moist with a light sheen of sweat, I was afraid my polyester dress would begin to smell. My feet numbed. I tried to remember why I had worn heels. "The only shoes that went with my dress," I thought idly.

These are the things I knew:

I knew that even if I were allowed to speak it would make no difference. The church chosen for the meeting was notoriously conservative, the first message sent by the powers that be. And I was an interloper: not born Southern, not raised Presbyterian, not heterosexual. And what about those dangly earrings? Presbyterians wear small studs or a single dropped pearl for eveningwear. And that cheap, purple, polyester dress. "For God's sake," I imagined them thinking, "she's not even *trying* to be one of us!"

I knew that while a moral issue was being debated, the unspoken larger issues were economics and fear. When women were admitted into ordained ministry, the fear was that there would be fewer jobs, fewer donations to seminaries that admitted women, fewer members because those who disagreed would leave the church. Nobody said it, and no one was saying it now, but if the ministry was flooded with those gays like it was with those women, there would be even fewer employment opportunities to go around. And no one was saying, "We are not going to trust God in this business of call and ministry." Even if it is what they were doing.

Ben Kline once told me, "They are afraid of you, Connie. Every man here is afraid you will go after his wife or daughter. They feel castrated."

So the net-net was that this is a 'ball' issue? I never felt like I was scary. I knew I had a lot more to fear then they did.

What mattered is that I was there. I was present, standing, and faithful. I had no idea what would come next, but everything so far led to this day. It mattered that I would exit the sanctuary and leave the church not knowing where Godde would call me next. I would keep wandering on this journey without maps. I was there not as a decorated general but as a private, a "pawn on the battlefield." My silence was a voice crying in the wilderness, a clumsy prophet challenging the people of Godde.

I hated that I was trembling. I struggled to stiffen up (while not locking my knees) and to appear stronger than I ought to be. The scent of laundry detergent and sweat rose from the armpits of my dress. My left earring tangled in my hair, which somehow was no longer orderly and brushed into submission, but transformed into a lions mane in the humidity.

I knew those gathered for this meeting thought I was the only gay person in the room.

What they didn't know is that some of their close friends and beloved clergy sat in silence, listening to their diatribes, crying inside. What they didn't know is that they amplified self-hatred and further isolated of some of their close friends and beloved clergy. What they didn't know is that some of their close friends and beloved clergy had hearts silently breaking for their sons and daughters, sisters and brothers. What they didn't know is that the moderator, herself, was a lesbian, put in an untenable position losing life-long friendships as well as her income, ministry, and security. And you know the sad part? She seemed more threatened by my silent witness than by all your vitriol.

"I cannot acknowledge anyone who is not an ordained or elected member of this meeting," the moderator admonished me for the second time.

I stood, angry with the moderator, not because she didn't call on me, but because she underestimated me. I'm pretty sure I'm not the one she would have chosen to represent gays and lesbians in the Presbyterian Church USA. But she assumed I didn't know better. She assumed I was a threat to her and others in the room. I gritted my teeth, not to keep silent, but to feel my anger, to clench it in my jaw, my powerful, silent, lion's jaw.

I knew that I was not enough like them to be taken seriously.

We are past the time in this nation and in this century where we reason together, where we listen for the leading of the Spirit, where we open ourselves to new understandings in the light of Love. Maybe we were never there.

I knew that power is never willingly shared.

I knew that even if I were allowed to speak I would not be heard.

I choked on my sadness. My throat swelled. If I had been allowed to speak, I feared only sobs would come out. Breathe. Breathe. *Pray.* Breathe. The room closed in and humid air pressed down with an unbearable weight that only I seemed to notice. And even though I couldn't imagine how being there might make a difference, I continued to stand, silent, outclassed and outnumbered, protected only by inbred civility. I trusted that I was where Godde called me to be and grieved that it was my last act as one of you.

I knew that my small act of standing would not matter.

Once, as I sat in much despair and with some gnashing of teeth in Ben Kline's top floor office, the light from the dormer window casting a halo behind his neat, gray head, he said, " Connie, you are like a pebble being tossed into the pond. You will sink to the bottom, never knowing the ripples you have caused to reach the shore."

With that, he summed up my entire spiritual journey. Each day I must learn to trust and remind myself that results are not the reason or the value of my faith. If ever a heart or mind has been changed, soothed, healed, opened, I may hear whispers of it years later, and be thankful for my faithfulness in that moment.

"Ben," I said, "Where do I go from here? The church won't have me and I can't hear God."

"Walk as far as you see the Light." he said. "And when you get a little further on the Light will be a little further on. Walk as far as you see the Light."

So I stood. A small stone sinking to the bottom of a very large pond.

The discussion ended. Still I stood. My only witness: the act of remaining erect. The vote was taken. The amendment to *The Book of Order* that would have affirmed the ordination of lesbian and gay candidates for the ministry failed.

Still I stood. Heart pounding, knees quaking, polyester stinking.

The meeting adjourned.

I stood until the last person filed out of the sanctuary.

# Epilogue

I asked God if it was okay to be melodramatic
And she said yes
I asked her if it was okay to be short
and she said it sure is
I asked her if I could wear nail polish
or not wear nail polish
and she said honey
she calls me that sometimes
she said you can do just exactly
what you want to
Thanks God I said
And is it even okay if I don't paragraph
my letters
Sweetcakes God said
who knows where she picked that up
what I'm telling you is
Yes Yes Yes

—*God Says Yes to Me*, Kaylin Haught

IN 1993 A GROUP of wayward women started an ecumenical, feminist, Christian, worshipping community and we call ourselves Circle of Grace. In 1995, at a large ecumenical service, Circle of Grace ordained me to be their pastor. I continue to be in discernment as to where and to what I am being called. I have no relationship with the Presbyterian Church (USA) or any other denomination. That has been both a blessing and a hardship. Telling this story and perhaps others is part of my response to where Godde is calling me now.

In June of 2012, at their annual General Assembly meeting, the Presbyterian Church (USA), announced that the necessary two-thirds majority of local presbyteries had voted to allow the inclusion of lesbians and gays to ordained ministry, forty years after the initial proposal in 1972 and twenty-six years after I graduated from Columbia Theological Seminary. Though some member churches have withdrawn from the denomination, the vote stands.

June 2018, the 223$^{rd}$ General Assembly of The Presbyterian Church (USA) approved two historic overtures. The first affirmed people of diverse gender identities, items 11-12 stating:

> "Standing in the conviction that all people are created in the image of God and that the Gospel of Jesus Christ is good news for all people, the 223$^{rd}$ General Assembly (2018) affirms its commitment to the full welcome, acceptance, and inclusion of transgender people, people who identify as gender non-binary, and people of all gender identities within the full life of the church and the world. The assembly affirms the full dignity and the full humanity of transgender people, their full inclusion in all human rights, and their giftedness for service. The assembly affirms the church's obligation to stand for the right of people of all gender identities to live free from discrimination, violence, and every form of injustice."

It goes on to call for General Assembly leaders to bear witness to these affirmations on matters of military inclusion, access to public accommodations, including gender-neutral restrooms, and Title IX protections. It also encourages congregations to expand their welcome to transgender and gender non-binary people.

In items 11–13 it further states that:

> "Celebrating the expansive embrace of the gospel of Jesus Christ and the breadth of our mission to serve a world in need, the 223$^{rd}$ General Assembly (2018) affirms the gifts of LGBTQIA+ people for ministry and celebrates their service in the church and in the world."

The resolution laments the suffering of LGBTQIA+ people who were hurt by the church's policies in the past, and gives thanks for the persistence of those who worked for change. It notes the ministries of those serving in many capacities in the church today with excellence, and it calls for greater openness, stronger social witness, and intentional effort in ecumenical and mission co-worker relationships to advocate for justice and equality for all people.

It is important to tell our stories. Our small acts of heroism are the conduits of change and a bold invitation to affirm the heresy of Godde's grace.

# Book Club Questions

1. Where does your religious tradition stand on LGBTQ issues? Has it changed over time? Have your opinions changed? If so, why?

2. If you are LGBTQ, are you currently part of a spiritual community? Where does it stand on LGBTQ issues and how does that stand affect your spiritual journey? Have you left the church/synagogue/mosque of your youth? Have you changed denominations or left organized religion for good? If so, why?

3. One of the themes of the memoir is the tension between righteousness and piety. How do you define the difference between the two? Does the idea of being righteous rather than pious change the way you look at being a spiritually driven person? Do you think of yourself as righteous or pious? Why?

4. Another theme is that of belonging. How do you experience belonging? What determines whether one belongs or not? Where do you belong spiritually, physically, and relationally? How does that belonging inform your actions and perspectives?

5. A premise of the book is that doctrine needs to be challenged by experience. Have you encountered doctrine that is contrary to your experience of the Holy? Has doctrine been a help or an impediment to your faith? Can doctrine become an idol?

6. In what way, if any, has your understanding of what it means to be a prophet been challenged? Does it help or hinder your spiritual understandings to see people of Godde as flawed and deeply human?

7. What do you consider to be spiritual success? What are the challenges to the author as she seeks to be faithful? What are your challenges?

8. Many traditions consider the body "an occasion for sin." The author explores the connection between her body and her experience of Godde. In what ways, if any, have you experienced the Sacred with your body?

9. The theme of integrity and authenticity is central to the author's call. Why is being authentic important to a spiritual journey? Is it difficult to be authentic? Is it worth it, given what can be lost and/or gained by being authentic?

10. The author seems to forgive herself her foibles. Is it important to be able to do that? Is she excusing bad behavior? Are you able to forgive yourself? Is Godde involved in that process? Does it change how you are able to move forward?

I hope you enjoyed reading *A Gracious Heresy: The Queer Calling of an Unlikely Prophet*. There is no greater honor for a writer than for a reader to take pleasure in their work. You can find updated information and my book-signing itinerary on my website: connietuttle.com. If you enjoyed this book, please tell others, like it on facebook, and if it meant a lot to you, review it on Amazon. Thank you!